Fenton Glass
The 1990s Decade

edited by James Measell

© Copyright 2000

The Glass Press, Inc.
dba Antique Publications
Post Office Box 553 • Marietta, Ohio 45750

Fenton Art Glass Co.'s website: www.fentonartglass.com

ALL RIGHTS RESERVED

PB ISBN 1–57080–078–2

HB ISBN 1–57080–079–0

CONTENTS

PUBLISHER'S INTRODUCTION 4

FOREWORD and ACKNOWLEDGEMENTS 5

Chapter Twenty-Nine
  THE FENTON MYSTIQUE 6

Chapter Thirty
  A QUIET WEEK AT FENTON 8

Chapter Thirty-One
  A DECADE OF GROWTH, 1990-1999 14

Chapter Thirty-Two
  THE FENTON LINE 19

NOTES ON THE COLOR PLATES 32

COLOR PLATES 33-144

DESCRIPTIONS OF COVERS 145

Chapter Thirty-Three
  HISTORIC COLLECTION COLORS 154

Chapter Thirty-Four
  CONNOISSEUR COLLECTION 166

Chapter Thirty-Five
  FAMILY SIGNATURE SERIES 175

Chapter Thirty-Six
  EASTER AND CHRISTMAS LIMITED EDITIONS 179

Chapter Thirty-Seven
  OTHER LIMITED EDITIONS 189

Chapter Thirty-Eight
  CARNIVAL GLASS 201

Chapter Thirty-Nine
  SPECIAL PRODUCTS 207

Chapter Forty
  FENTON AND QVC 211

Chapter Forty-One
  COLLECTING FENTON GLASS 215

INDEX 221

PUBLISHER'S INTRODUCTION

Over the past twenty–three years, I have helped produce four volumes on the Fenton Art Glass Company and the family that has kept the business alive. The latest of those four books was *Fenton Glass: The 1980s Decade,* and in it, I ended my publisher's introduction by wondering "Will I–or one of my sons–one day write an introduction to a fifth book on Fenton Glass?" And here we are.

Let me begin my musings by sharing some personal history. Twenty-five years ago I came out of the military and went to work in the family printing business. Soon afterwards, an employee quit to go into business for himself and I became a sales representative. As luck would have it, many of the accounts which I called upon were in the "table top" industry, i.e., companies which made products to be used as either functional or decorative items. For many years I regularly visited factories that produced china, pottery, porcelain and glass.

As the seventies ended and the eighties began, the American "table top" industry was in turmoil. A combination of events resulted in the disappearance of the traditional markets for these items. Perhaps you are wondering why I would include this information in an introduction of *Fenton Glass: The 1990s Decade*. The reason is that the Fenton family was astute enough to recognize they had to change. A conscious decision was made to pursue the collectibles market in addition to the "table top" market. Because of that decision, we can publish this book on the glass of the nineties. Fenton is still here, creating beautiful glass, because they were able to adjust to the marketplace. One of my reasons for asking the Fenton family to let us produce this book is to celebrate their continued healthy existence some ninety-five years after they started.

My personal opinion as to why they are still here can be illustrated by the following story.

Three or four years ago, I acquired an old mould, a compote with a holly pattern, commonly called the Christmas compote. The compote's maker had been highly debated for many years by Carnival glass collectors. Jim Measell encouraged me to have some "new" compotes made from this beautiful old mould. I knew there was only one place to get this done—The Fenton Art Glass Company!

I arranged a production date and made plans to bring the mould over a few days in advance. I was surprised by the number of people who came out to the curb to look at the mould and help bring it into the mould shop. The craftsmen were excited at the historical significance of the moment. They were equally fascinated with the mould itself and the intricacies involved in its creation. The professionals in the mould shop set about cleaning and preparing it for production once again.

A few days later, a "turn" was scheduled for ruby Christmas compotes. We felt the moment was so "momentous" that we videotaped the occasion. On this day, Jim (Measell) and I were there, as was Frank Fenton, but also several of Fenton's glassmakers who gathered to either watch or help in the production of this compote. I learned that day that making glass from an old mould is extremely difficult, especially when the mould has very thick metal and is carved with a deep pattern. This can best be summed up by quoting Frank Fenton: "The boys learned a few things about making glass today."

The result was an exquisite "re–creation" of an old collectible—a holly compote in ruby Carnival.

I relate this event because, in my opinion, it explains why the Fenton Art Glass Company is still a viable concern when so many others have failed. From the upper echelons of management and the craftsmen in the hot metal shop through the selectors and packers, Fenton has people who are genuinely interested in making a beautiful, high quality product. They all understand the historical significance in the old patterns and moulds and constantly seek new colors in which to "re–create" old collectibles. And, they make beautiful glass, really lovely glass pieces. The care that is taken with production, color selection, and hand decorating leads to pieces that people want to collect.

My collection has numerous Fenton pieces, old and new. I am a tremendous admirer of the glass and the men and women who create it. To Frank and Bill, their children and their children's children, from the bottom of my heart, I thank you for all the glass you have made and continue to make. This book is a celebration of one of the greatest decades of glass production in the history of Fenton. I hope you enjoy it and the glass it portrays.

David E. Richardson, Publisher
June, 2000

FOREWORD and ACKNOWLEDGEMENTS

Not long after *Fenton Glass: The 1980s Decade* was published in 1996, someone made this remark to me: "I hope you don't wait as long afterwards to do the 1990s decade!" After a bit of a chuckle, I managed this comeback: "I'll get started right away tomorrow morning, so the Fenton 1990s book will be ready just a few days after the 1990s decade is over!"

As it turns out, my facetious reply was not really far off the mark, for this book is scheduled to be published in late July of the year 2000, about seven months after the close of the 1990s decade. When I made the statement above, however, I didn't know everything that would happen.

In the course of doing the Fenton 1980s decade book in 1995-96, I was asked about the possibility of my coming to work for the Fenton Art Glass Company. After the book was published, this question became a serious consideration for me and my family.

Saying "yes" was easy, but accomplishing all the needed tasks took time. Finally, everything seemed to happen to my wife Brenda and me at once: sending our youngest child off to college; my retiring from a 27–year university teaching career; our selling and buying houses; and, best of all, my starting in as Fenton's Associate Historian.

Almost as soon as I joined the Fenton ranks in August 1997, I started to plan this book. I had ready access to files and records of all kinds. I had almost daily contact with three generations of Fentons and many company employees. The same cheerful, friendly folks who helped with the 1980s book were willing to search their memories and to answer questions about the 1990s decade. And, some of those whose employment started in the 1990s were among the most enthusiastic when they found out that "their history" was to be the subject of a new book for Fenton glass collectors.

First and foremost, I thank the members of the Fenton family–Bill, Christine, Don, Frank, George, Lynn, Mike, Nancy, Randy, Scott, Shelley, and Tom–for their help and encouragement. They helped get the facts right and the stories straight, and they offered many constructive suggestions and comments.

Many Fenton Art Glass Company employees and Fenton Gift Shop employees also contributed. Gayle Buckley, Pam Dick, Jeff Kelley, Jennifer Maston, and Ann Stull proofed the color page captions and helped solve a few mysteries.

Chris Benson, Tami Lane, and Joyce Sims searched the computer and the card files for elusive color codes and other data.

Sculptor Jon Saffell was always willing to talk about his work, past and present. Decorating designers Frances Burton, Kim Plauché, Martha Reynolds and Robin Spindler were very helpful in recalling the stories behind various decorations. Fenton retiree Howard Seufer loaned some photos and took others as needed.

Beth Hart's organizational skills made the research in Fenton catalogs and price lists go smoothly. When the time came to photograph glass, she packed (and unpacked!) and carried cartons. She prepared the first drafts of the captions for the color pages and the index.

The dealers at the Williamstown Antique Mall always let me "borrow" whatever was needed for a photo. Several Fenton glass collectors loaned the items we needed.

At The Glass Press, Nikki Strauss and Katie Thomson did the scanning, typesetting and layout with speed, skill, and good humor–even when deadlines were especially pressing.

James Measell
June 7, 2000

Chapter Twenty–Nine
THE FENTON MYSTIQUE

Fenton collectors from far and wide come to the Williamstown to browse in the Fenton Gift shop, tour the factory, and visit the Fenton Museum. Some of them bring their children, or their grandchildren, and they have a great time learning about Fenton glass.

Naturally, a few of these Fenton collectors are accompanied by reluctant companions in the form of friends or even spouses. In the midst of an extraordinarily warm day, one tired but patient soul uttered this question, "What is it about this Fenton stuff, anyway?"

That's a question worth rephrasing and repeating: "What is it about Fenton, anyway?" The answer to this question is the Fenton experience and, indeed, the Fenton mystique!

In 1904, the year before Fenton Art Glass was founded, there were about 399 establishments in various branches of the glass industry across the United States. About one–third made glass tableware by hand, and many of these were located in the Ohio River Valley, from Pittsburgh winding south to the western tip of West Virginia.

By 1920, the ranks had thinned. By 1950 or so, there were about two dozen hand plants remaining. Now, in the year 2000, you can count them all on your hands ... and have both thumbs and a few fingers left over. The Fenton Art Glass Company is a survivor ... and that's part of the Fenton mystique.

Collectors come to be associated with Fenton in different, but often deeply personal, ways. Many longtime Fenton glass collectors can trace their collection to a Fenton item from their parents' or grandparents' home. Others have a collection that began with a gift they received. And at least a few Fenton collections began by deciding to keep a gift item that was purchased with someone else in mind! Last but not least, sometimes people buy something simply because they like it, although they don't know much about it. Later, when they learn that their mystery item is Fenton glass, they seek further information and become avid Fenton glass collectors.

Perhaps the Fenton mystique could be captured in six letters: **F–E–N–T–O–N**

F = family. The Fenton family is far more extensive than the four Fenton generations who have owned and managed the company. It encompasses and embraces employees, sales reps and dealer accounts as well as the thousands who enjoy Fenton products.

This dramatic photo of glassblower Rick Snyder captures the skill, craftsmanship and pride that characterize each piece of Fenton glass.

E = energy. It takes physical strength and energy to make glass, of course, but it also takes energy and enthusiasm to track the trends and anticipate the wants of consumers and collectors alike. Despite the ups and downs over the years, Fenton maintains that vital energy.

N = niche. A niche is a special place or position. Throughout its 95 year history, Fenton has been able to find its place. There has been an evolution from utilitarian glassware to decorative giftware and collectibles, to be sure, but Fenton has always found its niche.

T = teamwork. Even a brief look at the factory floor will show anyone that glassmaking is a team sport. But there are many others less visible in the company. They see to everything from the raw materials and employee training to the temperatures of the furnaces and the readiness of packing materials. They are a team in every sense of the word.

O = obligation. This is a serious word at Fenton. There is an obligation to produce a quality product and to support all the efforts to market that product. And, there is a sense of obligation to the collectors who make it all possible.

N = novel. Throughout its history, Fenton glass has been novel. The firm which originated iridescent ware in late 1907 continues to innovate, creating distinctive glass colors and decorative treatments.

Why and how has Fenton succeeded and continued to succeed where others have not? The answer is no surprise ... it's the Fenton mystique!

Visit Fenton's website: www.fentonartglass.com

Chapter Thirty
A QUIET WEEK AT FENTON

Humorist Garrison Keillor always begins his weekly radio monologue with the same line: "It was a quiet week in Lake Wobegon." Keillor has yet to visit Fenton Art Glass, but here is what happens during a "quiet week" at Fenton.

At 4:15 am on Monday, the Fenton plant seems to be at rest in the early morning. The factory, which contains 290,000 square feet on four levels, sits on 11.2 acres in the city of Williamstown, West Virginia. With its complex systems for gas and electrical power, plus more than 600 employees working at various times, the plant is really a village within a city. Within two hours, employees will be at work in many different departments.

For collectors and those who take the Fenton factory tour, Hot Metal (glassmaking) and Decorating (a department in Cold Metal) may be the most apparent places of activity, but a piece of Fenton glass may go through many areas where it is touched by many hands and seen by numerous pairs of eyes.

In the pre–dawn hours, a half dozen cars or pickup trucks are already in the parking lot across from the guardhouse, where the night shift security officer is stationed. The vehicles belong to a crew of furnacemen and others who are beginning to prepare the Hot Metal working area for the first shift of the week. The ever–present roar of the furnaces is the first sound one hears upon entering the factory.

Sensitive monitors constantly record the temperature of individual units. Glass melting typically requires temperatures of more than 2500 degrees, The Fenton plant has a 12–pot furnace, with each pot holding about 2200 pounds of glass. There are also nine large day tanks and several portable tanks plus a continuous tank which produces a never–ending supply of crystal to feed two color cells and a crystal outlet.

Fenton glass is "made to order," both literally and figuratively. When a new product is approved, the company makes samples and creates printed catalogs or other sales materials. Manufacturers representatives throughout the country call on more than 9000 dealer accounts and take orders for Fenton glass. The orders come into Fenton's sales department, and daily inquires are made to see how many items are on order and what quantities remain in inventory. A list of "top 40" needs circulates weekly, and regular meetings each Wednesday among Fenton department heads and schedulers allow them to plan for the next Monday–Friday production time.

Scheduling is not an easy task. One scheduler likened the enterprise to "chess and a jigsaw puzzle combined with a tough crossword." The schedulers must anticipate the time and labor needed for many tasks, from glassmaking and decorating to a myriad of other essentials for various products–selecting, repairing, finishing (sawing, grinding and polishing), sandblasting, decorating, applying gold, firing, numbering, and packing for shipment. The goal (to ship on time to every customer) is elusive. Time studies and years of experience enable supervisors to determine how best to accomplish their department's many tasks.

During a "Quiet Week" Fenton...

- Needs 92,000 pounds of sand to make glass
- Consumes about $21,000 worth of natural gas
- Requires more than 400 ounces of pure gold for its distinctive colors
- Uses more than 20 miles of bubble wrap to pack glass.

Once the glass is made, it may be routed throughout the plant so that whatever is required for the final product can be done. More than a mile of flow racks and conveyors help move the glass from place to place and even level to level, but every ware tray (containing four or six to several dozen items depending upon the size of the articles) makes its way through the Fenton plant with a destination ticket attached.

Most of the glass to be used on a Monday morning has been melted over the weekend. Fenton chemists add just the right amounts of coloring ingredients to the basic batch of sand, soda ash, and lime. Cobalt oxide is used to make dark blue glass, and chromium produces green glass. Cranberry, Rosalene and Burmese contain pure gold. Glass technology many seem a textbook science, but the practical demands of making glass are many. Glassmaking is a unique blend of science and art–with some trial and error added!

In reflecting upon the 1990s decade, company President George Fenton made these observations: "When we develop new colors and glassmaking techniques for our Connoisseur Collection, surprises often happen–some with good results and some with bad." For example, Fenton made some beautiful Wild Rose glass for a Connoisseur piece in 1997, but, when the piece was decorated and fired, the handpainted floral motif turned an unpleasant color! Various solutions were tried–all to no avail–and quite a few pieces simply had to be scrapped. Finally, the proper color was achieved.

Subject to changes in the quality of chemicals as well as humidity and atmospheric pressure, molten glass is always a fickle substance. There are added demands relating to Fenton colors. If a pressed piece is relatively heavy and thick, the glass batch must not be as dark as it would be for a thinner, lightweight blown item. The proper colors for rings (Fenton's distinctive colored edges) and basket handles must be developed so that all elements of the final piece will match.

Since Fenton glassworkers may make colored items with crystal handles or other combinations of colors or opalescent effects, the glass needed must be located in melting units which are in reasonably close proximity to one another.

Blocker Mike Sine, Sr., uses a marver.

Presser Harvey Cottrill.

Glassmaking is a team activity. Groups of workers called shops make pressed or blown items, and each position in a shop requires procedures and tools that are designed for both efficiency and safety. Many Fenton shops are composed of glassworkers who have worked with one another for years or even decades.

The first shift of glassworkers in Hot Metal work for two four–hour "turns" per day. The first turn commences at 6:15 am and ends with a half–hour lunch break at 10:15. During this time, a crew takes the moulds to a cleaning area and brings out different moulds to be used on the next turn, which runs from 10:45 to 2:45. Within an hour, the work area has been swept clear and readied for a second shift of glassworkers. They work from 3:45 to 7:45, have a dinner break until 8:30 (during which the moulds are changed), and resume work from 8:30 to 12:30 a.m.

The moulds used for glassmaking are made of cast iron, and Fenton's Mould Shop is staffed with skilled mouldmakers and machinists. Their craft can be called "sculpture in reverse," and they are responsible for executing the patterns and designs which ultimately take on further beauty from Fenton's repertoire of glass colors. Moulds are among the company's most important assets, and moulds for a new item can represent an investment of $20,000.

Each piece of glass must pass through an annealing lehr after it has been pressed or blown and brought to its final shape. The entry point of the lehrs is hot enough to keep the glass from cooling too quickly.

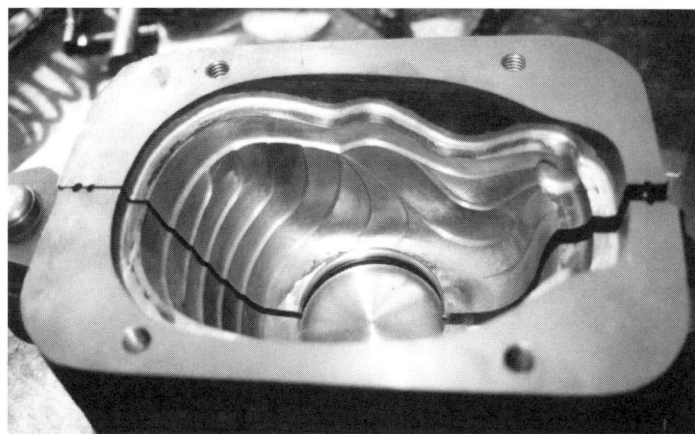

The mould for Fenton's Christmas sleigh (4695) was completed in 1996.

Greg Lauderman cleans the plunger for a press mould.

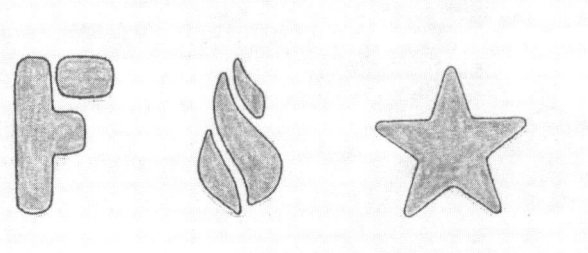

Line drawings of marks used on seconds.

The journey through the lehr on a chain link belt may take 2½ to 3 hours, as the piece cools slowly to room temperature. At the end of the lehrs, selectors examine each piece carefully. The selectors' vocabulary for various defects seems like another language. A blister, crizzle, lap, rocky bottom, seed, or stone may condemn an item to cullet, where it is broken up to be recycled by Fenton or taken away by a commercial cullet firm.

Selectors grade the acceptable glassware into three categories–good, repairs and seconds. Seconds are sold through the Fenton Gift Shop; currently, these are marked as seconds by sandblasting a small block "F" on the bottom of the item. Earlier in the 1990s decade, seconds were marked with a "flame" that resembles a calligraphy–style S. Later, seconds were marked with a five–pointed star. Sometimes, Fenton items that could be discarded as cullet are donated to local charitable organizations to use in dime–toss or other fundraising games (these items were often marked with two five–pointed stars).

Items sent to the repair area may need only a deft touch with a polishing wheel to remove a tiny black speck or other minor concern. If the repair cannot bring the item to the status of "good," it becomes a second or cullet as the case may be.

Standards are set for each and every item. The color, the size and the shape must be right. Frank M. Fenton often remarks that "there is no perfect piece of handmade glass, so it's a matter of deciding what kind and what degree of imperfections are to be tolerated." When items are first put into production, selectors and quality control supervisors set aside questionable pieces for further evaluation and discussion.

For example, Burmese glass must be reheated in order to "strike" the pink color that collectors so enjoy. No two pieces will strike exactly alike, so the employees in Quality Control may question the acceptance of pieces that seem to be too light, too dark or a bit uneven. Furthermore, many pieces are touched by one tool or another during the manufacturing process, and the acceptability of a particular "tool mark" may be a concern.

Quality decisions are made daily as top personnel from management, sales and quality control see glassware from the previous day's production. For questionable items, ballots are provided and the "accept" and "reject" votes are tallied. Often, adjustments or changes in some aspect of the Hot Metal production can alleviate or eliminate quality problems as the glassworkers gain experience in making the particular item.

Many items labeled "good" go directly to shipping as they do not require any finishing and they are not going to be decorated. Quite a few, however, must be sent to one or more of the Cold Metal finishing areas. Many figurines, for example, are produced by "pressing through a fount." The fount must be cut off with a diamond saw. Subsequently, the bottom of the figurine is made smooth in a succession of grinding and polishing steps. Similarly, lamp shades must be ground and polished after excess glass is sawed off, and the shade must sit properly on the lamp hardware.

Another active area in Cold Metal finishing is the "blaster," which imparts a soft satin–like texture to Burmese glass and is used for other items which require a similar finish.

The blaster uses aluminum oxide crystals under pressure to etch the surface of the glass. This softens the color gradations and gives the glass a nice feel to the touch. It also makes the glass especially suitable for decorating because the paint can bond easily, although Fenton does do considerable decorating on items which are not blasted.

The Decorating Department is quite a contrast to the hustle and bustle of the noisy Hot Metal area. There is almost a serene feeling in Decorating, as more than 95 women and men work quietly, seated at individual work stations, deftly handpainting intricate and beautiful designs. Most decorators arrive in the early morning and are in place for their eight-hour shift by 6:30 or 7 am.

Decorator Debra Cutshaw.

Many decorators enjoy their favorite music on headsets, and some prefer to listen to talking books. A separate area, called the "gold room," is equipped with powerful ventilating fans. The decorators in the gold room wear breathing masks as they apply 22k gold to items. Sometimes the gold must be fired separately, but on other occasions, the gold and the paint can be fired together.

Individual decorators are responsible for the entire handpainted motif, and each personally signs the completed piece (typically with the phrase "handpainted by" followed by a first initial and last name). The time required for each item varies with the size of the piece and the complexity of the decoration. Painting on glass is far from easy, as the decorator must adapt to the curved surface and be ever mindful of the relationships among the colors of the paint and the glass itself.

As new decorating designs are approved, the decorators who will paint them begin a training program to assure that quality standards are met. There is some room for variations, but elements such as butterflies and flowers must be sized properly and spaced according to the standard. Each decorator gains experience with the new items he or she learns to paint.

Workers called "bench hands" deliver the glassware to the decorators' work stations. The decorators get their paint from a common supply, assuring that the colors are the same when several different decorators are working individually on the identical item from the Fenton line or in a QVC order. Naturally, those who mix the paints each day must be sure that the color does not vary.

When the decorator has finished with a group of items, a bench hand takes the completed pieces to a decorating lehr (or, in some cases, a kiln) to be fired. This requires a slow temperature climb to 1000–1050 degrees F., followed by a gradual cooling. The paints change color during firing, and these changes have been anticipated by the decorating design team as they planned and tested the new decorations some time ago.

The Packing and Shipping Departments are closely related, especially in terms of inventory control. At first sight, everything seems to be a maze of shelves, flow racks and conveyors. Each Fenton item is a separately numbered "skew" (short for "stock keeping unit" or SKU), and a computer inventory system keeps track of both the progress through the plant and the quantities of every item in the Fenton catalogs and supplements.

The packers often use strips of "bubble wrap" to protect Fenton items as they are placed in cartons. Smaller items are usually wrapped tightly in plain paper before they are inserted in a small box. Most recently, Fenton has used attractive silver boxes with lettering in black for its products. These make for eye-catching displays in Fenton retail outlets, and they are attractive gift boxes as well.

The silver boxes come in various sizes, and, because of their modular design, they can be combined in a multitude of ways to fill a Fenton "large master" or "small master" carton. This modular combining feature allows Fenton to ship many different items using standard master containers. The silver boxes fit snugly, and potential problems in shipping are minimized.

Beyond the daily and weekly functions at Fenton which have already been described, there are plenty of "behind the scenes" activities which are likewise essential to the success of the company. For example, Safety Director Mike Fenton and others conduct periodic tours of the entire plant, looking for areas and employee working practices which can be made both safer and more efficient.

An internal program called Safety Partners provides both stimulus and support for employee efforts in this area. Another important company program is CIQ (Continuous Improvement of Quality). Over the years, employees have submitted hundreds of ideas, and many of them led directly to improvements in production, efficiency and communication among everyone involved.

The Fenton Art Glass Company purchases thousands of different things from outside suppliers. The tons of sand, soda ash and lime (plus coloring agents like gold, selenium and cobalt) which are needed to make glass are the most obvious, of course. But, every Birthstone Bear or Calendar Cat needs the right color jewel or necklace for its month, and all of these have to be purchased and maintained in inventory.

This t-shirt was designed for Fenton's "CIQ Day" in December, 1997.

Tour guide Susan Morriston explains the operation of a press shop to her group.

With over 600 employees, Fenton has its own personnel staff to deal with testing and hiring new employees as well as the administration of employee records and seeing to health insurance matters and retirement benefits. This staff also promotes wellness programs and other opportunities for employees.

When visitors come to Fenton, they generally browse in the Fenton Gift Shop and take the factory tour. After the tour, which includes both glassmaking and decorating, they may go upstairs to spend some time in the Fenton Museum. The Gift Shop is actually a separate organization from the glass company, and the Gift Shop also operates the Fenton Museum. The Gift Shop purchases its stock of Fenton glass from the company just like any other Fenton dealer. The Gift Shop also stocks many other collectibles and various gift items.

Fenton family members are active in many different areas of the Fenton Gift Shop and the Fenton Art Glass Company. Frank M. Fenton has the post of Historian, and he answers many questions from collectors and enjoys developing new displays for the Fenton Museum. Frank also works with Fenton's Special Orders Department on souvenirs and other special items for the collectors clubs. Bill Fenton is Chairman of the Board of the glass company and President of the Gift Shop, and he is always involved in creating new Fenton glass items for QVC.

Frank's son, George W. Fenton, is company President. Frank jokes that George "has to attend all the meetings I used to go to," and that is certainly true! George oversees all company activities, but many others have key roles. George might confer with Stan Vanlandingham, Fenton's Chief Financial Officer, on the company's financial status and then meet with American Flint Glass Workers Union offi-

The Fenton Museum displays more than 1000 examples of glassware from Fenton's past.

cers before heading for a New Product Development committee meeting. Later on, the weekly scheduling meetings will take up two hours or more.

Director of Design Nancy Fenton (George's wife) is in close contact with all the decorating designers (Frances Burton, Kim Plauché, Martha Reynolds, and Robin Spindler) as well as sculptor Jon Saffell. Nancy travels to trade shows and merchandise marts, and she tracks trends through trade publications and other important reference sources.

Tom Fenton is Vice-President of Manufacturing. A typical day finds him in touch with Hot Metal Superintendent Ken Moore as well as the supervisors and foremen on both shifts. The recent factory expansion and ongoing furnace construction and repairs during 2000 kept Tom busy with plant engineers and consultants. The Fenton CIQ (Continuous Improvement in Quality) is another of Tom's administrative responsibilities.

Vice–President of Sales Don Fenton likes to say that he is either "on the phone or on the road." Indeed, Don maintains close communication with Fenton sales reps and with many Fenton dealers. A newsletter called "The Fenton Connection" goes to Fenton Showcase Dealers, and regular Sales Bulletins are mailed to all accounts.

Mike Fenton holds the positions of Safety Director and Purchasing Manager. He is responsible for all aspects of safety in the work environment, including many recent efforts to study the ergonomics of various jobs in the plant. These studies have resulted in on–going training programs to encourage safety and to promote increased efficiency in job tasks.

Shelley Fenton Ash can often be found at her computer, hard at work designing the next Fenton catalog or supplement. If she's not there, it's a good bet that she's at the printer's office looking at color proofs or at the photographer's studio checking on the shots needed for the next publication.

Randy Fenton is Treasurer of the Fenton Gift Shop, and Christine Fenton is Data Processor there. Within the past few years, the Fenton Gift Shop has opened two new locations–Flatwoods, WV, and Grove City, PA. The Gift Shop also extended its traditional summer "Tent Event" to run for about six weeks (late June through early August).

Two fourth generation Fentons joined the company in the 1990s decade. Lynn Fenton Erb is involved with the company's Strategic Planning and CIQ programs, and she is also responsible for the administration of the quarterly Glass Messenger newsletter. Both Lynn and Scott Fenton, who came into the Sales Department in early 1998, are planners for the National Sales Meeting. Scott travels frequently to meet with Fenton sales organizations, and he has worked on numerous sales projects, ranging from national collectibles shows to iQVC and the export business.

The Fenton family gathers for a portrait in 1998. Laughter breaks out (inset) as the group begins to assemble for the photographer. Finally, everyone is in place. Standing, left to right: Don A. Fenton (Vice–President of Sales); George W. Fenton (President); Nancy G. Fenton (Director of Design); Lynn Fenton Erb (Assistant to the President and CIQ Coordinator); Christine Fenton (Data Processor, Fenton Gift Shop); Shelley Fenton Ash (Graphics Manager); Michael D. Fenton (Safety Director/Purchasing Manager); and Thomas K. Fenton (Vice–President of Manufacturing). Seated (left to right): Randall R. Fenton (Treasurer, Fenton Gift Shop); Wilmer C. "Bill" Fenton (Chairman of the Board); Frank M. Fenton (Historian); and Scott K. Fenton (Assistant National Sales Manager).

Chapter Thirty–One
A DECADE OF GROWTH, 1990–1999

The 1980s had been a roller–coaster decade for Fenton. The year 1981 saw record sales, but the next several years brought declines. Two longtime American glass companies, Fostoria and Imperial, closed their doors in the mid–1980s, and there was some genuine concern regarding the future of the hand glass business.

In the late 1980s, however, Fenton's "back–to–basics" approach was beginning to move the company forward. Giftware customers liked the Victorian and traditional styles that Fenton's skills could provide, and the Dusty Rose and Cranberry colors were selling well. Attempts at diversification (Fenton–from–Afar and Christine Victoria) and a home party plan (Gracious Touch) were winding down, and all of them would soon be gone.

In 1990, Fenton stockholders were told that "business ... has been good" and that "our biggest problem is an inability to make as much glass as we can sell." There were some short–lived difficulties early in the decade, but 1991–1999 witnessed generally steady growth and positive times for Fenton.

The Fenton logo, in use since the 1970s and throughout the 1980s, was changed  slightly to help identify pieces made during the 1990s decade. As pictured here, the name Fenton appears in script within an oval, and a small 9 was placed below Fenton (incidentally, the small 9 was replaced by a small 0 in 2000, and this logo will be used through 2009).

In 1990–91, giftware retailers faced some tough economic conditions, but Fenton glass was one of their most successful products. President George Fenton observed that "when the market is difficult ... the good performers get stronger." He was right. Many retailers increased their orders for Fenton glass, and the company was able to respond to increased demand for its products, although timely shipping was not always possible.

There were some other difficulties. Furnace rebuilding cut into the company's glassmaking capacity, and illnesses suffered by important skilled glassworkers held things back. New environmental guidelines affected Fenton's formulas for ruby glass, and there were so many problems with the Favrene treatment that some potential new product ideas were put aside until experiments could be carried out.

In a speech to Fenton sales representatives in late 1999, President George Fenton reflected that the term "collectible" had become increasingly important to the company during the past decade. In 1991, for example, Fenton began to take steps to "develop our current independent base into a stronger dealer network" and to "make Fenton more important in the collectible market."

During 1992, Fenton advertising appeared in Collectors Mart and Glass Collector's Digest, and feature articles on Fenton glass were carried in several publications. Fenton glass was exhibited at one of the first national collectible shows (held in South Bend, Indiana). Sales of Fenton's Valentine's Day and Easter offerings increased in strength yearly between 1989–1993, and Fenton regular line colors such as Dusty Rose were in keeping with consumer trends.

When The Beaumont Company of Morgantown, West Virginia, shut down in the early 1990s, Fenton acquired numerous moulds for lighting goods, and several former Beaumont glassblowers and other workers found employment at Fenton. During the 1990s decade, Fenton also acquired moulds from the Chicago Art Glass Company and from the L. G. Wright Glass Company.

The Family Signature Series was launched in early 1993, and collectors soon began to acquire these special pieces with an enthusiasm similar to that which they had developed for the Fenton Connoisseur Collection or some of the Historic Collection colors. Family Signature Series pieces are made with colors and treatments from the regular Fenton line, but they are individually numbered and dated with the year of issue.

This attractive yet functional display unit was an important part of the Fenton Showcase Dealer program when it began in 1994.

NEW IMPRESSIONS

The watercolor look of the French Impressionists highlights the Fenton Art Glass and Christine Victoria 1990 collection. Contrasting in black satin, antique rose and a silvertone blue is an array of delicate pieces of glassware and handmade accessories.

The subtle combination adds bold distinction to a new era of craftsmanship. Share the dawn of a decade with the "Impressions of a New Era," unique, handcrafted accessories and Fenton quality glassware.

Christine Victoria is a subsidiary of The Fenton Art Glass Company

FENTON

700 Elizabeth St. Williamstown, WV 26187

Created with Love.
Handcrafted with Pride.
★ Made In America ★

The Fenton Showcase Dealer program, begun in 1994, spurred growth in sales of limited editions later in the 1990s. Fenton Showcase Dealers carry the entire line of Fenton products, and they receive some special incentives from the company. Many Fenton Showcase Dealers often work closely with collectors, and many are "Fenton fanatics" themselves.

The positive sales figures for Fenton glass increased the ranks of Fenton employees. There were 235 employees in mid–1986, and the number increased to 350 in mid–1990. After a brief fallback to about 325 in 1991, the workforce steadily increased, reaching 405 in late 1993 and rising to 533 by the end of 1996. In 1999, the employee count surpassed 600.

In addressing Fenton sales reps in December, 1994, President George Fenton spoke of the tradition behind the company's success: "[There] is a constant effort to develop new and beautiful glass. The success of this effort is born out of our love of the product we make. We don't just look at these pieces as a way to make a living. We look at them as an expression of our values–the source of our pride."

This foil seal was used during 1995.

Rain didn't dampen spirits at the 1995 company picnic. Ken Scott holds the umbrella over wife Martha and sons Eric and Andrew (hiding from the camera).

The year 1995 marked the 90th anniversary of Fenton Art Glass. Expansion plans were in the works to increase melting capacity and to deal with other concerns. Fenton products were firmly established in three areas: gifts/sentiments; decorative accessories; and limited edition collectibles.

The 90th anniversary year of 1995 was marked by growth, particularly in decorating (where the number of artists doing handpainting grew to 51 from 36 just a year earlier) but also in melting capacity. One of the Historic Collection colors, a group of five decorated items in Burmese glass, was marketed as a numbered limited edition. A five–year strategic plan was in place, and the company was soon to publish the premier issue of a quarterly subscriber newsletter for collectors, the Fenton Glass Messenger.

During the summer of 1997, Fenton embarked upon an ambitious and costly series of capital improvements: the closure of a former disposal area and the construction of a basement storage area. Other improvements included the construction of new glass melting units and the rebuilding of others, including the large continuous tank.

Because the old disposal area for glass cullet contained cadmium and selenium, studies and testing were undertaken during the first half of the 1990s. Working closely with the West Virginia Division of Environmental Protection and consultants, Fenton engineers developed a plan to "cap" the area, which had not been in use for about ten years.

The plan was announced on July 24, 1997, and several West Virginia newspapers quoted company President George W. Fenton: "Our priority is to get the job done safely and in an environmentally sound manner that protects our workers, neighbors, and visitors." The cullet pile was relocated and compacted, and a bentonite clay liner sandwich within woven fabric was used. Several feet of soil then covered this cap. A drainage system with monitoring points assures the integrity of the environmental cap.

A new basement area was constructed after the disposal area project was complete. This area, serviced by a loading dock, provides storage space for Fenton's extensive inventory of moulds. The top of the new basement and the concrete cover over the disposal area were at the same level. This provided enough area so that Fenton's Hot Metal facilities could be expanded by about 10,000 square feet.

In 1998–99, trade publications such as *Giftbeat* often listed Fenton products among the most popular as reported by retailers across the country in the gift, home accessories and collectibles areas. The

The environmental cap is put in place.

"Fenton brand" was taking hold, and newly designed silver gift boxes added to the prestige of the product. The authors of *Watch It Made in the USA* ranked the Fenton factory tour in its "top ten," and an article in the *USA Today* newspaper (July 10, 1998) was illustrated with a photo of Fenton glassblower Chuck Handell.

Handell retired later in 1998, and he joined the ranks of many longtime Fenton employees who retired during the 1990s decade or early in the year 2000.

The retirement cake has become a Fenton tradition.

Packer Ernestine Dulaney cuts her retirement cake in 1998 as Becky Hendershot looks on.

GLASSWARE

Rating	Vendor/Line
#1	**Fenton**–vases, various
#2	Joan Baker–suncatchers
#3	Crystal Clear–bowls, various
#4	Mikasa–bowls, vases, various
#5	Glass Baron–figurines
#6	Ganz–various
#7	Durand–toasting glasses
#8	M. Block & Sons–glasses, various
#9	Fashion Forty–Worry Box

From *Giftbeat*, December 1999.

HOME DECOR

Rating	Vendor/Line
#1	Manual Wood–throws, wall hangings
#2	Goodwin Weavers–throws, Pooh
#3	**Fenton**–vases, various
#4	Pacific Rim–lamps, various
#5	Toland–rugs
#6	Figi–various
#7	CBK–various
#8	Crystal Clear–vases
#9	Rug Barn–throws
#10	Riverdale–pillows

From *Giftbeat*, September 1997.

COLLECTIBLES

Rating	Vendor/Line
#1	Roman–Seraphim Classics
#2	Dept. 56–Heritage Village
#3	Enesco–Precious Moments
#4	**Fenton**–art glass
#5	Swarovski–crystal, various
#6	Lladro–general line
#7	Coynes & Co.–Williraye
#8	Harbour Lights–lighthouses and Willitts Ebony Vision (tie)

From *Giftbeat*, April 2000.

GENERAL GIFT

Rating	Vendor/Line
#1	Burnes–frames
#2	Fetco's frames and NCE's chimes, various (tie)
#3	Ganz–fish, art candles, various
#4	Boyd's Bearstone and Yankee's candles (tie)
#5	Lasercraft–frames
#6	**Fenton**–general line
#7	Whispering Winds–chimes
#8	Joan Baker–suncatchers, various

From *Giftbeat*, April 2000.

Some recent national rankings as compiled by the trade publication *Giftbeat*.

Frank M. Fenton congratulates retirees Sonny Burdette (left) and Ron Bayles in March 2000.

Jenny Fenton Hukill poses with Fenton President George Fenton (left) and Vice President of Sales Don Fenton.

When the L. G. Wright Glass Co. of New Martinsville, WV, liquidated its assets in May 1999, Fenton acquired several hundred moulds. Some of these were used for products which went into the Fenton line for the year 2000. In keeping with Fenton's practice, these are marked with a script F in a vertical oval and a small 0 just outside the oval.

For its National Sales Meeting in December 1999, Fenton chose the theme "Charting Our Course for a New Millennium." The focus was on the future, of course, but the company honored both individual sales representatives and entire organizations for their achievements. Sales reps Craig Archer and Joe Buck were recognized in their respective categories, and sales rep Jenny Fenton Hukill (Tom Fenton's daughter) was "Newcomer of the Year" for 1999. The Seattle–based firm of Dick Gibson & Associates was "Organization of the Year" for 1999. A special award for "Organization of the Decade" went to The Weikels group of Greensboro, North Carolina.

As this is being written in June 2000, the Fenton Art Glass Company is looking back on a successful decade and reflecting on 95 years of its history. Just as important, the Fenton Art Glass Company is eagerly looking forward to its centennial in 2005 ... and to the years beyond.

Chapter Thirty–Two
THE FENTON LINE

Broadly speaking, the "Fenton line" includes everything the company produces and markets through more than 9000 retail dealers, ranging from independent gift shops to Hallmark shops and Old Country Stores in Cracker Barrel restaurants.

The line can be divided into two segments, limited and unlimited. Limited editions–such as the Historic Collection, the Connoisseur Collection, the Family Signature Series, and Easter and Christmas limited editions as well as others–are discussed elsewhere in this book (see Chapters 33–37); these areas of Fenton glass production are "limited," either by number or by a time period during which orders are accepted from Fenton dealers.

The balance of the Fenton line consists of "unlimited" colors and decorative treatments which may be offered over a long period of time. In fact, the longevity of anything in the Fenton line is determined by two factors: (1) its sales success; and (2) the company's ability to produce the item consistently. A good seller that is very hard to make may be more of a liability than an asset because the profit margin is small and because it consumes the production time of skilled glassworkers whose talents are needed for other items which have tight shipping deadlines.

Over the years, some patterns and colors in the Fenton line have been remarkable success stories. The Hobnail pattern, in various colors and in Milk Glass, was popular for over four decades beginning in the 1940s. Some Hobnail items were made during the 1990s, and the close of the 1990s decade and the year 2000 were marked by a stir of new interest in the Fenton Hobnail pattern. Indeed, Fenton Hobnail has achieved the status of a "classic" pattern among collectors of American glass.

The Dusty Rose color, introduced in the Fenton line during 1984, sold briskly throughout the last half of the 1980s decade and continued to sell strongly in the 1990s. When sales of Dusty Rose seemed to be diminishing somewhat during the mid–1990s, Fenton chemists reformulated the pink color to create Empress Rose (CP), which was introduced in 1998 and continues to sell well in the year 2000.

Long before the Fenton General Catalog is published in January, careful consideration goes into planning the Fenton line for the year. Director of Design Nancy Fenton is especially interested in tracking color trends in other industries and in developing glass colors and decorative treatments which display well together and coordinate with one another in decorative schemes. The New Product Development Committee meets regularly to keep track of both new ideas and projects which are in various stages of approval as they move toward becoming part of the Fenton line. During the 1990s decade, the Fenton line was both extensive and varied, as historic moulds saw new life in contemporary Fenton colors and new moulds (and new shapes) were created to add to the richness of the products offered to those who enjoy fine glass.

At the outset of the 1990s decade, Fenton issued a 40–page catalog. Catalog supplements (consisting of four to eight pages) appeared in June 1990, as well as in January and June 1991. Other mailings to Fenton dealers dealt with Collector's Extravaganza (see Chapter 33), the 85th Anniversary Burmese grouping (see Chapter 34) or such seasonal offerings as Easter and Christmas.

The 1990–91 catalog displayed a wide range of Fenton glass colors and decorative treatments. Some of these were illustrated in a previous book, *Fenton Glass: The 1980s Decade:* Antique Rose (p. 138); Copper Rose (p. 135); Country Scene (p. 136); Cranberry Opalescent (p. 142); Dusty Rose (p. 143); Elizabeth Collection (p. 142); Handpainted Tulips (p. 139); Hearts and Flowers (p. 138); Lilac (p. 141); and Salem Blue (p. 141). Cranberry Opaline and Cased Jade Opaline from the June 1990 supplement are also illustrated (p. 144).

It might be tempting to say that Fenton's success in the 1990s was propelled by its colors, such as Cranberry and the various shades of pink, blue, and green. Colors, however, are just part of the story. One must also consider the many decorations which graced articles in the Fenton line. Furthermore, there were several innovative combinations, such as handpainting on Cranberry glass, which had not been in the Fenton line previously.

The concept of "shape" must be added to color and decoration in the equation which explains Fenton's success during the 1990s decade. Designer Jon Saffell came to Fenton in 1994, and he created a number of new shapes for Fenton baskets and vases as well as a variety of interesting figurines and other products. Moreover, skilled workers in Fenton's Hot Metal department mastered new crimping techniques and developed some innovative handles for both baskets and bells.

New Fenton colors or decorative treatments are often introduced in the general catalog which is distributed to Fenton sales reps in December and mailed to Fenton dealers in January. On other occasions, the new colors and treatments debut in a mid–year catalog supplement. Sometimes a new color is introduced and then a decorative treatment on that color comes along shortly thereafter.

Collectors should note that some colors or decorative treatments in the Fenton line beginning in 1993 have been used for limited edition Family

Signature Series items. This occurs when a color or decorative treatment is used for a piece which is then inscribed with the year and the signature of a Fenton family member (see Chapter 35).

Rather than discuss each Fenton catalog and supplement in chronological order, the remainder of this chapter will detail the key color trends of Fenton glass during the 1990s decade as well as those portions of the line directed at Easter, Christmas and other gift–giving occasions.

Without doubt, the continuous presence of Cranberry and the pervasiveness of various pink hues are among the top stories. There were other episodes, however, ranging from greens and blues to some other treatments, which left their respective marks in Fenton history.

Constantly Cranberry

"Year in and year out," as Don Fenton said in 1991, "Cranberry is our number one color among those who purchase Fenton glass for themselves or as a gift." The 1990s decade is a strong testimony to Don's statement, for this gold–based color remained in the Fenton line during every year of the 1990s decade (see pp. 34–35, 45, 52, and 74–75). The shapes varied from year to year, and the color code (CC) remained the same, although the 1990–91 name "Country Cranberry" became simply "Cranberry" for the rest of the decade. Cranberry Opalescent was also in the Fenton line during 1990–93 (see p. 36) and again during 1995–97.

In the 1993 Fenton General Catalog, three Cranberry items (including the 1640 C1 Family Signature Series item) were shown with a hand-painted decoration (see Figs. 209–211). No name was given for the decoration, and it was not described in the catalog. In 1994, however, Fenton unveiled four items called "Pansies on Cranberry," a decoration developed by Frances Burton. The Fenton catalog explained it this way: "For over 100 years Americans have been carrying on a love affair with Cranberry glass. We've added a new dimension to our most collectible glass by applying pure gold pansies with velvety touches of cream and violet. each flower is then touched with crystal ice for its sparkling finale."

The Pansies on Cranberry (CW) decoration caught on reasonably well with collectors, and it remained in the line throughout the 1990s, as the number of pieces offered grew from four in 1994 to ten in 1998 (see pp. 52 and 74). Eight pieces remained in the line in 1999, and Pansies on Cranberry was replaced by a new decoration, Provincial Floral on Cranberry, for the year 2000.

Rose Garden (EG), a decorated motif designed by Frances Burton for opal satin glass, was closely associated with Cranberry in Fenton catalogs during 1995 and thereafter. Indeed, Fenton dealers often display Rose Garden and Cranberry pieces together, and the articles complement each other quite well (see p. 75). The 1999 catalog called Rose Garden "one of Fenton's most popular handpainted patterns" and noted the balance of design in which "blushing and pinstriping offset the delicate roses."

In the 1994 Fenton General Catalog, Rose Garden was shown with Fuschia (EH), a vivid, new Fenton color that a novice collector might mistake for Cranberry Opalescent (see Figs. 294–301). Fuschia was produced by covering gold ruby glass with Rose Magnolia, an opalescent glass color. The Fuschia items were blown and quite difficult to make, so this color was in the line only during 1994.

Persistent Pinks

As mentioned earlier, Dusty Rose (DK) was one of the most popular Fenton colors in both the 1980s and the 1990s. Even though Empress Rose (CP) replaced it in 1998, Dusty Rose was at the forefront of several pink hues which defined much of Fenton glass in the 1990s (see p. 72). The strength of the pink colors was augmented by handpainted decorations featuring pink as well as an opalescent effect called Trellis, which was a strong seller following its introduction in 1995.

A soft opaque color, Shell Pink, and its decorated counterpart, Pearly Sentiments (PT), which has applied porcelain roses (see Figs. 1–12), were in the Fenton line in the early 1990. A short–lived decoration called Watercolors (PF) on satin–finished pink was in the Fenton line during 1990 (see Figs. 13–22). Several new pink colors were soon to come.

In 1990–91, a new transparent color called Petal Pink (PN) made its debut (see p. 39). More shapes

This Cranberry Opalescent five–piece Fern water set (1804 CR) was shown in the 1992 Fenton General Catalog and listed as "retired" the following year. Note the nine curved petals in the daisy on the pitcher.

Cranberry items from the 1993 Fenton General Catalog. Note the three decorated items in the upper right.

were added to the grouping in 1991, and a decorated version, Arbor Blossom on Petal Pink (JY), was also produced (see p. 39). Both remained in the Fenton line for the next two years, and, in 1994, the Arbor Blossom decoration was replaced by Violas on Petal Pink (PU). Violas lasted just a year, and Petal Pink was out of the line at the end of 1995 (see p. 50).

An iridized version of the Petal Pink color, Pink Pearl (HZ), was in the line during 1992. An iridized version of Dusty Rose, the color Rose Pearl (DN) was in the line during 1993; a decorated version called Vining Hearts (DW) was created by Martha Reynolds (see p. 47).

In 1994, Rose Magnolia (RV) entered the Fenton line after having been offered in the Hobnail pattern as an Historic Collection color in 1993. Rose Magnolia (see Figs. 314–325) is a strong opalescent pink made with neodymium, a rare earth element. A new decoration, Primrose (DS) was on the facing page in the Fenton catalog (see Figs. 326–338).

Beginning in 1995, four Trellis (DX) pieces in blown glass combined an opalescent lattice effect

Trellis makes its debut.

with crests and/or handles in Dusty Rose and a handpainted floral motif in light fuschia. Two animal figurines in French Opalescent with handpainted decoration completed the Trellis grouping. Items were added in 1996, and Trellis continued to grow in 1997–98 as some items were dropped and others added. More than a dozen different items were available in 1999, making Trellis one of Fenton's major successes of the last half of the 1990s.

Dusty Rose was also used as an overlay color with Milk Glass in 1996–97, and these items were decorated. At first, there were three items in Martha Reynold's Asters on Rose Overlay (DP), but three others, including a lamp, were pictured in the 1997 Fenton General Catalog.

Another pink hue (see p. 67) of the 1990s was Champagne Satin (PQ), an opalescent color which was introduced in 1996. A decorated version, Field Flowers on Champagne Satin (PI), came into the line in 1997. Martha Reynolds designed Field Flowers on Champagne Satin, and it remained in the line until the close of 1998. Champagne Satin continued through 1999 and some items were still in the Fenton line during the year 2000.

Great Greens

The were no green hues in the 1990–91 Fenton catalog, but the January 1991 Catalog Supplement featured Vining Garden on its front cover. The first two pages of the catalog were devoted entirely to three new treatments: a transparent light green called Sea Mist Green (LE); a decorated version named Vining Garden (FP); and Sea Mist Opalescent (LO). Sea Mist Green coordinated well with Meadow Blossom (SF), an opal satin blushed with pink and decorated with handpainted green leaves and floral blossoms (see Figs. 157–168).

Frances Burton's innovative Vining Garden motif on transparent Sea Mist Green features dark green leaves and flowers with relatively large petals. The petals are handpainted by applying two different colors simultaneously using a round brush. The decorators make this technique look almost effortless, and the result is a remarkably smooth, lifelike blend of colors on the delicate flowers (see Fig. 468-469).

A satin–finished color, Sea Mist Green Satin (ZL) appeared in Fenton advertising during the spring of 1991 and was shown in the June 1991 Fenton Catalog Supplement (see Figs. 88–93). This color was discontinued in late 1992.

Sea Mist Opalescent was also in the line only through 1992, but both Sea Mist Green and Vining Garden proved hardy indeed. The Vining Garden decoration was replaced by Morning Glories (L3) on Sea Mist Green in January 1997. Both Morning Glories and Sea Mist Green were discontinued at the end of 1997 (see p. 67).

Green lived on during 1998 as crests and handles for the handpainted Meadow Beauty glassware. The Meadow Beauty (PD) decoration was designed by Robin Spindler. The floral motif was set off nicely by French Opalescent glass, and rib or swirl optic effects added to the interest of the blown items.

In 1995, the Vining Garden motif was also used

Sea Mist Opalescent items from a 1991 Fenton Catalog Supplement.

on three blown items in a new color, Thistle (FS). The color was created by covering a bud of gold ruby glass with Sea Mist Green so as to hold the ruby color at the top of the item when blowing the item to its final shape. One of the Thistle items, a graceful pitcher (1566 FS) with a French curl handle, was part of the Family Signature Series.

Although Thistle was soon discontinued due to difficulties in production, the color ultimately led to the limited edition Historic Collection color Rubina Verde, which was introduced in mid–1997. The development of these glassmaking procedures helped pave the way for other colors using the "fade" technique which were in the Fenton Historic Collection groupings later in the 1990s decade.

As discussed later in this chapter, Spruce Green was an important part of Fenton's regular line for Christmas beginning in 1995. This color was also used to make Carnival glass (see Chapter 38). Opaque Sea Green Satin was a Fenton Historic Collection color for 1998 (see Chapter 33).

Beautiful Blues

Blues have long been an important part of the Fenton color story, and the blues of the 1990s decade are no exception, for several new blue colors were developed. Both Salem Blue and Blue Royale were shown in the 1990–91 Fenton General Catalog, and they are pictured in *Fenton Glass: The 1980s Decade* (pp. 135 and 141).

Twilight Blue (TB) and its decorated counterpart, Twilight Tulips (TT), led off the 1992 Fenton General Catalog (see Figs. 169–178). Many of the same shapes appeared in the 1993 and 1994 General Catalogs, along with some additional items. A group of pressed Twilight Blue items was pictured with Martha Reynolds' Cottage Scene (Z8) decoration in the 1994 catalog. The blue sky in the handpainted scene on satin–finished milk glass coordinated nicely with the dark Twilight Blue.

Blue was a major color statement for Fenton in 1995. Celeste Blue Stretch was an Historic Collection offering, and the 1995 General Catalog featured Cobalt (KN) and its decorated counterpart, Golden Flax on Cobalt (KG), which was designed by Frances Burton (see p. 58). These were continued into 1996, and new shapes were added. Burton also designed the Mountain Berry (KT) decoration on the three items in Gold Overlay glass (see p. 61), which were illustrated with Cobalt in the 1996 Fenton General Catalog

Iridescent Misty Blue Satin (LR) was introduced in 1997, and the catalog described the color as a "soft, feminine blue." A decorated version, Irises on Misty Blue Satin (LS), which was created by Martha Reynolds, was also available (see p. 66). Misty Blue Satin was produced for some Easter items in 1997, too. Both Misty Blue Satin and Irises on Misty Blue Satin remained in the Fenton line through 1999.

A transparent color called Ice Blue with Bellflowers decoration (LH) was introduced in 1999 (see p. 73). The color and Martha Reynolds' decoration went nicely with Misty Blue Satin, and they were shown together in the 1999 General Catalog.

Cobalt Blue (KN) made its reappearance in the 1999 Fenton General Catalog, for collectors wanted

(text continued on p. 27)

The short–lived Thistle color appeared only in the 1995 Fenton General Catalog where it was shown with Sea Mist Green items.

Twilight Blue and Twilight Tulips from the 1992 Fenton General Catalog.

Bellflowers

Clear icy blue is decorated to coordinate with Misty Blue Satin. The clean crisp look of clear water offsets the satin shimmer of Misty Blue adding a new texture and interest to the grouping. Designed by Martha Reynolds, each fresh Spring bouquet features tiny enameled beads for added depth.

6702 LH
Lamp, Paisley, 20"

7682 LH
Vase, Melon, 11"

6864 LH
Bell, Melon, 6"

2777 LH
Basket, 7"

7565 LH
Vase, Reverse Melon, 8"

3272 LH
Pitcher, Melon, 5½"

5136 LH
Elephant, 3½"

5151 LH
Bear, 3½"

Save 3%!
0853 AS
9 Pc. Bellflowers Assortment

New Handpainted "Bellflowers" coordinates with Misty Blue Satin

FENTON — Handcrafted Glass Artistry Since 1905

Bellflowers items from the 1999 Fenton General Catalog.

more of this popular color and the company responded. A blue–green hue called Aquamarine (AA) was introduced at the same time, although a few gift items, such as trinket boxes, had been made in Aquamarine during 1998.

The Aquamarine and Cobalt colors were combined in yet another new Fenton creation, Tranquility (see p. 73). The blown Tranquility items (AL) have a fade effect because Aquamarine is gathered over Cobalt prior to blowing the item to its final shape. Other Tranquility items (AK), featured a Cobalt edge produced by spinning a ring or crest on the edge of the article before finishing.

Plum

The 1993 Fenton General catalog devoted two of its first three pages to the new Plum (PL) and its decorated counterpart, Vintage (PV), which was designed by Frances Burton (see p. 46). Plum glass was also used as a crest on Milk Glass, and these items were decorated for a new grouping called Handpainted Lilacs (PJ). The decoration, designed by Martha Reynolds, featured subtle changes in color within the clusters of delicate flowers (see p. 46).

Plum, Vintage, and Lilacs sold reasonably well in 1993–95. In 1996, Plum remained in the line while Vintage and Lilacs dropped out, but a new decoration, Pansies (PF), was created to coordinate with Plum (see p. 63). They were joined in 1997 by Frances Burton's handpainted Sweetbrier (P9) decoration on Plum Overlay glass (see p. 68), and all three of these continued through 1998. Still another Plum treatment, Plum Carnival (PX), was in the Fenton line during 1998 (see Chapter 38).

Closely related to Plum are Violet Satin, an Historic Collection color for 1999 (see Chapter 33) and Violet, which went into the Fenton line for the year 2000.

Milk Glass

As mentioned earlier in this chapter, Milk Glass was one of the most popular colors in Fenton history. Indeed, the Hobnail pattern in Milk Glass could be called Fenton's "flagship" line for the 1950s and 1960s, and some Hobnail Milk Glass items continued to be available in both the 1970s and the 1980s. Another Fenton staple was Silver Crest, which has an edge of pure crystal on Milk Glass items in generally plain shapes.

The lone Milk Glass item in the Fenton General Catalog for 1990–91 was a Gone with the Wind lamp in Hobnail (3808 MI). In 1992, however, the General Catalog pictured eleven items in Silver Crest, including three decorated with a handpainted blue floral motif (these have color code ES and were from the Elizabeth Collection introduced in 1990–91). Furthermore, a Fenton sales sheet (see p. 44) offered more than a dozen items in Milk Glass Hobnail; these were also available in 1993, as were some pieces called Royal Hobnail (SC), which featured the crystal edge characteristically found on Silver Crest.

In 1994–95, Milk Glass Hobnail and Royal Hobnail appeared in Fenton catalog supplements with some Cranberry Opalescent items (see pp. 56–57). Except for the 3808 MI lamp, Milk Glass Hobnail was not in the Fenton catalogs for 1996–98.

A decorated Milk Glass grouping called Morning Mist (CG) made its debut in 1999 (see Figs. 672–675). Some of these items had the crystal edge associated with Silver Crest, and all were decorated with blue and green leaves "dappled with dew drops." Robin Spindler created this decoration.

In late 1999 and into the year 2000, responding to requests from collectors, the Fenton Gift Shop had some items produced in Milk Glass Hobnail through Fenton's Special Products department.

Other Colors and Decorations

A key element of Fenton's success over the years has been the company's ability to develop interesting glass colors and decorative treatments. The 1990s decade is noteworthy both for those mentioned above and those described in this section.

Mulberry (MG), a recreation of a Fenton color from the early 1940s, came into the Fenton line in 1989 and remained through 1992. The color was produced using techniques similar to that of Fenton's Cranberry. A small bud of gold ruby glass was covered with azure blue. The glassblowers sought to keep the cranberry color in the top half of the item so that the color would appear to blend smoothly into the rich blue below (see p. 37). This "fade" technique was employed to make the Mulberry color for the Fenton Historic Collection (mid–1996), as well as for Thistle, Rubina Verde, Gold Amberina, and some others during the 1990s.

Fenton's "Crackle Glass" in 1992 was a re–creation of a longstanding treatment whereby the gather of hot glass on a blowpipe is plunged into cold water (producing fine fractures in the glass) and then

Crackle items from 1992.

Silver Crest (SC) and Elizabeth Collection (ES) items from the 1992 Fenton General Catalog.

Morning Mist

Silvery blue and green leaves dappled with dew drops on a crisp white background. The peaceful simplicity we crave is captured in this creation from Robin Spindler. A pure crystal ring floats on the edge to complete its charm.

Morning Mist coordinates beautifully with Tranquility, Aquamarine and Cobalt.

3280 AL Pitcher, 9"
6548 CG Vase, 11"
4560 AK Bell, 6 3/4"
6530 CG Basket, Diamond, 7"
4769 CG Bell, 6 1/2"
5151 CG Bear, 3 1/2"
7484 CG Covered Box, 5"
6833 CG Basket, Ribbed, 8"
6505 CG Lamp, Student, 18"
5163 CG Bird, 4"
5290 CG Slipper, Cat, 6"
4566 CG Pitcher, 6" Family Signature Series Piece (Scott Fenton)

Save 3%! 0903 AS 18 Pc. Cobalt/Morning Mist Assortment

Morning Mist (CG) from the 1999 Fenton General catalog.

reheated to seal the cracks on the surface. Fenton added to the tradition of this classic treatment by employing an iridescent finish after the item was blown and finished to its final shape. Fenton's products–called Pink Crackle, Sea Mist Crackle, and Twilight Crackle–sold well in early 1992, and new shapes were added at mid–year (see p. 43).

Two rich colors, Autumn Gold (AM) and Autumn Gold Opalescent (AO), were introduced in the 1994 General Catalog (see pp. 54–55). All of the Autumn Gold items were made as pressed glass, and this color was also used for the handles and edges of three Hobnail baskets in French Opalescent. The blown Autumn Gold Opalescent items were made by gathering French Opalescent over Autumn Gold, inserting the gather into a ribbed optic mould, chilling the glass followed by reheating, and, finally, blowing the piece to its final shape. These treatments were short–lived in the Fenton line, and in retrospect, they may have been a bit ahead of their time.

At several times during the 1990s, black glass with vivid handpainted decorations was part of the Fenton line. Copper Rose (KP), which was in the General Catalogs from 1990–91 through 1993, featured a pink floral and copper bands (see *Fenton Glass: The 1980s Decade*, p. 135). A new decorative creation from Martha Reynolds, Autumn Leaves on Black (AW), came into the line in 1994 (see Figs. 256–267) and was shown with both Autumn Gold and Autumn Gold Opalescent, both of which were discussed in the previous paragraph in this chapter.

In 1995, several of the shapes used for Autumn Leaves on Black, along with other items, were used for Victorian Bouquet (BT), a new decoration on black glass (see p. 60). The 1996 Medallion Collection contained two decorated animal figurines, the 5226 Fox and 5258 Owl, which were made of black glass. The 5165 Cat was added in 1997, as well as a vase (7565 X5) which was in both the Medallion Collection and the Family Signature Series (see Fig. 1007).

There are also some noteworthy Fenton decorations from the 1990s decade. Many of these have already been mentioned in the discussion of Fenton colors or because they were coordinated with key Fenton colors.

Kristen's Floral (YB) was introduced in 1995. Martha Reynolds created this decoration, which featured raised peach and pink enameled flowers and 22k gold highlights on satin–finished Ivory glass (see p. 59). The decorating process requires separate firing steps for the paint and the gold. The shapes from 1995 were continued through 1996, and the grouping was then discontinued.

In 1999, a new decoration called Martha's Rose (AZ) was introduced. Like Trellis and Meadow Beauty, Martha's Rose is French Opalescent and the blown pieces feature crests and handles from a color in the Fenton line (in this case, Aquamarine). The floral motif (see Figs. 670–671) was created by Martha Reynolds to coordinate with Fenton's Champagne Satin glass.

LifeStyles

In mid–1998, Fenton launched a special area of the Fenton line called "LifeStyles." For the most part, these were relatively large items (such as vases) or accessories intended for home decor (see p. 70).

The twelve–page Fenton LifeStyles catalog led with items in Sea Green Satin and Royal Purple,

This postcard was used to publicize the Fenton LifeStyles line.

which were also the two Fenton Historic Collection colors initiated in January 1998. Martha Reynolds created a decoration called Watercolors for some of these Sea Green Satin items, and Robin Spindler developed a stylized motif called Leaves for three of the nine Royal Purple items.

Satin–finished French Opalescent (called the "Pinstripe Collection") and Cranberry rounded out the LifeStyles grouping. All told, there were some 38 different items in the LifeStyles offering (see p. 70 for some of these). Fenton sales reps were challenged to broaden Fenton's market by soliciting orders for LifeStyles from stores which specialized in home decor. As it turned out, however, Fenton collectors were the major purchasers of LifeStyles pieces, and few accounts were secured specifically in the home decor area.

Easter and Christmas

During the 1990s decade, Fenton produced quite a few items for the Easter and Christmas holidays. Some of these were limited editions (see Chapter 36), but many Easter and Christmas items in the Fenton line were intended as decorative accessories or for gifts.

(text continued on page 146)

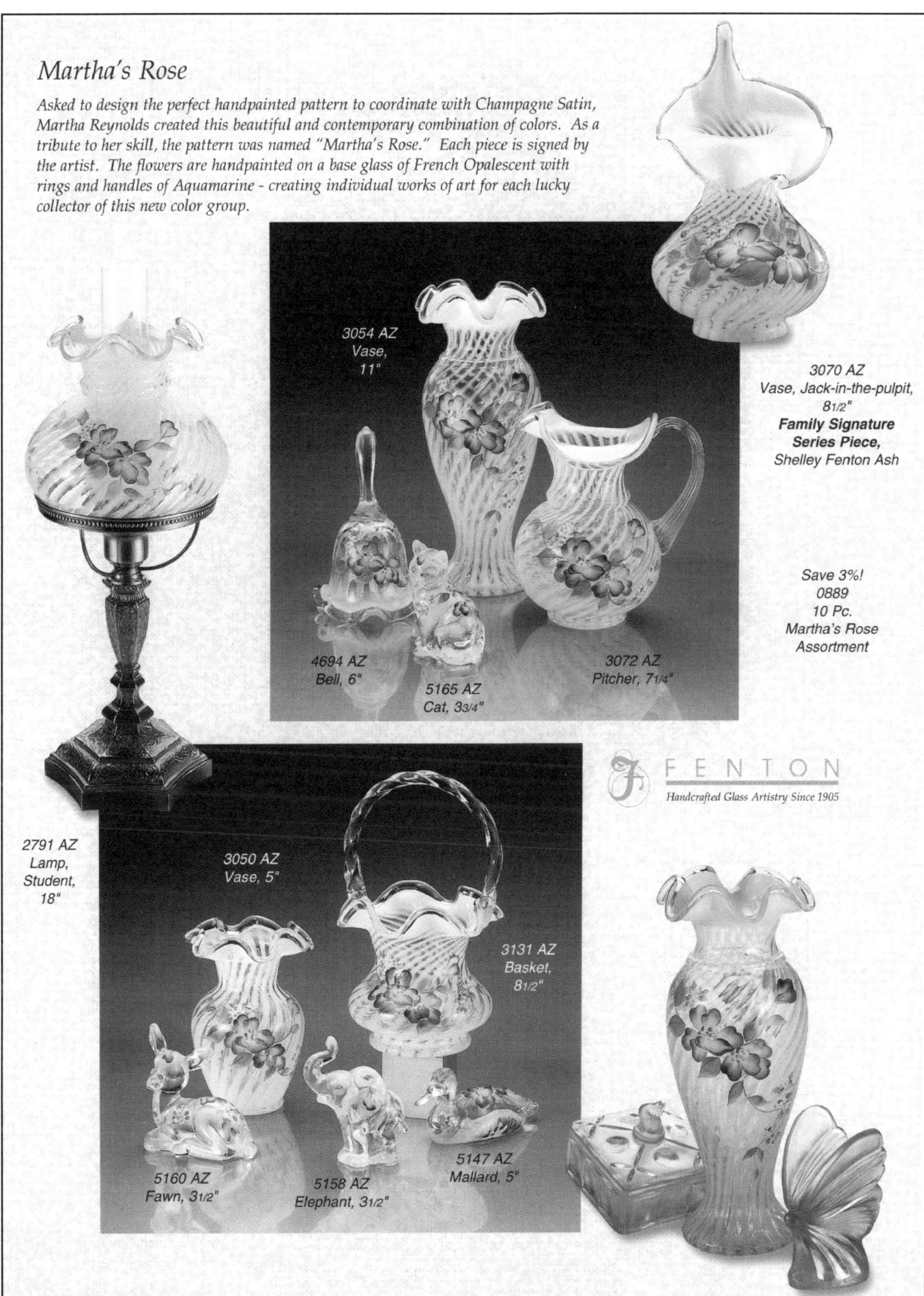

Martha's Rose (AZ) from the 1999 Fenton General Catalog.

(Chapter 32 continued on page 146)

NOTES ON THE COLOR PLATES

The 112 color pages in this book capture the breadth, depth, diversity, and beauty of Fenton glass in the 1990s decade.

You will see more than seven hundred items from the Fenton line (pp. 33–77) in a wide variety of colors. You will also see many limited edition items: Historic Colors (pp. 78–96), Connoisseur Collection (pp. 97–108), Family Signature Series (pp. 109–112), and Designer Series Bells (p. 121) as well as limited editions for occasions such as Easter, Mother's Day or Christmas. Also pictured are many other interesting items such as Fall Lamp Specials, the Millennium Collection, Fenton Showcase Dealer Exclusives, Family Signing Event pieces, and Glass Messenger Subscriber Exclusives. Several pages are devoted to Fenton items made for QVC (pp. 137–142), including the Diamond Jubilee Collection and the New Century Collection.

Almost all of the glass pictured was drawn from Fenton's own storage archives. Additionally, some Fenton glass collectors loaned items for the photography sessions, which required several days at the Fenton plant and at The Glass Press photo studio in Marietta.

Original color transparencies from Fenton catalogs, catalog supplements and other promotional materials made it possible to include some items or treatments that would not otherwise have been available. Because these transparencies were taken separately for various purposes, you will notice somewhat different size characteristics and "props" (flowers, candy, etc.).

The captions on each page identify the articles pictured and provide Fenton's ware numbers and color codes. Dates given generally reflect the time when the piece was first listed in a Fenton catalog or catalog supplement or was being made for a special promotion. Consult the Index in this book to locate discussions of specific items or colors in the various chapters or the locations of other illustrations.

These Pearly Sentiments (PT) items are from the 1990-91 Fenton General Catalog.

1. 9763 PT 3½" petite Heart bell.
2. 9764 PT 5½" large Heart bell.
3. 9539 PT 7" h. Leaf basket.
4. 5160 PT 3½" Fawn.
5. 5165 PT 3¾" Cat.
6. 5151 PT 3½" Bear cub.
7. 5163 PT 4" Bird.
8. 5197 PT 6" Happiness Bird.
9. 5780 PT 3¾" Heart box.
10. 5119 PT 4" Kitten.
11. 5233 PT 4" reclining Bear cub.
12. 9295 PT 6" Rose slipper.

These Watercolors (PF) items are from the 1990-91 Fenton General Catalog.

13. 7630 PF 7" Aurora basket.
14. 9667 PF 6" Aurora bell.
15. 7250 PF 8" tulip vase.
16. 5165 PF 3½" Cat.
17. 9589 PF 4½" oval trinket.
18. 7662 PF 4½" petite bell.
19. 8691 PF 4½" alarm clock.
20. 7620 PF 4" Aurora vase.
21. 9229 PF 7" Empress comport.
22. 7410 PF 20" student lamp.

These Cranberry (CC) items were in the Fenton line in 1990-91.

23. 1400 CC 20" Coin Dot lamp.
24. 8251 CC 9½" Mandarin vase.
25. 9666 CC 5" Sandwich pitcher.
26. 2001 CC 17" Feather lamp.
27. 3108 CC 30" Spiral pillar lamp.

28. 9500 CC 3" Leaf salt and pepper shakers.	**33.** 9050 CC 5½" Flute and Dot vase.
29. 8252 CC 7½" Empress vase.	**34.** 9754 CC 6¼" Caprice vase with bow.
30. 1478 CC 8½" Coin Dot vase.	**35.** 1860 CC 4¼" Fern pitcher.
31. 2557 CC 6" Daisy vase.	**36.** 3132 CC 8¾" basket.
32. 9752 CC 7¾" Daffodil vase.	**37.** 1432 CC 32 oz. Coin Dot pitcher.

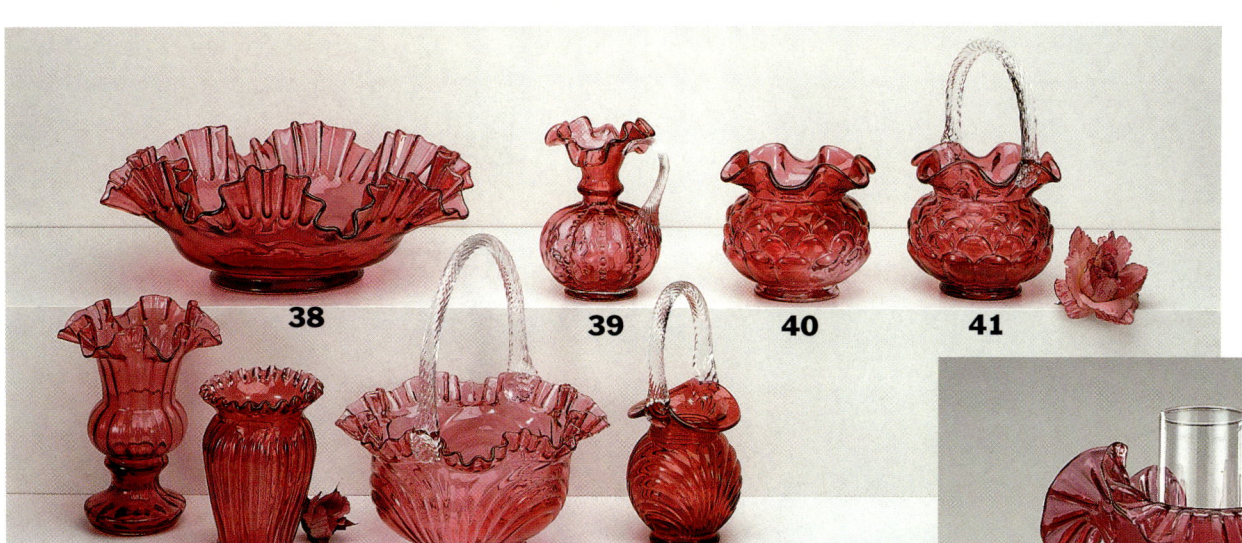

These Cranberry (CC) items were in the Fenton line in 1990-91.

- **38.** 1728 CC 10" Diamond bowl.
- **39.** 2566 CC 6" Daisy handled jug.
- **40.** 9452 CC 4½" Jacqueline vase.
- **41.** 9434 CC 8¼" h. Jacqueline basket.
- **42.** 1553 CC 6½" rib urn vase.
- **43.** 9055 CC 5½" ribbed vase.
- **44.** 9730 CC 9½" Caprice basket.
- **45.** 9732 CC 8½" Caprice basket.

46. 9218 CC 20" Rose student lamp.

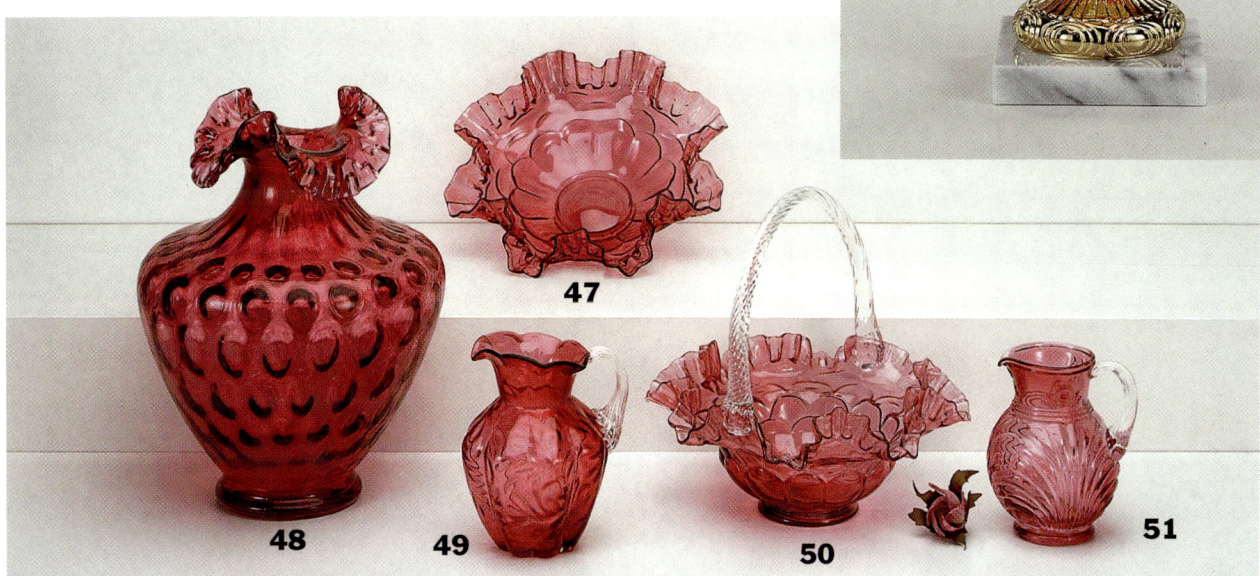

- **47.** 9442 CC 9½" Jacqueline bowl.
- **48.** 1443 CC 10½" Coin Dot vase.
- **49.** 1866 CC Fern pitcher.
- **50.** 9464 CC 8½" h. Jacqueline basket.
- **51.** 9760 CC 4½" Caprice pitcher.

These Cranberry Opalescent (CR) items were in the Fenton line in 1991.

52. 1840 CR 10 oz. tumbler.
53. 1874 CR 70 oz. pitcher.

54. 1852 CR 11" Fern optic vase.

55. 8354 CR 9" Basketweave vase.
56. 1872 CR 32 oz. Fern pitcher.
57. 2071 CR 4½" pitcher.
58. 1784 CR 4" vase.
59. 1800 CR 23½" Gone with the Wind Lamp.

These Cranberry Opalescent (CR) items were in the Fenton line during 1990-91.

60. 1726 CR 10" diamond optic bowl.
61. 2095 CR drapery optic cruet with stopper.
62. 1353 CR 10" fine dot tulip vase.
63. 1354 CR 7" dot optic vase.
64. 1739 CR diamond optic basket.
65. 1799 CR 6" diamond optic vase.
66. 3133 CR 6" spiral basket.
67. 3163 CR 16 oz. spiral pitcher.
68. 3161 CR 11" spiral vase.

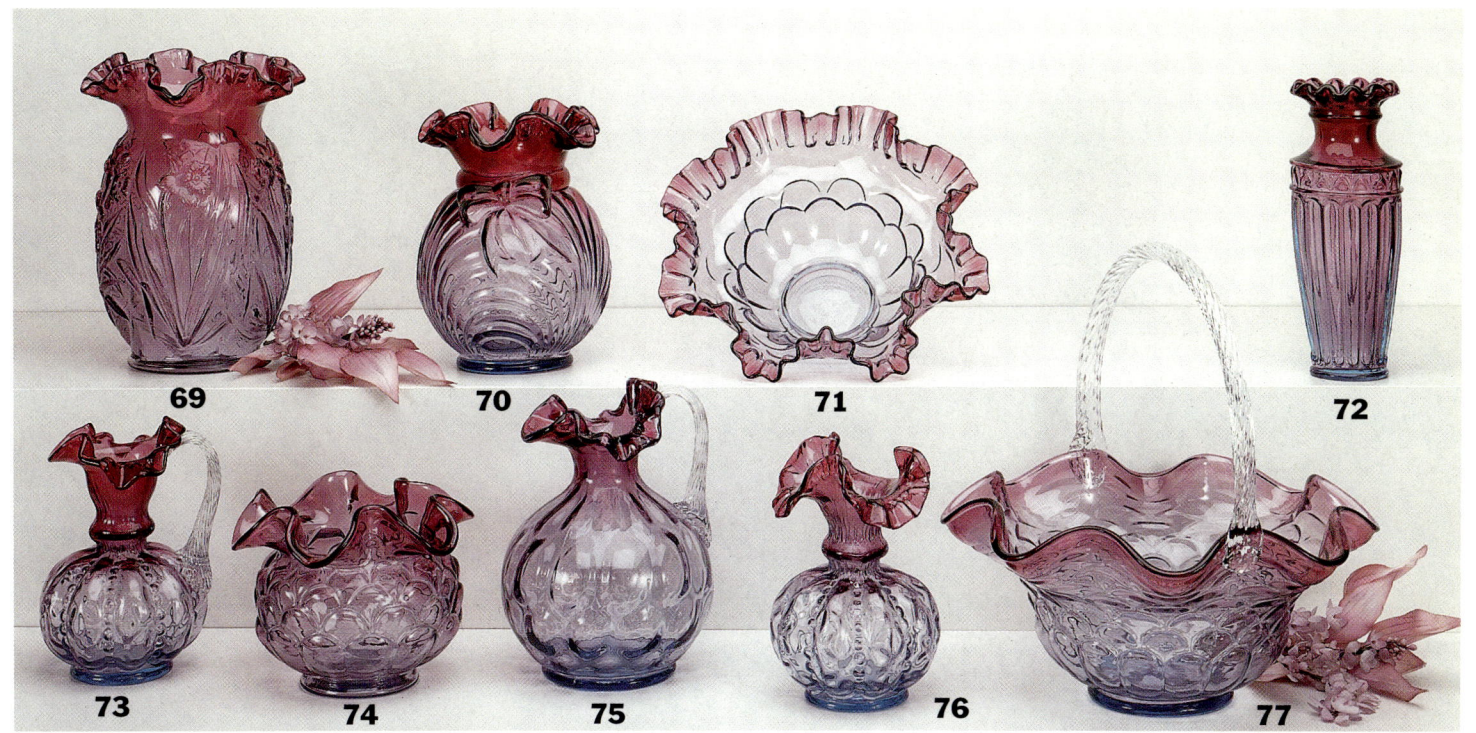

These Mulberry (MG) items are from the 1990-91 Fenton General Catalog.

69. 9752 MG Daffodil vase.
70. 9754 MG 6" Caprice vase with bow.
71. 9442 MG 9½" Jacqueline bowl.
72. 9655 MG 7½" vase.
73. 2566 MG 6" handled Daisy jug.
74. 9452 MG 4½" Jacqueline vase.
75. 1432 MG 32 oz. Coin Dot pitcher.
76. 2557 MG 6" Beaded Melon vase.
77. 9139 MG 10½" h. Jacqueline basket.

78. 3108 MG 30" h. Spiral pillar lamp.
79. 9218 MG 20" Rose student lamp.

These Mulberry (MG) items are from Fenton's January, 1991, Catalog Supplement.

80. 2095 MG cruet with stopper
81. 9464 MG 8½" Jacqueline basket.
82. 3161 MG 11" Spiral vase.
83. 1784 MG 4" vase.
84. 1738 MG Diamond basket
85. 2071 MG 4½" pitcher.
86. 1705 MG 21" lamp with prisms.

This Sea Mist Opalescent (LO) vase appeared in Fenton's January, 1991, Catalog Supplement.

94.   8354 LO 9" Basketweave vase.

These Jade Opaline (AP) items were shown in Fenton's June, 1990, Catalog Supplement.

95.   7536 AP 8½" square basket.
96.   9758 AP 8" stylized vase.

These Sea Mist Green Satin (ZL) items were shown in Fenton sales materials from May, 1991.

87.   3210 ZL 21" student lamp.
88.   3254 ZL 11" vase.
89.   3233 ZL 8" basket.
90.   1556 ZL 10" tulip vase.
91.   3221 ZL 9½" bowl.
92.   3231 ZL 6" basket.
93.   3265 ZL 32 oz. pitcher.

These Petal Pink (PN) and Arbor Blossoms on Petal Pink (JY) items are from the 1992 Fenton General Catalog.

- **97.** 8379 PN 6" Valencia comport.
- **98.** 3231 JY 6" basket.
- **99.** 1556 JY 10" tulip vase.
- **100.** 3234 JY 7¾" basket.
- **101.** 9667 JY 7" Aurora bell.
- **102.** 3263 JY 6" vase.
- **103.** 5197 PN 6" Happiness Bird.
- **104.** 3265 JY 32 oz. pitcher.
- **105.** 9071 PN 8½" candleholders.

These Petal Pink (PN) items are from the 1990-91 Fenton General Catalog.

- **106.** 9780 PN 5½" Heart comport.
- **107.** 9764 PN 5½" Heart bell.
- **108.** C9240 PN 6½" Rose basket with bath items.
- **109.** C9237 PN 8½" large Rose basket with bath items.
- **110.** 5240 PN 6½" open Bird.
- **111.** 5239 PN 4" Bear cub.
- **112.** 5151 PN 3½" sitting Bear cub.
- **113.** 9763 PN 3¼" Petite Heart bell.
- **114.** 5233 PN 4" reclining Bear cub.
- **115.** 9295 PN 6" Rose slipper.

39

These items in Shell Pink (PE), Iridized Jade Opaline (EZ), and handpainted White Pearlized (BT) were for Easter, 1991.

116. 5186 EZ 5½" Hen on nest.
117. 4685 EZ 3½" h. Chick out of egg.
118. 4680 EZ 8½" l. Covered rooster box.
119. 5213 EZ 2½" Mini chick.
120. 5212 EZ 2½" Mini duckling.
121. 5211 TZ 2½" Mini hen.
122. 4670 EZ 8" Rabbit tray.

123. 4670 PE 8" Rabbit tray.
124. 5213 PE 2½" mini Chick.
125. 5211 PE 2½" mini Hen.
126. 5212 PE 2½" mini Duckling.
127. 4680 PE 8½" Rooster covered box.
128. 4685 PE 3½" Chick out of egg.
129. 5186 PE 5½" Hen on nest.

130. 4680 EZ 8½" l. covered Rooster box.
131. 5140 PM 3½" Egg on stand.
132. 4683 BT 7" Bunny covered box.
133. 5162 PM 3¾" Bunny.
134. 5163 PM 4" Bird.
135A. 5169 PM 3¼" Duckling.
135B. 5212 EZ 2½" mini Duckling.
136. 5186 PE 5½" Hen on nest.

These items in Jade Pearl (EZ) and Violets on Iridized Opal (Q6) were made for Easter, 1992.

- **137.** 4683 C9 7" handpainted Bunny covered box.
- **138.** 4680 EZ 8½" Rooster covered box.
- **139.** 4683 EZ 7" Bunny covered box.
- **140.** 5186 EZ 5½" Hen on nest.
- **141.** 4685 EZ 3½" Chick out of egg.
- **142.** 5163 Q6 4" Bird.
- **143.** 5213 EZ 2½" mini Chick.
- **144.** 5211 EZ 2½" mini Hen.
- **145.** 5162 Q6 3½" Bunny.
- **146.** 5212 EZ 2½" mini Duckling.
- **147.** 5169 Q6 3" Duckling.

These items in Pink Pearl (HZ) and handpainted White Pearlized (BT) were made for Easter, 1992.

- **148.** 4680 BT 8½" handpainted Rooster covered box.
- **149.** 5257 HZ standing Rooster (not in line; samples only).
- **150.** 4680 HZ 8½" Rooster covered box.
- **151.** 5211 HZ 2½" mini Hen.
- **152.** 5213 HZ 2½" mini Chick.
- **153.** 5186 HZ 5½" Hen on nest.
- **154.** 4683 HZ 7" Bunny covered box.
- **155.** 5212 HZ 2½" mini Duckling.
- **156.** 4685 HZ Chick out of egg.

These Meadow Blossom (SF) items were shown in the January, 1991, Fenton Catalog Supplement.

157.	7662 SF 4" bell.	**161.**	5119 SF 4" Kitten.	**165.**	5233 SF 4" reclining Bear.
158.	7250 SF 8" tulip vase.	**162.**	5197 SF 6" Happiness Bird.	**166.**	4638 SF 5" Victorian alarm clock.
159.	5163 SF 4" Bird.	**163.**	6761 SF 7" Paisley bell.	**167.**	9589 SF 4½" oval trinket.
160.	1628 SF 6" comport.	**164.**	9295 SF 6" Rose slipper.	**168.**	9238 SF 6½" Panelled basket.

These Twilight Tulips (TT) and Twilight Blue (TB) items were shown in the 1992 Fenton General Catalog.

169.	3260 TT 10½" vase.	**171.**	6572 TT 10½" footed basket.	**175.**	5152 TB 5" Whale.
170.	6780 TB 7" Paisley candy with cover.	**172.**	9295 TT 6" Rose slipper.	**176.**	3265 TT 32 oz. pitcher.
		173.	6761 TB 7" Paisley bell.	**177.**	5151 TB 3½" sitting Bear.
		174.	4655 TB 7½" Daffodil vase.	**178.**	9071 TB 8½" candleholders.

These are Sea Mist Crackle (L4).

179. 7648 L4 4" pitcher.
180. 7644 L4 5" vase.
181. 7643 L4 8" basket.
182. 7649 L4 9½" vase.
183. 7647 L4 8½" Pinch vase.
184. 7645 L4 4½" vase.

Fenton offered "Crackle glass" in three colors in the June, 1992, Catalog Supplement.

These are Pink Crackle (P8).

185. 7476 P8 14½" vase.
186. 7479 P8 10½" vase.
187. 7483 P8 10½" pitcher.
188. 7477 P8 14" vase.
189. 7576 P8 11" basket.

These are Twilight Crackle (T6).

190. 7643 T6 8" basket.
191. 7649 T6 9½" vase.
192. 7645 T6 4½" vase.
193. 7644 T6 5" vase.
194. 7648 T6 4" pitcher.
195. 7647 T6 8½" Pinch vase.

These Milk Glass Hobnail items were in the Fenton line in 1992.

196.	3807 MI 21" Student lamp.	**202.**	3336 MI 6½" basket.
197.	3365 MI 6" pitcher.	**203.**	3638 MI 8½" basket.
198.	3752 MI 11" vase.	**204.**	3355 MI 6" Hand vase.
199.	3734 MI 12" basket.	**205.**	3995 MI slipper.
200.	3000 MI pitcher and bowl set.	**206.**	3335 MI basket with looped handle.
201.	3356 MI 7½" jack-in-the-pulpit vase.	**207.**	3645 MI 6" bell.
		208.	3907 MI 26" Pillar lamp.

These decorated Cranberry items were in the Fenton line in 1993.

209. 1749 C1 9" diamond optic pinch vase.
210. 1640 C1 11" rib vase (George Fenton signature).
211. 1748 C1 Beaded Melon basket.

These Cranberry items were in the Fenton line in 1992.

212. 9752 CC 7¾" vase.
213. 2557 CC 6" Daisy vase.
214. 3167 CC 6½" ribbed vase.
215. 1434 CC 8" Coin Dot basket.
216. 1443 CC 10½" Coin Dot vase.
217. 9442 CC 9½" Jacqueline bowl.
218. 1432 CC 32 oz. pitcher.
219. 6590 CC 6" spiral bell.
220. 3183 CC 6½" tulip vase.
221. 9754 CC 6¼" Caprice vase with bow.

These handpainted Lilacs (PJ) items were shown in the 1993 Fenton General Catalog.

222. 6730 PJ 8½" Paisley basket.
223. 9229 PJ 6½" Empress comport.
224. 6570 PJ 4½" Panelled Grape puff box.
225. 5151 PJ 3½" Bear.
226. 2746 PJ 7" Paisley bell.
227. 5163 PJ 4" Bird.
228. 9295 PJ 6" Rose slipper.

These Plum (PL) and handpainted Vintage (PV) items appeared in the 1993 Fenton General Catalog.

229. 7630 PV 7" Aurora basket.
230. 1792 PL 11" Diamond vase.
231. 1789 PL 6" Melon vase.
232. 1785 PV 8" Diamond vase.
233. 1706 PV 17" Diamond lamp.
234. 7620 PL 4" Aurora vase.
235. 9229 PV 6½" comport.
236. 7463 PV 6" bell.
237. 9578 PL 4¼" two-way candleholder.
238. 9295 PV 6" Rose slipper.

These Rose Pearl (DN) and handpainted Vining Hearts (DW) items were shown in the 1993 Fenton General Catalog.

239. 8466 DN 7" Fabergé bell.
240. 7630 DW 7" handpainted Aurora basket.
241. 6564 DN 8" Elite vase.
242. 9229 DW 6½" handpainted comport.
243. 1992 DN 2½" Daisy and Button hat.
244. 7620 DW 4" handpainted Aurora vase.
245. 5786 DN 3¾" Hummingbird trinket box.
246. 5243 DW 3½" handpainted Cat.
247. 9185 DN 9" Panelled Daisy candy with cover.

These Rose Pearl (DN) and handpainted Vining Hearts (DW) items were shown in the 1993 Fenton General Catalog.

248. 9120 DN 6" Fine Cut and Block comport.
249. 6572 DW 10½" handpainted footed basket.
250. 9137 DN 8" Fine Cut and Block basket.
251. 2731 DN 6" Lamb's Tongue basket.
252. 1940 DN 8½" perfume with stopper.
253. 1995 DN 6" Daisy and Button slipper.
254. 9667 DW 7" handpainted Aurora bell.
255. 9102 DN 6" Fine Cut and Block fairy light.

These handpainted Autumn Leaves on Black (AW) items were shown in the 1994 Fenton General Catalog.

256. 2756 AW 9½" vase.
257. 7380 AW 8½" covered candy (Don Fenton signature).
258. 6572 AW 10½" footed basket.
259. 8600 AW 6" clock.
260. 2758 AW 8" vase.
261. 2757 AW 5" vase.
262. 9667 AW 7" Aurora bell.
263. 5226 AW 6" Fox.
264. 2759 AW 6" rose bowl.
265. 9295 AW Rose slipper.
266. 5253 AW 5" Unicorn.
267. 9071 AW 8½" candleholders.

These handpainted Cottage (Z8) items were shown in the 1993 Fenton General Catalog.

268. 7661 Z8 9" vase (Shelley Fenton signature).
269. 2735 Z8 7¾" basket (samples only; the production basket was 3234 Z8; see Fig. 100 for the shape).
270. 7662 Z8 3½" petite bell.
271. 7668 Z8 6" bell.
272. 2751 Z8 5" vase.
273. 7204 Z8 16" Colonial hammered lamp.

These items in Rose Pearl (DN), Ocean Blue (OB), and handpainted Iridized Opal (BT and CD) were made for Easter, 1993.

274.	4683 CD 7" Bunny box.	**277.**	5163 CD 4" Bird.
275.	5186 BT 5½" Hen on nest.	**278.**	5169 CD 3" Duckling.
276.	4680 BT 8½" Rooster box.	**279.**	5162 CD 3½" Bunny.

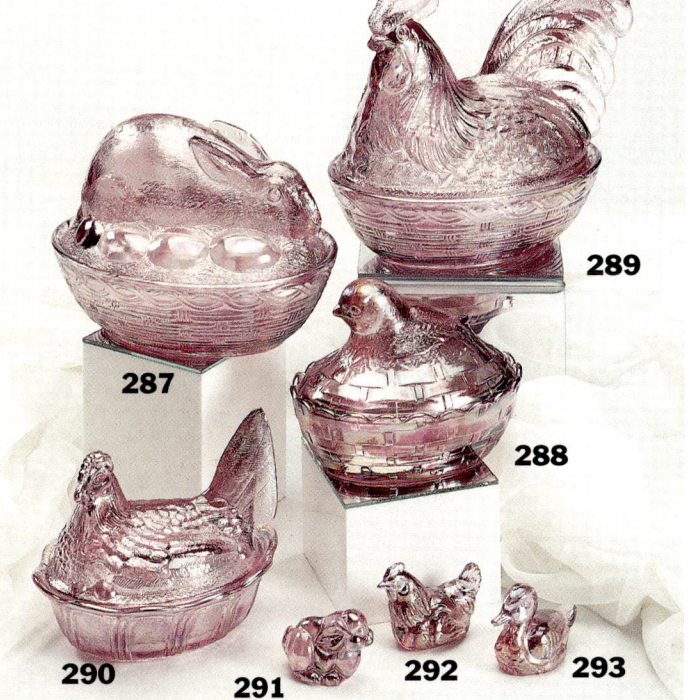

280.	4680 OB 8½" Rooster covered box.	**284.**	5211 OB 2½" mini Hen.
281.	5185 OB 5" Chick on nest.	**285.**	5209 OB 2½" mini Bunny.
282.	4683 OB 7" Bunny covered box.	**286.**	5186 OB 5½" Hen on nest.
283.	5212 OB 2½" mini Duckling.		
287.	4683 DN 7" Bunny covered box.	**291.**	5209 DN 2½" mini Bunny.
288.	5185 DN 5" Chick on nest.	**292.**	5211 DN 2½" mini Hen.
289.	4680 DN 8½" Rooster covered box.	**293.**	5212 DN 2½" mini Duckling.
290.	5186 DN 5½" Hen on nest.		

49

These Fuschia (EH) items are from the 1994 Fenton General Catalog.

294. 2001 EH 17" Drapery lamp.
295. 3077 EH 11" Spiral basket.
296. 2025 EH 10" Drapery bowl.
297. 2059 EH 8½" Jack in the pulpit vase.
298. 2052 EH 7" Drapery vase.
299. 2058 EH 6" Drapery vase.
300. 2031 EH 8" Drapery basket.
301. 1215 EH 6" Spiral pitcher.

These Petal Pink (PN) and Violas on Petal Pink (PU) items are from the 1994 Fenton General Catalog.

302. 1218 PU 9½" Feather vase.
303. 3265 PU 32 oz. pitcher.
304. 9763 PN 3¼" Heart bell.
305. 6572 PU 10½" footed basket.
306. 6702 PU 20" Paisley lamp.
307. 9295 PU 6" Rose slipper.
308. 2767 PU 4" vase.
309. 9144 PN 3" ringholder.
310. 1765 PU 6" bell.
311. 5165 PU 3¾" Cat.
312. 9596 PN 4¼" two-way candleholder.
313. 5151 PU 3½" sitting Bear.

50

These Rose Magnolia (RV) items are from the 1994 Fenton General Catalog.

- **314.** 2742 RV 5" Grape comport.
- **315.** 9754 RV 6" vase with bow.
- **316.** 8265 RV 6" bell.
- **317.** 8460 RV 8" basket.
- **318.** 8453 RV 5½" Rose bowl.
- **319.** 8450 RV 6"-8" handkerchief vase.
- **320.** 6570 RV 4½" puff box.
- **321.** 2731 RV 6" basket.
- **322.** 9295 RV 6" Rose slipper.
- **323.** 5151 RV 3½" Sitting bear.
- **324.** 6556 RV 4" basket.
- **325.** 5165 RV 3¼" Cat.

These handpainted Primrose (DS) items are from the 1994 Fenton General Catalog.

- **326.** 2739 DS 6½" Empress comport.
- **327.** 7250 DS 8" tulip vase.
- **328.** 9335 DS 7" Basketweave basket.
- **329.** 2751 DS 5" vase.
- **330.** 9295 DS 6" Rose slipper.
- **331.** 4605 DS 20" Basketweave lamp.
- **332.** 9589 DS 4½" oval trinket.
- **333.** 7662 DS 4½" bell.
- **334.** 2737 DS 7" basket.
- **335.** 9462 DS 6" Basketweave bell.
- **336.** 5165 DS 3¾" Cat.
- **337.** 9357 DS 4" Basketweave vase.
- **338.** 5233 DS 4" reclining Bear.

These Cranberry (CC) and decorated Cranberry with Pansies (CW) items were in the Fenton line in 1994.

- **339.** 3161 CC 11" spiral vase.
- **340.** 9655 CC 7½" vase.
- **341.** 1639 CW 8" basket.
- **342.** 1559 CW 9½" vase (Bill Fenton signature).
- **343.** 1728 CC 13" diamond bowl.
- **344.** 1214 CC 6" Melon vase.
- **345.** 5151 CC 3½" Bear.
- **346.** 1700 CW fairy light.
- **347.** 1685 CW 7½" tulip vase.
- **348.** 6590 CC 7" spiral bell.
- **349.** 3132 CC 8¾" basket.

350. 1158 FT 7" basket.
351. 3638 FD 8½" basket.
352. 1158 FR 7" basket.
353. 3834 FD 4½" basket.

These ducks were in a group called Puddle Parade.

354. 5169 J5 "Miss Daphne" 3" duck.
355. 5169 J7 "Ditsy" duck.
356. 5169 J3 "Delbert" duck.
357. 5169 J8 "Daffodil" duck.
358. 5169 J6 "Dolly Sue" duck.
359. 5169 J4 "Dugan" duck.

360. 4683 FK 7" handpainted Bunny covered box.

These items, including Sea Mist Slag (2A) and Plum Slag (8A), were made for Easter, 1994.

360A. 4683 8A 7" Bunny box.
361. 4680 8A 8½" Rooster box.
362. 5212 8A 2½" Duckling.
363. 5211 8A 2½" Hen.
364. 5186 8A 5" Hen on nest.
365. 5209 8A 3½" Bunny.

366. 4680 2A 8½" Rooster covered box.
367. 4683 2A 7" Bunny covered box.
368. 5212 2A 2½" Duckling.
369. 5186 2A 5" Hen on nest.
370. 5211 2A 2½" Hen.
371. 5209 2A 3½" Bunny.

These Autumn Gold (AM) and Autumn Gold Opalescent (AO) items are from Fenton's 1994 General catalog.

- **372.** 1569 AO 32 oz. pitcher.
- **373.** 1217 AO 11" Basket (Frank M. Fenton signature).
- **374.** 1559 AO 9½" vase.
- **375.** 1520 AO 21" student lamp.
- **376.** 1531 AO 8" basket.
- **377.** 5165 AM 3¾" Cat.
- **378.** 9544 AM 8" Vulcan basket.
- **379.** 1995 AM 6" Daisy and Button slipper.
- **380.** 9050 AM 5½" Flute & Dot vase.
- **381.** 7620 AM 4" vase.

These Autumn Gold (AM) and Autumn Gold Opalescent (AO) items are from Fenton's 1994 General catalog. The French Opalescent Hobnail baskets (FT) have Autumn Gold edges and handles.

382. 1558 AO 8" Vase.
383. 3638 FT 8½" Hobnail basket.
384. 1158 FT 7" Hobnail basket.
385. 8369 AM 6" Barred Oval bell.
386. 1218 AO 9½" Feather vase.
387. 3834 FT 4½" Hobnail basket.
388. 5163 AM 4" Bird.
389. 8388 AM 7½" candy with cover.
390. 2731 AM 6" basket.
391. 1549 AO 7" vase.
392. 9229 AM 6½" comport.
393. 1599 AO 5" vase.

55

These Milk Glass Hobnail pieces were in the Fenton line during 1994-95.

394. 3752 MI 11" vase.
395. 3907 MI 26" Pillar lamp.
396. 1174 MI 22" Student lamp with prisms.
397. 3808 MI 23½" Gone with the Wind lamp.
398. 3356 MI 7½" jack-in-the-pulpit vase.
399. 3734 MI 12" basket.
400. 3645 MI 5½" bell.
401. 3784 MI footed candy box.
402. 3995 MI 4½" slipper.
403. 3938 MI 12" bowl.
404. 3335 MI basket with looped handle.
405. 3606 MI cream and covered sugar set.
406. 3336 MI 6½" basket.
407. 3802 MI candy (or butter) with cover.
408. 3974 MI 4½" candleholders.
409. 3700 MI slipper candy box with cover.
410. 3806 MI salt and pepper set.
411. 5171 MI Butterfly on branch (not Hobnail).

These Milk Glass Royal Hobnail (note the crystal edge) and Cranberry Opalescent Hobnail items were in the Fenton line in 1995.

412. 3701 SC four pc. epergne set.
413. 3907 CR 26" Pillar lamp.
414. 1174 CR 22" Student lamp with prisms.
415. 3308 CR 25" Gone with the Wind lamp.
416. 3314 SC footed comport.
417. 3346 CR 8½" basket.
418. 3356 CR 7½" vase.
419. 3344 SC 8½" basket.
420. 3345 SC 10½" basket.
421. 3380 CR three-pc. fairy light.
422. 3733 SC handled heart bonbon.
423. 3861 CR 4¼" rose bowl.
424. 1167 SC three pc. fairy light.
425. 3366 CR 5½" pitcher.
426. 3328 SC lily bowl.
427. 3348 CR 10½" basket.
428. 3357 SC 6" footed vase.

These Golden Flax on Cobalt (KG) items were in Fenton's 1995 General Catalog.

429. 7380 KG 9½" footed candy with cover.
430. 1649 KG 9½" Feather vase (Shelley Fenton signature).
431. 2766 KG 8" basket.
432. 2953 KG 9" hexagonal vase.
433. 1540 KG 23½" Lamp.
434. 9229 KG 6½" Empress comport.
435. 1133 KG 7" basket.
436. 5109 KG 4½" Polar Bear.
437. 5165 KG 3¾" Cat.
438. 9667 KG 7" Aurora bell.
439. 3265 KG 32 oz. pitcher.
440. 5136 KG 3½" Rearing Elephant.

These Kristen's Floral (YB) items were in Fenton's 1995 General Catalog.

- **441.** 3522 YB 7½" Spanish Lace comport.
- **442.** 3559 YB 7" Spanish Lace vase.
- **443.** 5151 YB 3½" Sitting Bear.
- **444.** 2788 YB 7½" basket.
- **445.** 2791 YB 21" lamp.
- **446.** 9295 YB 6" Rose slipper.
- **447.** 9266 YB 4½" bell.
- **448.** 8691 YB 4½" clock.
- **449.** 5780 YB 3¾" heart trinket box.
- **450.** 3535 YB 7" basket.
- **451.** 5158 YB 3½" Elephant.
- **452.** 7241 YB 4" vase.
- **453.** 6761 YB 7" Paisley bell.

These handpainted Victorian Bouquet on Black (BT) items were shown in the 1995 Fenton General Catalog.

454. 2756 BT 9½" Feather vase.
455. 7380 BT 9½" covered candy.
456. 6585 BT 10½" basket.
457. 5165 BT 3¾" Cat.
458. 7691 BT 7" Aurora vase.
459. 8600 BT 6" clock.
460. 2958 BT 8½" Jack-in-the-pulpit vase.
461. 2757 BT 5" vase.
462. 9071 BT 8½" candleholders.
463. 2759 BT 3½" rose bowl.
464. 9589 BT 4½" oval trinket.
465. 9667 BT 7" Aurora bell.
466. 9295 BT 6" Rose slipper.

Fenton products from the mid-1990s: Vining Garden on Sea Mist Green (FP); Pansies (PF); Trellis (DX); Asters on Dusty Rose Overlay (DP); Mountain Berry on Gold Overlay (KT); and Meadow Beauty (PD).

467.	1683 DP 7" Aurora vase.		**477.**	1213 PD 4½" vase.
468.	3265 FP 6½" pitcher.		**478.**	1145 PF 6" bell.
469.	1689 FP 9½" vase.		**479.**	1219 PD 7½" basket.
470.	6006 FP 2½" salt and pepper set.		**480.**	5136 DX 3½" Elephant.
471.	2766 FP 8" basket.		**481.**	1212 PD 7" pitcher.
472.	1683 KT 7" Aurora vase.		**482.**	5163 DX 4" Bird.
473.	1145 DX 6½" bell.		**483.**	3076 DP 8" basket.
474.	3127 KT 7½" basket.		**484.**	5165 DX 3¾" Cat.
475.	5563 PF 5" pitcher.		**485.**	1132 DX 7" Diamond Optic pitcher.
476.	5585 DX 5½" Melon box with cover.			

These Sea Mist Green (LE) items were in the Fenton line in 1996.

486. 9071 LE 8½" candlesticks.
487. 2925 LE 9¾" Revere bowl.
488. 1686 LE 10½" pitcher.
489. 6761 LE 7" Paisley bell.
490. 9551 LE 6½" candy with cover.
491. 5186 LE 5" Hen on nest.
492. 1674 LE 7½" cruet.

493. 5257 LE 8½" rooster.
494. 5292 LE 5½" Folk Art Rooster.
495. 5136 LE 3½" Elephant.
496. 5165 LE 3¾" Cat.
497. 2775 LE 4½" Diamond Fan basket.
498A. 9144 LE 3" ringholder.

These Handpainted Pansies (PF) items were in the Fenton line in 1996.

498B. 6701 PF 20" Paisley lamp.
499. 6585 PF 10½" basket.
500. 9450 PF 8½" Melon vase.
501. 9295 PF 6" slipper.
502. 5165 PF 3¾" Cat.

503. 5563 PF 5" pitcher.
504. 1145 PF 6" bell.
505. 2739 PF 6½" Empress comport.
506. 5148 PF 3" Mouse.
507. 5585 PF 5½" covered box (Family Signature Series).

Introduced in 1996, the Fenton Medallion Collection was intended as gifts for men. Items were made in dark colors as indicated, and each came with a wooden base as shown. In 1997, a vase was added (see Fig. 1007), while the 5165 Cat was produced in black (X7) and the 5147 Mallard in dark Plum (Y9).

508. 5243 Y7 3½" Cat (dark cobalt).
509. 5258 Y8 6" Owl (black).
510. 5197 Y5 Happiness Bird (dark Plum).
511. 5163 Y4 Bird (dark Plum).
512. 5160 Y3 Fawn (dark green).
513. 5226 Y6 Fox (black).
514. 5147 X9 5" Mallard (dark green).
515. 5136 X8 3½" Elephant (dark cobalt).

These items are from the new Romance Collection in 1997.

516. 8267 RW 7" bell.
517. 8288 RW 8½" candy box with cover.
518. 4639 RW 7½" basket.
519. 5780 RW 4" trinket box.
520. 9357 RW 4½" vase.
521. 5197 RW 5½" Happiness Bird.

These baskets in Misty Blue Iridescent (LK) and Champagne Iridescent (PY) were made for Easter, 1997.

522. 6539 LK 10" Leaf basket.
523. 4634 LK 8" Peacock basket.
524. 4634 PY 8" Peacock basket.
525. 6539 PY 10" Leaf basket.
526. 6558 PY 4½" Diamond basket.
527. 6563 LK 4½" footed basket.
528. 2776 LK 4½" Teardrop basket.
529. 2778 PY 6½" Strawberry basket.
530. 2778 LK 6½" Strawberry basket.
531. 6563 PY 4½" footed basket.

65

These Misty Blue Satin (LR) and Irises on Misty Blue Satin (LS) items are from Fenton's 1997 General Catalog.

532. 9451 LR 7"-8½" Fabergé bud vase.
533. 8484 LR 9" Lily of the Valley candy with cover.
534. 1535 LR 9½" Diamond Panel basket.
535. 9752 LR 7¾" Daffodil vase.
536. 8450 LR 7"-8" Lily of the Valley vase.
537. 5170 LR 4" Butterfly with stand.
538. 8453 LR 5½" Lily of the Valley rose bowl.
539. 8265 LR 6" Lily of the Valley bell.
540. 5165 LR 3¾" Cat.

541. 2782 LS 11" Feather vase.
542. 5440 LS 7½" pitcher (Don Fenton signature).
543. 6700 LS 18" Paisley lamp.
544. 1683 LS 7" Aurora vase.
545. 1538 LS 8" basket.
546. 5163 LS 4" Bird.
547. 9295 LS 6" Rose slipper.
548. 6830 LR 7½" Silverton basket.
549. 9667 LS 7" Aurora bell.
550. 5151 LS 3½" sitting Bear.

These Champagne Satin (PQ) and Field Flowers on Champagne Satin (PI) items were in the 1997 Fenton General Catalog.

551. 8475 PQ 4" candleholders.
552. 4751 PI 6" Vase (Shelley Fenton signature).
553. 9303 PQ 20" Poppy lamp.
554. 8257 PQ 8" Peacock vase.
555. 3429 PQ 5½" Cactus comport.
556. 2948 PI 8" basket.
557. 5151 PI 3½" Bear.
558. 1145 PI 6½" bell.
559. 5148 PI 3" Mouse.
560. 1214 PI 6" Melon vase.
561. 9451 PQ 7-8½" Fabergé bud vase.

These Sea Mist Green (LE) and Morning Glories on Sea Mist Green (L3) items were in the 1997 Fenton General Catalog.

562. 1693 L3 9" vase.
563. 2766 L3 8" basket.
564. 1600 L3 20" lamp.
565. 9408 LE 10" Welcome light.
566. 9551 LE 6½" candy with cover.
567. 9667 L3 7" bell.
568. 3265 L3 6½" pitcher.
569. 8450 LE 6"-8" Lily handkerchief vase.
570. 5290 LE 6" Cat slipper.
571. 2776 LE 4½" Teardrop basket.
572. 9144 LE 3" ringholder.
573. 2731 LE 6" Lamb's Tongue basket.
574. 5148 L3 3" Mouse.
575. 5170 LE 4" Butterfly with stand.
576. 5165 LE 3¾" Cat.

These Plum (PL) and Sweetbriar on Plum Overlay (P9) items were in the 1997 Fenton General Catalog.

- **577.** 1648 P9 9" hexagonal vase.
- **578.** 1562 P9 7½" pitcher.
- **579.** 2800 P9 20" lamp.
- **580.** 4648 P9 9" Melon basket (Lynn Fenton signature).
- **581.** 9229 PL 6½" Empress comport.
- **582.** 2787 PL 8" basket.
- **583.** 1560 P9 7" vase.
- **584.** 6558 PL 4½" Diamond basket.
- **585.** 1789 PL 6" Melon vase.
- **586.** 5170 PL 4" Butterfly with stand.
- **587.** 9578 PL 4½" 2-way votive.
- **588.** 6761 PL 7" Paisley bell.
- **589.** 9295 PL 6" Rose slipper.

These items were made for Easter, 1997.

590. 5292 LR 5½" Folk Art Rooster.
591. 4680 PQ 8½" Rooster covered box.
592. 4680 LR 8½" Rooster covered box.
593. 5292 PQ 5½" Folk Art Rooster.
594. 4683 LR 7" Bunny covered box.
595. 4683 PQ 7" Bunny covered box.
596. 5186 LR 5" Hen on nest.
597. 5275 PY 2¾" mini Bunny.
598. 5265 LK 2¾" mini Rooster.
599. 5265 PY 2¾" mini Rooster.
600. 5275 LK 2¾" mini Bunny.
601. 5186 PQ 5" Hen on nest.

These items in Aquamarine (AA), handpainted French Opalescent (JB) and Champagne Satin (PY) were made for Easter, 1999.

602. 5292 AA 5¾" Rooster.
603. 5265 AA 2¾" Rooster.
604. 5275 PY 2¾" Bunny.
605. 5169 JB 3½" Duckling.
606. 5275 AA 2¾" Bunny.
607. 5265 PY 2¾" Rooster.

These items appeared in Fenton's "LifeStyles" catalog in 1998.

608. 9866 WX Leaves on Royal Purple 8" square vase.
609. 3254 XH Watercolors on Sea Green Satin 11" vase.
610. 8807 WX Leaves on Royal Purple 9" urn.
611. 1699 CC Cranberry 18" vase.
612. 9873 XG 12¾" Sea Green Satin Pigeons bowl.
613. 1544 FZ Pinstripe 7" w. covered box.
614. 8722 FZ 10" Leaf bowl.
615. 1615 CC Cranberry 14" bell lamp.

These Christmas items were in Fenton's regular line in the year noted.

616. 5535 XI Rose Pearl 6¼" Christmas Tree with Partridge, 1995.

617. 5535 V5 Ruby 6½" Christmas Tree with gold angel topper, 1994.

618. 5558 GL 3" Golden Glow Ornament with Ice, 1993.

619. 5556 ZN Misty Blue Iridescent 4" Christmas Tree with gold squirrel, 1998.

620. 5535 VK Spruce Green 6½" Christmas Tree with gold bow, 1999.

621. 5700 SO Spruce Green sugar and creamer, 1998-99.

622. 1127 SE Magnolia and Berry on Spruce 6½" bell, 1996-97.

623. 6839 SE Magnolia and Berry on Spruce 10½" Basket, 1996-97.

624. 6190 RU Ruby 7" Swirl candlestick, 1999.

625. 5535 XE Crystal Satin Iridized 6½" Christmas Tree with bird, 1993.

626. 7669 DB 6" Musical Bell ("White Christmas"), 1991.

627. 5535 CY Crystal 6½" Christmas Tree, 1992.

628. 5557 ZT Crystal Iridized Christmas Tree with cardinal, 1997.

629. 5160 SB Snowberry 3½" Fawn, 1992.

630. 5109 FE Woodland Frost 4½" Polar Bear, 1999.

631. 5261 JX Twining Berries 8" Reindeer, 1999.

632. 4695 P7 Poinsettia Glow 7½" Sleigh, 1997.

633. 9335 SB Snowberry 7" Basketweave basket, 1992.

634. 9869 FE Woodland Frost 5" vase, 1999.

635. 5265 WI Crystal Iridized Madonna candlelight, 1991.

636. 8930 WH Crystal Satin 2" iceberg votive, 1998.

637. 5135 XL "Baby's First Christmas" 3" Hobby Horse, 1992.

638. 8931 WH Crystal Satin 3" iceberg votive, 1998.

639. 9071 JX Twining Berries 8½" candlestick, 1998.

640. 6865 P7 Poinsettia Glow 9" pitcher, 1996.

641. 7463 P7 Poinsettia Glow 6½" bell, 1996.

Dusty Rose (DK) was in the Fenton line from 1984 to 1997. Empress Rose (CP) entered the Fenton line in 1998.

642.	5750 DK 9" Rose vase.		**650.**	9262 DK 6" Rose bell.
643.	3258 CP 11" Melon vase.		**651.**	9223 DK 6½" Rose comport.
644.	7653 CP 7½" Daffodil vase.		**652.**	1995 CP 6" Daisy and Button slipper.
645.	6630 CP 8½" ribbed basket.		**653.**	5163 DK 4" Bird.
646.	9256 DK 11" swung bud vase.		**654.**	5065 CP 5" Cat.
647.	2751 DK 5" Radiance light.		**655.**	6558 DK 4½" basket.
648.	9265 DK 7" Butterfly bell.		**656.**	4838 CP 5" Diamond Lace basket.
649.	9237 DK 7½" Rose basket.		**657.**	9144 CP 3" ringholder.
			658.	8691 DK 4½" clock.

All of these were in the Fenton line during 1999: Aquamarine (AA); Cobalt (KN); Ice Blue with Bellflowers (LH); Martha's Rose (AZ); Morning Mist (CG); and Tranquility (AK or AL).

659.	5371 KN 6" rose bowl set.		**668.**	6864 LH 6" Melon bell.
660.	3280 AL 9" pitcher.		**669.**	5137 AA Dolphin.
661.	6480 KN 9" trumpet basket.		**670.**	4694 AZ 6" bell.
662.	6630 AA 8½" ribbed basket.		**670a.**	5165 AZ 3¾" cat.
663.	2973 KN 8½" pitcher.		**671.**	3131 AZ 8½" basket.
664.	5939 AK 7" basket.		**672.**	6530 CG 7" Diamond basket.
665.	4560 AK 6¾" bell.		**673.**	6833 CG 8" ribbed basket.
666.	7565 LH 8" Reverse Melon vase.		**674.**	5163 CG 4" Bird.
667.	2777 LH 7" basket.		**675.**	7484 CG 5" covered box.

73

Cranberry (CC) and handpainted Pansies on Cranberry (CW) items.

676.	9464 CC 8½" Jacqueline basket.	**682.**	1700 CW two-piece fairy light.
677.	2964 CC 7" pitcher.	**683.**	1567 CW 7" Aurora vase (George Fenton signature, 1995).
678.	2782 CC 11" Feather vase.		
679.	1218 CC 9½" Feather vase.	**684.**	1557 CW 4" vase.
680.	3239 CW 6" Hat basket.	**685.**	1589 CC 5" box with metal cover.
681.	1554 CW 9" Rib vase.	**686.**	3290 CC 6½" Rib vase.
		687.	7793 CC 5½" Daffodil vase.

Cranberry (CC) and handpainted Rose Garden (EG) items.

688.	1646 CC 8" Reverse Melon vase.	**695.**	5165 EG 3¾" Cat.
689.	3240 CC 10½" vase.	**696.**	9126 CC 3½" Poppy rose bowl.
690.	1353 CC 10" tulip vase.	**697.**	9050 CC 5½" Flute and Dot vase.
691.	1478 CC Coin Dot vase.	**698.**	3271 CC 6½" bell (note handle).
692.	7139 CC 7½" Melon basket.	**699.**	9295 EG 6" Rose slipper.
693.	5158 EG 3½" Elephant.	**700.**	1773 EG 6½" bell.
694.	5065 EG 5" Cat.	**701.**	2566 CC 6" Daisy jug.

These pieces were marketed as gifts for men in 1998.

702. 1502 JU handpainted Golf Scene on 12½" lamp.
703. 8600 JU handpainted Golf Scene on 6" table clock.
704. 1502 JW handpainted Fish Scene on 12½" lamp.

These are often given as birthday gifts for children (BP items are decorated with blue, and GU items are decorated with pink).

705. 5151 BP 3½" Bear.
706. 5151 GU 3½" Bear.
707. 5113 BP 5¾" Angel.
708. 5114 GU 5¾" Angel
709. 5273 BP 4" Praying Boy.
710. 5272 GU 4" Praying Girl.
711. 5040 BP 4½" Ball Cap.
712. 5040 GU 4½" Ball Cap.
713. 4610 BP 4¼" Baby Shoe.
714. 4610 GU 4¼" Baby Shoe.
715. 5135 BP 3" Rocking Horse.
716. 5135 GU 3" Rocking Horse.

Bells are among the most popular Fenton collectibles of the 1990s decade.

717.	6761 PL Plum 7" Paisley bell, 1994.	**730.**	7665 2H Dusty Rose "Happy Anniversary" mini bell, 1994.
718.	6864 KN Cobalt Melon bell, 1999.	**731.**	1760 1E Gold with floral mini bell, 1999.
719.	9265 AA Aquamarine Butterfly bell, 1999.	**732.**	9262 DK Dusty Rose 6" Rose bell, 1992.
720.	9665 KK Cobalt Beauty bell, 1990.	**733.**	6761 LE Sea Mist Green Paisley 7" bell, 1991.
721.	9560 CP Empress Rose Templebells bell, 1998.	**734.**	1145 PF Pansies on Milk Glass 7" bell, 1996.
722.	9667 AW Autumn Leaves 7" bell, 1994.	**735.**	6761 SC Silver Crest Paisley 7" bell, 1992.
723.	9764 RU Ruby Heart 6¼" bell, 1990.	**736.**	1773 EG Rose Garden 6½" bell, 1994.
724.	9763 PL Plum Heart 3¼" mini bell, 1993.	**737.**	7664 XA "Christmas Cactus" 3½" mini bell, 1992.
725.	9265 DK Dusty Rose Butterfly 7" bell, 1995.	**738.**	9266 YB Kristen's Floral 4½" mini bell, 1995.
726.	8265 LR Misty Blue Lily of the Valley bell, 1997.	**739.**	7664 XF "Christmas Rose" mini bell, 1992.
727.	9265 RN Red Carnival Butterfly 7" bell, 1996.	**740.**	7662 JW "Baby's First Christmas" mini bell, 1990.
728.	9667 FP Vining Garden 7" bell, 1991.	**741.**	7664 XG "Winterberry" mini bell, 1992.
729.	9266 SR Salem Blue Bow and Drape mini bell, 1990.		

These Sapphire Blue Opalescent items were made in 1990.

742. 1826 BX Fern 10" bowl.
743. 1832 BX Fern 7" basket.
744. 1860 BX Fern cruet with stopper.
745. 1830 BX Fern 5½" basket.
746. 1853 BX Fern 10" tulip vase.

747. 1802 BX 7 Pc. Water Set, Fern

748. 8229 BX Hearts and Flowers, 10" bowl.
749. 8489 BX Lily of the Valley candy with cover.
750. 8437 BX Lily of the Valley oval basket.
751. 8453 BX Lily of the Valley rose bowl.
752. 8265 BX Lily of the Valley bell.
753. 9651 BX Regency 3½" vase.
754. 8458 BX Lily of the Valley 10" bud vase.

All of these items are Stiegel Blue Opalescent (1991).

755. 4605 JU Basketweave lamp with handpainted grape pattern.
756. 9560 BO Templebells bell.
757. 4653 BO Paneled Grape 9" tulip vase.
758. 4632 BO Wildflower basket.
759. 4602 JU Diamond urn with cover, hand-painted grape pattern.
760. 4651 JU Colonial 10" bud vase with hand-painted grape pattern.
761. 4603 BO Innovation lamp.
762. 4633 BO Paneled Grape 6" basket.

763. 4672 BO Ring and Petal open edge candlesticks.
764. 4627 BO Ring and Petal open edge 10½" bowl.
765. 4601 BO Paneled Grape 14 pc. punch set (bowl, base, and 12 cups).
766. 4671 BO Ring and Petal open edge 11¼" cake plate.
767. 4693 BO Colonial comport.

These items are Stiegel Blue Opalescent (1991).

768. 4612 BO Saw Tooth covered comport.
769. 4650 BO Paneled Grape 5 pc. water set.
770. 4673 BO Peacock cream and sugar.
771. 4667 BO Paneled Grape covered butter.
772. 4613 BO single crimp basket.
773. 4614 BO mini 5 pc. water set.

These items are Light Amethyst Carnival (1991).

774. 4619 DT Good Luck bowl.
775. 4601 DT Panelled Grape punch bowl set (bowl, base, and 12 cups).
776. 4679 DT Eagle covered box.
777. 9065 DT Sable Arche bell.
778. 9799 DT Fenton logo.
779. 4644 DT Diamond and Panel toothpick.
780. 4617 DT Innovation three-toed basket.

Gold Pearl (GP) was made in 1992 and Persian Pearl (XV) was made in 1992-93.

781.	5252 GP Gold Pearl 7" Owl.
782.	5526 GP Gold Pearl 4" candlestick.
783.	5483 GP Gold Pearl 10½" h. cupped basket.
784.	5526 GF Star Flowers on Gold Pearl 4" candlestick.
785.	5480 GP Gold Pearl 12" swung vase.
786.	3784 XV Persian Pearl footed Hobnail candy box, 1992.
787.	8454 XV Persian Pearl Drapery bowl, 1993.

All of these items are from Fenton's "Rose Magnolia in Hobnail" Historical Collection (1993).

788.	3712 RV 14 pc. punch set (bowl, base, and 12 cups).	**794.**	3356 RV 7½" tulip vase.
789.	3701 RV 10" three-horn epergne.	**795.**	3784 RV candy with cover.
790.	3908 RV five-pc. water set (54 oz. pitcher and four 9 oz. tumblers).	**796.**	9799 RV Fenton rectangular logo.
791.	3313 RV Student lamp with prisms.	**797.**	3337 RV 7" basket.
792.	3834 RV 4½" basket.	**798.**	3645 RV 5½" bell.
793.	3854 RV 4½" vase.	**799.**	3863 RV cruet with stopper.

These Stiegel Green Stretch items were made in 1994.

- **800.** 7601 SS five pc. epergne set.
- **801.** 5551 SS 9" footed basket.
- **802.** 5552 SS 12" bowl.
- **803.** 5560 SS five pc. water set.
- **804.** 5526 SS candlesticks.
- **805.** 5554 SS comport.
- **806.** 2759 SS rose bowl.
- **807.** 5559 SS 8" handkerchief vase.
- **808.** 9667 SS Aurora bell.
- **809.** 5555 SS 7" footed basket.
- **810.** 9799 SS Fenton rectangular logo.
- **811.** 5553 SS 7" jack-in-the-pulpit vase.

These Stiegel Green Stretch items were made in 1994.

- **812.** 4602 SS Diamond urn with cover.
- **813.** 2787 ST 8" basket with handpainted decoration (Bill Fenton signature piece).
- **814.** 2773 SS 8" Open Edge bowl.
- **815.** 4802 SS Diamond Lace epergne.
- **816.** 4381 ST Lamb's Tongue candy box and cover with handpainted decoration.
- **817.** 5559 ST 8" handkerchief vase with handpainted decoration.
- **818.** 2759 ST rose bowl with handpainted decoration.
- **819.** 5259 ST Sparrow with handpainted decoration.
- **820.** 9667 ST Aurora bell with handpainted decoration.
- **821.** 5526 SS candlesticks.

These five Burmese items are from Fenton's 90th Anniversary Historical Collection (1995); numerical limits are given in parentheses.

822. 2932 UL Burmese Butterfly basket (790).

823. 2955 UU Burmese Hummingbird vase, inscribed with 11 Fenton family signatures (790).

826. 7502 UQ Burmese Daybreak 33" pillar lamp (300).

824. 2968 UN Burmese Cherry Blossom 10" pitcher (790).

825. 2909 UK Burmese Vintage Border bowl with black base (790).

These Opaline (TG) and Opaline with Blush Rose (TE) items were made in 1996.

827. 5357 TE 8½" vase (George Fenton signature piece).
828. 4854 TG Diamond Lace comport.
829. 4808 TG Diamond Lace epergne.
830. 4835 TG Diamond Lace basket.
831. 4806 TG Diamond Lace mini epergne.
832. 9499 TG Fenton oval logo.
833. 4833 TG 6" basket.

These Opaline (TG) and Opaline with Blush Rose (TE) items were made in 1996.

- **834.** 1147 TE 8" basket.
- **835.** 4568 TE bell.
- **836.** 3463 TG Cactus cruet with stopper.

- **837.** 1180 TE two-piece tumble-up set.
- **838.** 1795 TE 11" Feather vase. 
- **839.** 7701 TE cruet with stopper.
- **840.** 1705 TE 24" lamp.
- **841.** 1146 TE 7" pinch vase.
- **842.** 5367 TE pitcher.

These Mulberry items are from the 1996 Historic Collection; numerical limits are given in parentheses.

843. 5581 MD Evening Blossom with Ladybug 21" lamp (500).

844. 1531 MS Hummingbird and Wild Rose basket (1250).

845. 1671 MD Evening Blossom with Ladybug pitcher (1250).

846. 2750 MS Hummingbird and Wild Rose melon herringbone vase (1250).

847. 1689 MS Hummingbird and Wild Rose 9½" vase (1250).

87

These Topaz Opalescent (TS) and Topaz Opalescent with Hydrangeas (TP) items were made in 1997.

848. 7601 TS five-piece epergne.
849. 2000 TP 20" lamp with prisms.
850. 2033 TP 8" basket.
851. 2040 TP three-piece fairy light (Frank M. Fenton signature piece).
852. 2048 TP 9½" vase.
853. 9295 TS Rose slipper.
854. 2072 TP pitcher.
855. 9665 TS Beauty bell.

These Topaz Opalescent (TS) and Topaz Opalescent with Hydrangeas (TP) items were made in 1997.

856. 9550 TP 8" fan vase (Tom Fenton signature piece).
857. 2919 TS Paneled Grape basket.
858. 5197 TP Happiness Bird.

859. 9750 TS punch set (bowl with metal base and eight cups.
860. 2851 TS Wildrose vase.
861. 5150 TS Atlantis vase.
862. 8248 TS Scroll nut dish.
863. 1158 TS 8½" Hobnail basket.
864. 9499 TS Fenton oval logo.

These Rubina Verde items were made in 1997; numerical limits are given in parentheses.

865. 1581 BW Melon box with handpainted decoration (1750).

866. 1507 BW 24" lamp with hand painted decoration (650).

867. 7458 BW 11" Melon vase with handpainted decoration (1750).

868. 7139 BW Melon basket with handpainted decoration (1750).

869. 7565 BW 8" reverse Melon vase with handpainted decoration (1750).

870. 3066 BW 6" pitcher with handpainted decoration (1750).

These Sea Green Satin pieces were made in 1998.

871. 7511 GG Gone with the Wind lamp.
872. 9071 GE 8½" candlesticks.
873. 7601 GE five-piece epergne.
874. 5290 GE Cat slipper.
875. 5301 GE oval perfume.
876. 6840 GE Butterfly bon bon with cover.

These Sea Green Satin pieces were made in 1998.

877. 8252 GE Empress vase.
878. 9080 GE 4" square box.
879. 5167 GE Sunfish.
880. 9458 GE Swan 8" vase.
881. 5197 GG Happiness Bird.
882. 7255 GG 11" tulip vase (Nancy and George Fenton signature piece).

883. 6854 GG Aurora 7" vase.
884. 8251 GE Mandarin vase.
885. 5430 GG Lily basket.
886. 2731 GE Lamb's Tongue basket.
887. 8450 GE Lily handkerchief vase.
888. 5165 GG Cat.
889. 9499 GE Fenton oval logo.
890. 7768 GG 6½" bell.

These Royal Purple items were made in 1998; numerical limits are given in parentheses.

891. 1617 N4 8" basket (2950).
892. 1689 N4 9½" vase (2950).
893. 3265 N4 pitcher (2950).
894. 1610 N4 three-piece fairy light (2950).
895. 3290 N4 perfume bottle (2950).
896. 1509 N4 20" student lamp (1450).
897. 6470 UF 6½" vase (2950).

These Violet Satin items were made in 1999.

898. 5405 XP fairy light.
899. 7255 XP 11" tulip vase.
900. 5065 XP Cat.

901. 1602 XP 24" Gone with the Wind lamp.

902. 5290 XK Cat slipper.
903. 5320 XK perfume bottle with stopper.
904. 9499 XK Fenton oval logo.
905. 4650 XK five-piece Paneled Grape water set.

These Violet Satin items were made in 1999.

906. 7601 XK five-piece epergne.

907. 4106 XP Heart trinket box.
908. 7568 XP Legacy bell.

909. 5151 XP Bear.
910. 2963 XK Jack-in-the-Pulpit vase.
911. 2777 XP 7" basket.

912. 4559 XK Lance vase.
913. 9560 XK Templebells bell.

These Gold Amberina items were made in 1999; numerical limits are given in parentheses.

- **914.** 6150 AV lamp (950).
- **915.** 1533 AV 11" hexagonal basket (2500).
- **916.** 3075 AV cruet with stopper (2500).
- **917.** 3047 AV 6½" vase (2500).
- **918.** 3240 AV 11" vase (2500).
- **919.** 1211 AV 9½" pitcher (2500).

All of the items on this page are from Fenton's 1990 85th Anniversary Offering of Burmese glass, which took the place of the Connoisseur Collection for that year. These were limited to sales in May-November, 1990.

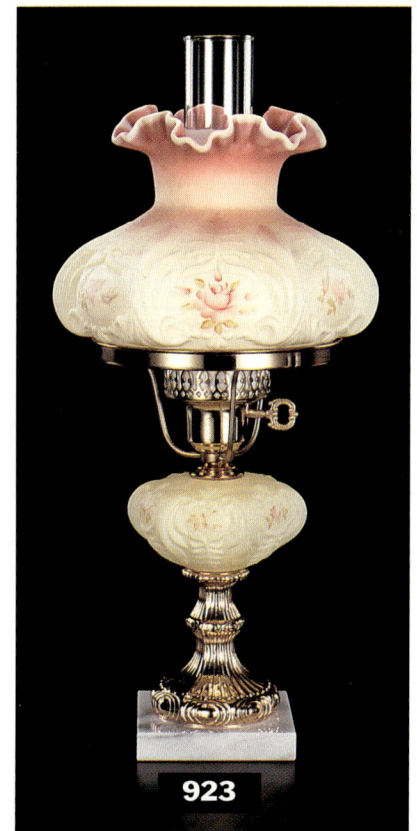

920.	7731 QH 7" basket with raspberries.	**925.**	7701 QJ cruet and stopper with Petite Floral.
921.	7412 QH 21" student lamp with raspberries.	**926.**	7792 QD 9" vase with Trees Scene.
922.	7700 QH 7-pc. water set with raspberries.	**927.**	7732 QD 5½" basket with Trees Scene.
923.	9308 RB 20" lamp with roses.	**928.**	7791 RB 6½" vase with roses.
924.	7202 QJ 2 pc. epergne with Petite Floral.	**929.**	7790 RB 6" vase with roses.

All of these items are from the 1991 Connoisseur Collection; limits are given in parentheses.

930. 8812 FQ Favrene 10½" vase with floral decoration (850).

931. 9394 FN Favrene 3-pc. Ogee candy box (1000).

932. 8812 G1 Favrene 10½" vase with fruit decoration (850).

933. 4647 MD Rosalene Empress basket (1500).
934. 6701 RB Burmese 20" Paisley lamp with roses (500).
935. 6761 UZ Rosalene Paisley bell (2000).
936. 7252 QH Burmese 7½" vase with raspberries (1500).
937. 5193 RE Rosalene Fish paperweight (2000).

All of these items are from the 1992 Connoisseur Collection; limits are given in parentheses.

938. 8817 QZ Seascape 8¼" vase (750).
939. 6080 RH Wave Crest covered box with marbelized lustre (1250).
940. 1684 RP Rosalene Twining Floral 7" vase (950).
941. 5531 QP Burmese 4½" pitcher with berries (1500).
942. 1211 RW Cranberry 9" Empire pitcher (950).
943. 5541 QH Burmese 6½" tulip vase with raspberries (1500).

All of these items are from the 1993 Connoisseur Collection; limits are given in parentheses.

944. 2747 RX Ruby Stretch rolled rim bowl (1250).

945. 1710 R5 Rosalene perfume bottle with Rose Trellis decoration (1250).

946. 8805 X3 iridized Plum 9" vase with sandcarved Leaves of Gold decoration (950).

947. 7661 P4 Persian Blue Opalescent vase with Victorian Roses decoration (950).

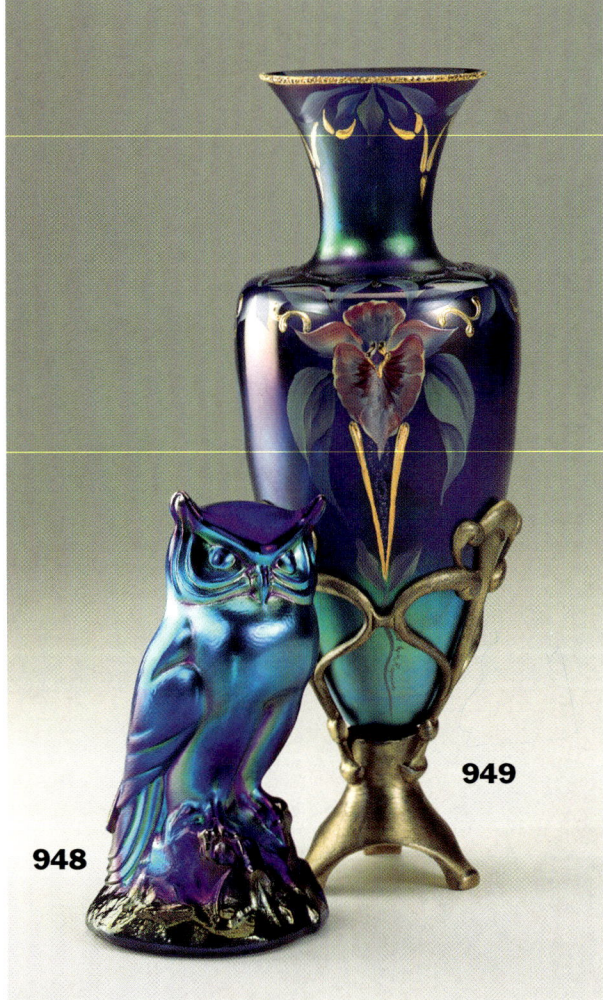

948. 5258 FN Favrene 6" owl (1500).

949. 2748 FW decorated Favrene amphora vase with stand (850).

950. 2780 CX Spring Woods reverse painted lamp (500).

All of these items are from the 1994 Connoisseur Collection; limits are given in parentheses.

951. 5580 JB Hummingbird reverse painted lamp (300).

952. 3161 JQ Gold Amberina 11" decorated vase (750).

953. 2729 JI Burmese Lattice Rose pitcher (750).

954. 7727 JC Cranberry Cameo sandcarved 14" bowl (500).

955. 2744 JK Plum Opalescent vase with scrollwork decoration (750).

956. 2743 JP Favrene 7" vase with coralene decoration (850).

957. 8691 JV Favrene decorated clock (850).

All of these items are from the 1995 Connoisseur Collection; limits are given in parentheses.

958. 2796 AM Victorian Art Glass pitcher (490).
959. 2950 VN Favrene 3-pc. ginger jar (790).
960. 2947 US Royal Purple decorated amphora with metal stand (890).
961. 5486 VU Butterfly and Floral reverse painted lamp (300).
962. 7691 WF Wild Rose Aurora 7" vase (890).

All of these items are from the 1996 Connoisseur Collection; limits are given in parentheses.

963. 3254 QJ Burmese Queen's Bird vase (1350).

964. 2782 DD Wild Rose 11" vase with berries (1250).

965. 2960 WQ Burmese Dragonfly 8" pitcher (1450).

966. 9855 EV Favrene vase with cut-back decoration (1250).

967. 6805 EA Poppies reverse painted lamp (400).

968. 6584 CD Mandarin Red decorated box with metal lid (1250).

969. 9866 TR Burmese Trout 8" vase (1450).

103

All of these items are from the 1997 Connoisseur Collection; limits are given in parentheses.

970. 2961 BY Burmese Trillium 9½" vase (1750).
971. 7632 BQ Burmese Fenced Garden 11½" basket (1750).
972. 7939 BJ Scenic Floral reverse painted lamp (550).
973. 9866 FX French Opalescent Tranquility 8" vase (1500).
974. 2965 UD Opaline Floral vase (1500).
975. 8966 ZJ Wild Rose pitcher with rose decoration (1350).
976. 8807 FR Favrene sandcarved Daisy vase with metal lid (1350).

These items are from the 1998 Connoisseur Collection; limits are given in parentheses.

- **977.** 5359 WP Leaves and Vines 9" vase (950).
- **978.** 6802 SV Trysting Place reverse painted lamp (750).
- **979.** 9259 FY Favrene Seasons 9" vase (1350).
- **980.** 8817 DJ French opalescent After the Rain 8" vase (2250).
- **981.** 4604 BZ Wild Rose Alhambra 6" vase (1500).

These items are from the 1998 Connoisseur Collection; limits are given in parentheses.

982. 7139 NP Burmese Blackberry Bouquet 7½" basket (2250).

983. 7557 UW Burmese Papillon 10" vase (2500).

984. 2998 YZ Burmese Bountiful Harvest 7" pitcher (2250).

985. 4505 WD Burmese Jacobean Floral lamp (750).

These items are from the 1999 Connoisseur Collection; limits are given in parentheses.

986. 6831 U5 Burmese Bluebird 9½" basket (2950).

987. 6359 WS Burmese Poppies 13" vase (2500).

988. 1862 VV Burmese Golden Gourds 7" ewer (2500).

989. 6200 HW Burmese Memories lamp with hibiscus and scrollwork decoration (950).

These items are from the 1999 Connoisseur Collection; limits are given in parentheses.

990. 3090 ZF Mulberry Mystical Bird amphora with metal stand (1250).

991. 7139 YC Peach Crest basket with roses decoration (1750).

992. 7488 FH Favrene ginger jar with orchid decoration (1750).

993. 6250 DR Tulips reverse painted lamp (750).

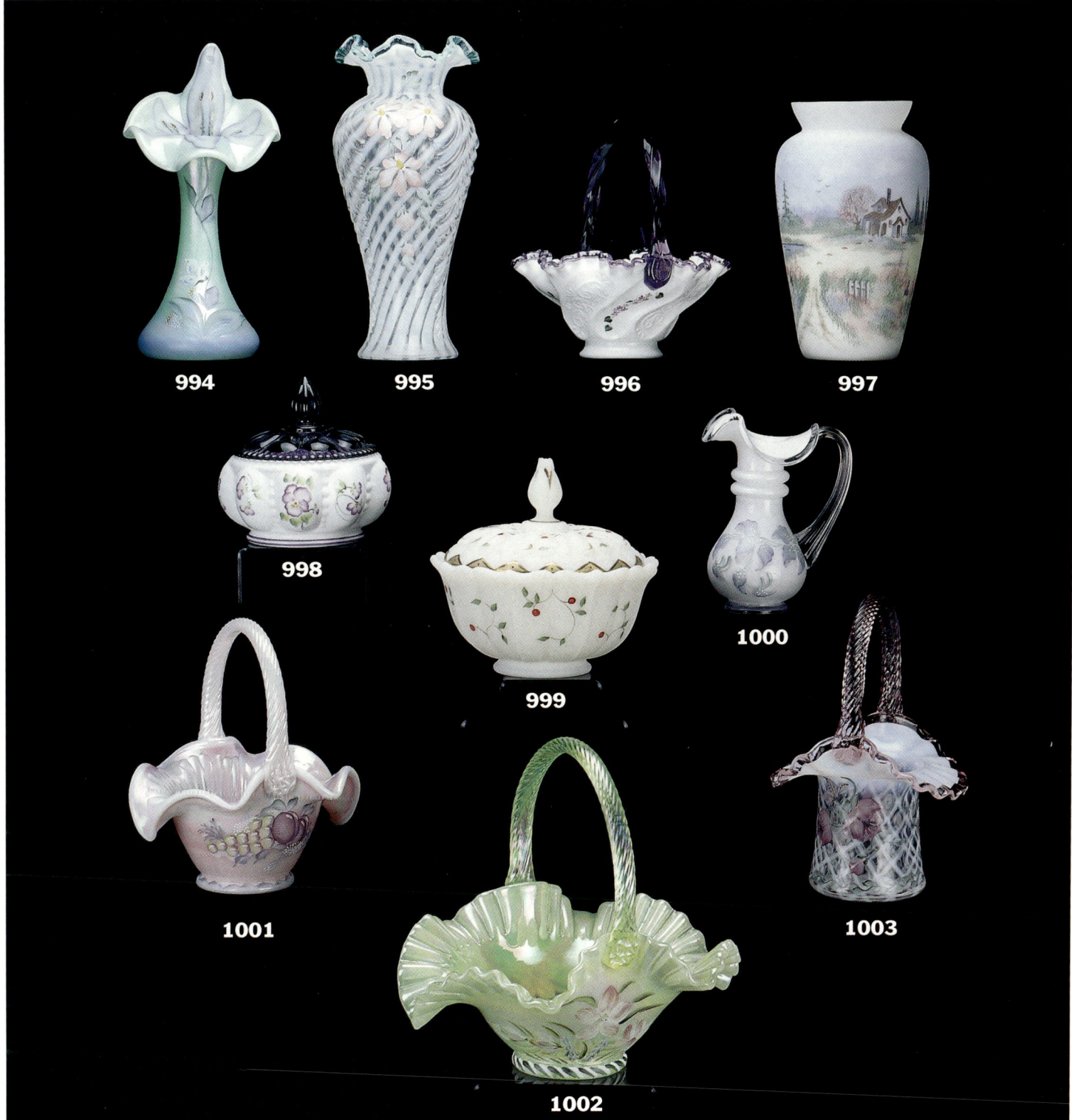

All of these items are from the Family Signature Series.

994. 7255 GG 11" Floral Interlude on Sea Green Satin Tulip vase (Nancy and George Fenton signatures, 1998).

995. 1563 PD Meadow Beauty 11" Feather vase (Nancy Fenton signature, 1996).

996. 6730 PJ handpainted Lilacs 8½" Paisley basket (Bill Fenton signature, 1993).

997. 7661 Z8 Cottage 9" vase (Shelley Fenton signature, 1993).

998. 5585 PF 5" Pansies on Milk Glass covered box (Shelley Fenton signature, 1996).

999. 9333 JX 7" Twining Berries covered box (Tom Fenton signature, 1999).

1000. 4566 CG Morning Mist 6" pitcher (Scott Fenton signature, 1999).

1001. 6833 HH handpainted Rosalene 8" basket (Lynn Fenton signature, 1999).

1002. 2039 SF handpainted 10½" basket (Shelley Fenton signature, 1998).

1003. 4830 DX Trellis 9½" Hat basket (Tom Fenton signature, 1998).

All of these items are from the Family Signature Series.

1004. 3127 NG Starflowers on Cranberry Pearl basket (Mike Fenton signature, 1996).

1005. 4957 SE White Magnolia on Spruce Green 10" vase (Tom Fenton signature, 1996).

1006. 4648 P9 Sweetbrier on Plum Overlay 9" basket (Lynn Fenton signature, 1997).

1007. 7565 Reverse Melon 8" black vase (Mike Fenton signature, 1997).

1008. 2040 TP Hydrangeas on Topaz Opalescent 3-pc. fairy light (Frank M. Fenton signature, 1997).

1009. 5540 LS Irises on Misty Blue pitcher (Don Fenton signature, 1997).

1010. 4751 PI Field Flowers on Champagne Satin 6" vase (Shelley Fenton signature, 1997).

1011. 1559 CW Pansies on Cranberry 9½" vase (Bill Fenton signature, 1994).

1012. 1566 FS Thistle 9" pitcher (Don Fenton signature, 1995).

1013. 9550 TP Hydrangeas on Topaz Opalescent 8" fan vase (Tom Fenton signature, 1997).

All of these items are from the Family Signature Series.

1016. 1216 EH Fuschia 10" Spiral vase (George Fenton signature, 1994).

1017. 3070 AZ Martha's Rose 8½" vase (Shelley Fenton signature, 1999).

1014. 1554 S9 9" Spruce Green hexagonal vase (Don Fenton signature, 1995).

1015. 1567 CW Pansies on Cranberry 7" vase (George Fenton signature, 1995).

1019. 4695 JX Twining Berries sleigh (Mike Fenton signature, 1998).

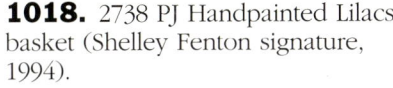

1018. 2738 PJ Handpainted Lilacs basket (Shelley Fenton signature, 1994).

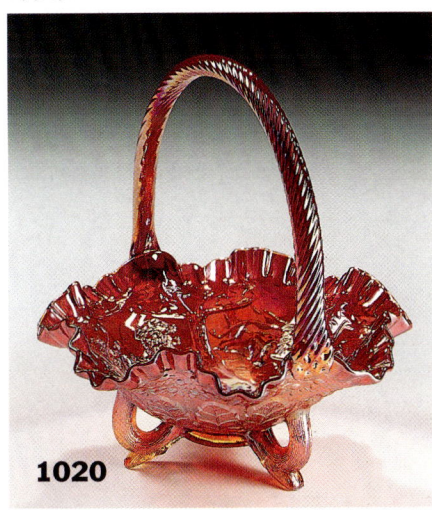

1020. 2779 RN Lion/Leaf 8½" Red Carnival basket (Tom Fenton signature, 1994).

1021. 1217 AO Autumn Gold Opalescent 11" basket (Frank M. Fenton signature, 1994).

1022. 7380 AW Autumn Leaves on Black 9½" candy with cover (Don Fenton signature, 1994).

1023. 4602 SE Magnolia and Berry on Spruce Green 13" urn with cover (George Fenton signature, 1997).

All of these items are from the Family Signature Series.

1024. 1689 LN Tranquility 9½" handpainted vase (Bill and Don Fenton signatures, 1999).

1025. 1640 C1 handpainted Cranberry 11" Rib vase (George Fenton signature, 1993).

1026. 5357 TE Blush Rose on Opaline 8½" vase (George Fenton signature, 1996).

1027. 2752 RN Red Carnival 9" Alpine Thistle vase (Frank M. Fenton signature, 1993).

1028. 1786 PV Vintage 10" Diamond Melon vase (Don Fenton signature, 1993).

1029. 3076 KT Mountain Berry on Gold Overlay 8" basket (Don Fenton signature, 1996).

1030. 3065 DP Asters on Dusty Rose Overlay 6½" pitcher (Lynn Fenton signature, 1996).

1031. 1135 JE Coralene Floral on Celeste Blue Stretch 9½" Diamond basket (Frank M. and Bill Fenton signatures, 1995).

1032. 8691 LS Irises on Misty Blue Satin 4½" clock (Lynn Fenton signature, 1998).

1033. 3271 N4 Colonial Scroll on Royal Purple 6½" bell (Don Fenton signature, 1998).

1034. 7484 XP Violet Satin 5" covered box (George Fenton signature, 1999).

1035. 5188 YZ Covered Hen egg plate (1995; limited to 950).

1036. 8405 YZ Egg fairy light (1995).

These blown eggs were made in 1993.
1037. 5031 WJ Ocean Blue egg.
1038. 5031 WE Plum egg.

These blown eggs were made in 1991.
1039. 4½" 5031 WD.
1040. 3½" 5030 QB.

These blown eggs were made in 1994.
1041. 5031 FU.
1042. 5031 FV.

These blown eggs were made in 1992.
1043. 5031 Q2.
1044. 5031 Q3.

These blown eggs were made in 1996.
1045. 1642 JO.
1046. 1642 JM.

These blown eggs were made in 1995.
1047. 5031 YW.
1048. 5031 YX.

These are from the Birth of A Savior Christmas Series; year of issue and numerical limits are in parentheses.

1049. 7300 KP The Announcement 5" Fairy Light, 1999 (2500).

1050. 3205 KP The Announcement 11" Hurricane Candle, 1999 (1750).

1051. 5146 KP The Announcement 3¾" egg, 1999 (2500).

1052. 7610 XS The Arrival 9" plate, 1998 (2500).

1053. 7566 XS The Arrival 7" oval bell, 1998 (2500).

All of these are from the Christmas Star Series; year of issue and numerical limits are in parentheses.

1054. 7418 VS Silent Night 8" plate, 1994 (1500).

1055. 7418 VT Our Home is Blessed 8" plate, 1995 (1500).

1056. 7418 SN Star of Wonder 8" plate, 1996 (1750).

1057. 7418 RX The Way Home 8" plate, 1997 (1750).

All of these are from the Christmas at Home Series; year of issue and numerical limits are in parentheses.

1058. 8600 HJ Christmas Eve 6" clock, 1991 (1500).

1059. 7300 HQ Family Traditions 5" Fairy Light, 1992 (3500).

1060. 7418 HT Family Holiday 8" plate with stand, 1993 (3500).

1061. 7668 HD Sleigh Ride 6½" bell, 1990 (3500).

These items were for Christmas in the year indicated. If applicable, numerical limits are given in parentheses.

1062. 6864 RY Ornamental Magic 6" Melon bell, 1998.
1063. 5146 RH Poinsettias 3¾" egg, 1999.
1064. 1145 GV Lenten Rose 6½" bell, 1998.
1065. 5146 GM Iced Pinecones egg, 1999.
1066. 7300 KE Jolly Snowman fairy light, 1999.
1067. 7768 KE Jolly Snowman bell, 1999.
1068. 9463 N7 Nativity bell, 1996 (1500).
1069. 5146 AC Golden Winged Angel egg, 1996 (1500).
1070. 7669 ZX 6½" musical bell, 1992 (950).
1071. 5145 QP 3½" Golden Partridge egg, 1996 (1500).
1072. 6662 CH Holly Berries 6½" bell, 1996 (1500).
1073. 5242 WU 4½" Renaissance Angel ornament, 1999.

Note the different bases on the various Collectible Eggs; numerical limits are given in parentheses.

1074. 5140 7W Butterflies on Black, 1992 (2500).
1075. 5140 7V Pink Rose and gold on white opal, 1992 (2500).
1076. 5140 ZN sandcarved Favrene, 1993 (1500).
1077. 5140 D5 Cottage on White Satin, 1993 (2500).
1078. 5145 F2 Hummingbird on Crystal Iridized, 1996 (2500).
1079. 5145 F7 Fish on Spruce Green, 1996 (2500).
1080. 5145 F5 Lake Scene on Ivory Satin, 1996 (2500).
1081. 5145 F5 Floral on Cobalt Blue, 1996 (2500).

All of these Collectible Eggs were made in 1999 and were limited to 3000 each.

1082. 5146 A1 Butterfly on Sea Green.
1083. 5146 A2 Floral and Scroll on Blue Burmese.
1084. 5146 A3 Floral on Empress Rose.
1085. 5146 A4 Floral on Crystal Iridized.
1086. 5146 A5 Lighthouse on Aquamarine Satin.
1087. 5146 A6 Fish on Cobalt.
1088. 5146 A7 Mary Gregory on Ruby.
1089. 5146 A8 Dragonfly and Flower on Champagne.

These Fenton limited edition Santas and Angels were issued in various years (if applicable, numerical limits are given in parentheses). The smaller angel figurines (without numbers) were made in 1985.

1090. 5542 TA 7½" Radiant Angel, 1995 (900).
1091. 5542 QB 7½" Radiant Angel, 1996 (1000).
1092. 5542 PU 7½" Radiant Angel, 1999.
1093. 5279 JM 7" Enchantment Santa, 1999 (4750).
1094. 5144 HN 5¾" Gold Feathered Angel girl, 1998.
1095. 5144 BM 6" Angel bell, 1997.
1096. 5144 JX 5¾" Twining Berries Girl Angel bell, 1998-99.
1097. 5299 VL 8" Northern Lights Santa, 1998.
1098. 5249 JN 8½" Golden Age Santa, 1999.
1099. 5299 JO 8" Bejeweled Santa, 1999.
1100. 5249 VP 8½" Patriotic Santa, 1998 (4750)
1101. 5299 I2 8" Olde Worlde Santa, 1997 (3750).

These "First Edition" pieces in the Fenton Nativity Set were made in groups (three pieces per year) between 1997-2000.

1102. 5055 NS Shepherd set (6½" standing Shepherd, 4¼" kneeling Shepherd, 2¾" Lamb), First Edition, 2000.

1103. 5289 WM Wise Men set (5½" Melchior, 7" Gaspar, 6¾" Balthazar), First Edition, 1998.

1104. 5280 NF Holy Family set (5" Mary, 6¼" Joseph, 2½" l. Baby Jesus), First Edition, 1997.

1105. 5050 NA Gloria Angel set (6¾" Angel, 5½" l. Camel, 4¼" l. Donkey), First Edition, 1999.

1106. FG118 22k goldplated 11¾" Star background (1998).

These "second edition" pieces were made in subsequent years; note the changes in the handpainted decorations when compared with the corresponding First Edition items.

1107. N5050 NA Gloria Angel set.

1108. N5280 NF Holy Family set.

1109. N5289 WM Wise Men set.

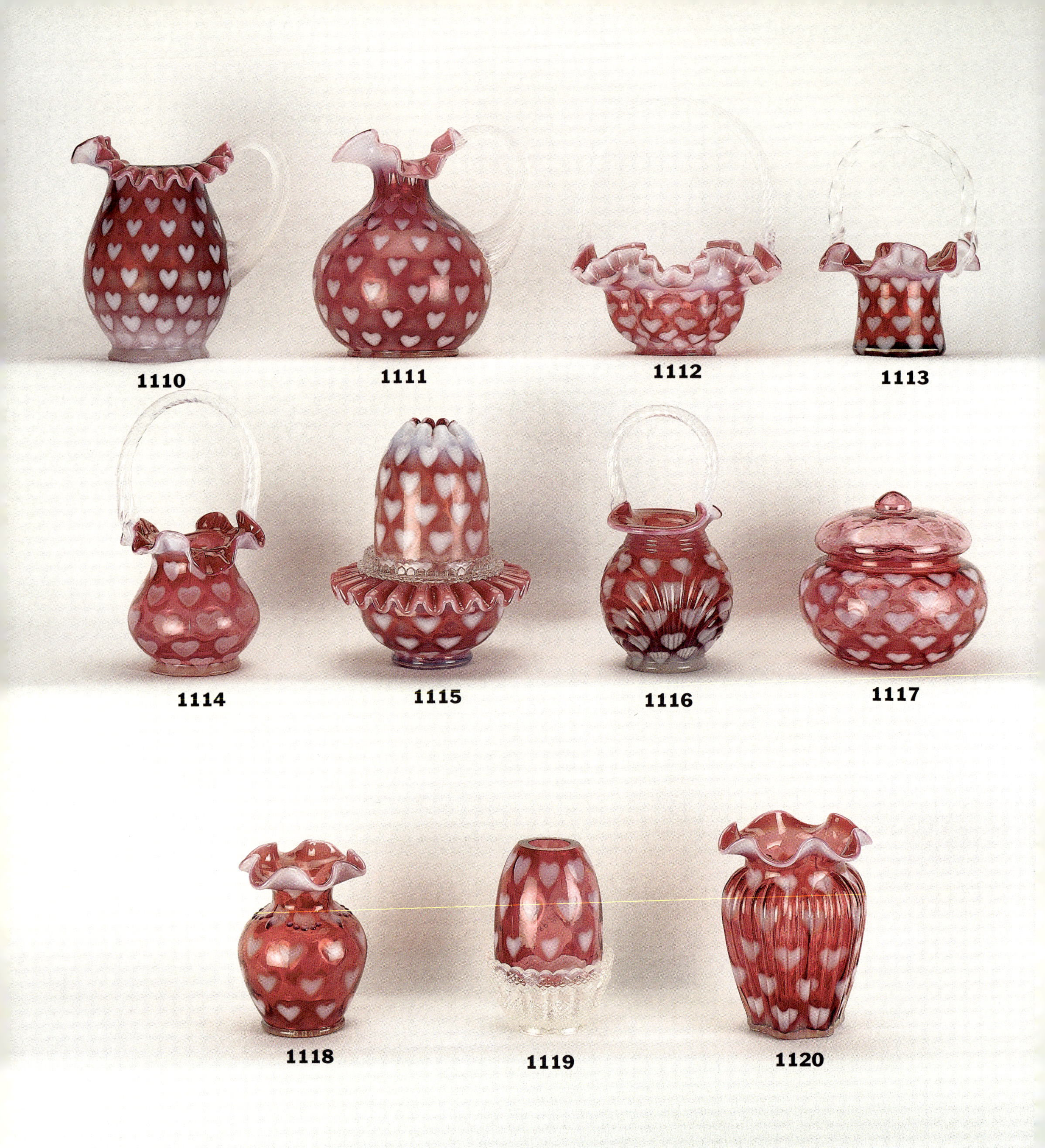

These Heart Optic items in Cranberry Opalescent were made at various times during the 1990s.

1110. Sample pitcher, 1996.
1111. 2169 CR 6½" pitcher, 1997.
1112. 7122 CR Melon basket, 1996.
1113. 4965 CR 7" hat basket, 1997.
1114. 2736 CR 7" basket, 1994.
1115. 2903 CR 3 piece fairy light, 1996.
1116. 2732 CR 7" Caprice basket, 1993.
1117. 4990 CR 4½" covered box, 1998.
1118. 4955 CR 5" vase, 1998.
1119. 4905 CR 5" fairy light, 1998.
1120. 2755 CR 5½" ribbed vase, 1995.

These Mary Gregory pieces were made by Fenton at various times in the 1990s decade. Dates are given for each item, and the limits for numbered limited editions are shown in parentheses.

1121. 1500 DI Breezy Day guest set, 1997 (1500).
1122. 1533 DI Breezy Day 11" hex basket, 1998 (1950).
1123. 3201 RK The Swan 13" lamp, 1999 (1250).
1124. 1554 RP Daydreaming 9" vase, 1996 (1500).
1125. 1539 DQ Girl Swinging 8" basket, 1997 (1500).
1126. 3275 DM 6½" Pitcher, 1998 (1950).
1127. 5145 RG 4" egg on stand, 1995.
1128. 1613 R8 8" basket, 1999 (2250).
1129. 3249 R8 5" vase, 1999 (2500).
1130. 1532 RK The Swan hat basket, 1996 (2000).
1131. 7463 OG Dusty Rose bell, 1992.
1132. 2906 RK 5½" perfume, 1998 (1950).

With the exception of Fig. 1146, these items are from a Fenton "Folk Art" grouping limited to sales through the end of March. The year of issue is given for each piece.

1133.	4683 NU 7" Bunny box, 1997.	**1141.**	5186 NH 5" Hen on nest, 1996.
1134.	4683 CQ 7" Bunny box, 1999.	**1142.**	5292 NO 5½" Rooster, 1997.
1135.	4683 FG 7" Bunny box, 1998.	**1143.**	5292 FV 5½" Rooster, 1998.
1136.	4683 NB 7" Bunny box, 1996.	**1144.**	5186 FK 5" Hen on nest, 1998.
1137.	4680 FK 8½" Rooster box, 1998.	**1145.**	5186 NE 5" Hen on nest, 1997.
1138.	5257 FV 8½" Standing Rooster, 1998.	**1146.**	5188 TJ 12" Hen Egg Plate, 1997 (limited to 950).
1139.	4680 NA 8½" Rooster box, 1996.	**1147.**	5292 CB 5½" Rooster, 1999.
1140.	4680 NJ 8½" Rooster box, 1997.		

Each year since 1996, Fenton's decorating designers have showcased their talents in the Designer Bell Series (each bell is numbered and limited to 2500).

These were designed by Frances Burton.
1148. 4568 EB Gilded Berry 6½" bell, 1996.
1149. 8267 CF Forest Cottage 7" Medallion bell, 1997.
1150. 3279 GN Hibiscus 6½" ribbed bell, 1998.
1151. 1145 EY Butterfly 7" bell, 1999.

These bells were designed by Kim Plauché.
1152. 7667 HW Wild Rose 5½" bell, 1996.
1153. 4629 AF Roses on Ribbons 6½" bell, 1997.
1154. 1145 QW Fairy Roses 6" bell, 1998.
1155. 7562 AG Deco Fuschia bell, 1999.

These bells were designed by Martha Reynolds.
1156. 4564 IN Floral Medallion 6" bell, 1996.
1157. 1145 GF Butterflies 6" bell, 1997.
1158. 2962 YD Topaz Swirl 7" Paisley bell, 1998.
1159. 7566 HT Iridescence 7" oval bell, 1999.

These bells were designed by Robin Spindler.
1160. 7562 PP Gardenia 7" bell, 1996.
1161. 9862 BF Feathers 6¾" Whitton bell, 1997.
1162. 9667 UJ Bleeding Hearts 7" Aurora bell, 1998.
1163. 6662 NI Gilded Daisy bell, 1999.

All of these are Fenton limited edition items (if applicable, numerical limits are given in parentheses).

1164. 5228 WB 7" doll with musical wooden base, 1996 (2500).

1165. 5141 BG 8" handpainted Burmese 8" girl figurine, 1997.

1166. 5328 XP handpainted floral on Violet Satin 6¾" doll, 1999 Showcase Dealer Exclusive (Nancy Fenton signature).

1167. 1960 PT Champagne Satin miniature five-piece water set (4½" pitcher with Plum Iridescent ring), 1998.

1168. 4807 PT Champagne Satin with Plum Iridescent ring, 4½" mini epergne, 1998.

1169. 6800 EZ Spruce Green Carnival, five-piece 3¾" Hobstar and Feather miniature punch bowl set, 1997.

1170. 6801 PT Champagne Satin with Plum Iridescent ring, 3¾" five-piece miniature punch bowl set, 1998.

1171. 6800 DZ Dusty Rose Iridized five-piece miniature punch bowl set, 1996.

1172. 7199 WB handpainted Milk Glass and crystal four piece vanity set, 1993 (1500).

1173. 8901 N9 handpainted English Daisy on iridized crystal, miniature table set with 10½" tray, 1999 (1500).

1174. 5575 FI limited edition lamp for Fall, 1995.

1175. Burmese 5575 5X limited edition lamp for Fall, 1996.

1176. Spring Woodlands 9509 XQ limited edition lamp for Fall, 1997.

1177. Wild Rose 9872 XF limited edition lamp for Fall, 1998.

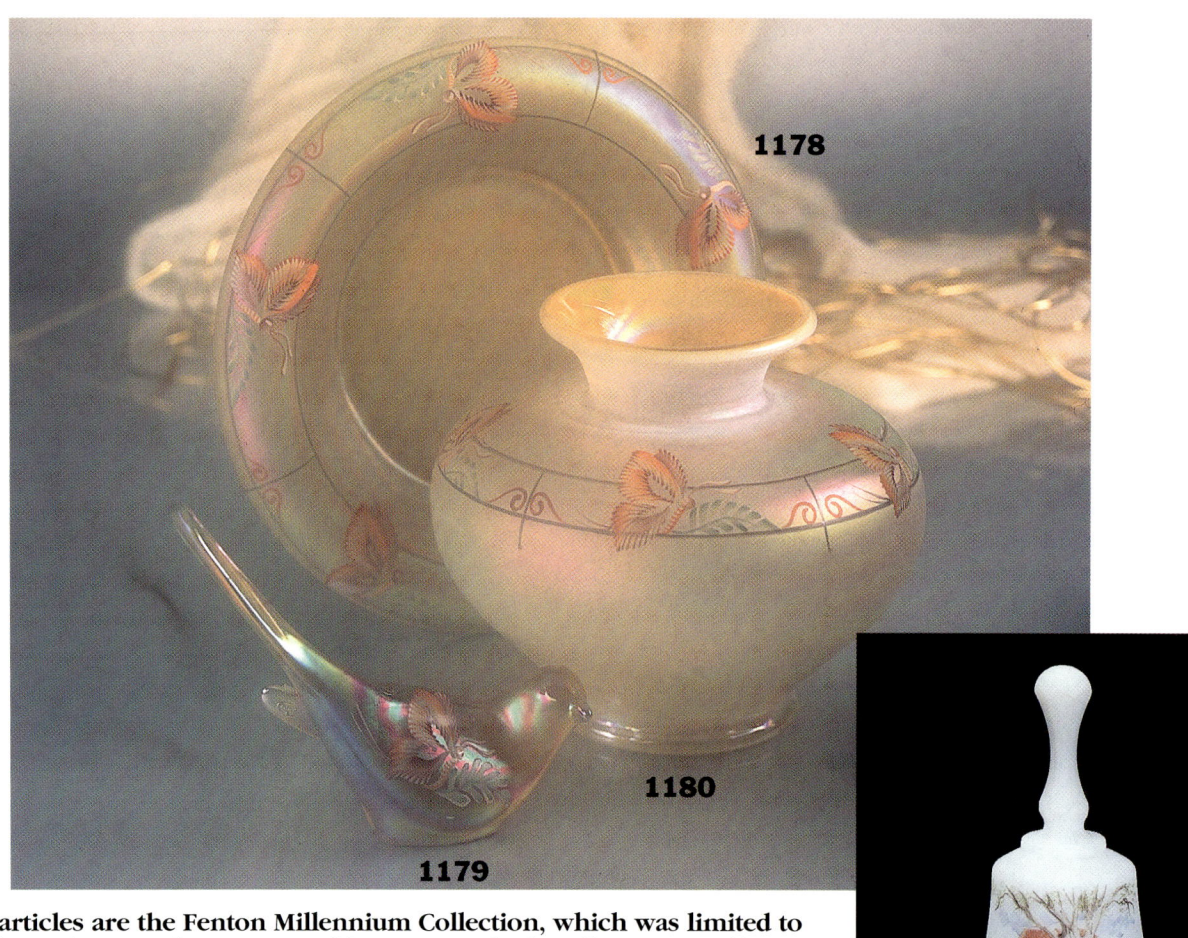

These articles are the Fenton Millennium Collection, which was limited to sales through November 15, 1999 (they are marked "Millennium Collection" on the bottom).

1178. 2747 JE 10" rolled rim bowl.
1179. 5197 JE 6" Happiness Bird.
1180. 6470 JE 6½" vase.

The Yellow Ribbon bell was produced during the first half of 1991. The reverse side has these words: "In honor of our men and women who served their country well for a peaceful world."

1181. 7668 YQ bell, 1991 (limited to 1000).

These bells were made to celebrate the Columbus Quincentennial--the 500th anniversary of the discovery of America. Separate panels feature a bust of Columbus, a sailing ship, and the wording "Discovery of America 1492-1992."

1182. 6571 TZ Cobalt Carnival Columbus Quincentennial bell.
1183. 6571 RN Red Carnival Columbus Quincentennial bell.
1184. 6571 WI White Carnival Columbus Quincentennial bell.

Showcase Dealer Exclusives

1185

1186

1187

1185. Periwinkle on Blue Burmese 7501 TA three-piece fairy light (Fall, 1999, Showcase Dealer Exclusive).

1186. Fields of Gold 1559 HC Rubina Verde 9½" vase (Fall 1998, Showcase Dealer Exclusive).

1187. French Opalescent 3185 ER pitcher with Sea Mist Green ring and handle (Spring 1997, Showcase Dealer Exclusive).

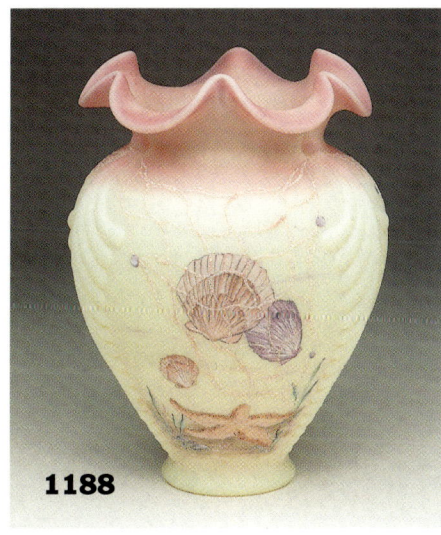
1188

1189

1188. Burmese Sea Dreams 1649 UY vase (Fall, 1995, Showcase Dealer Exclusive).

1189. 1649 MZ Mulberry vase (Fall, 1997, Showcase Dealer Exclusive).

1190

1191

1190. Cranberry Opalescent 3558 CR Buttons and Braids vase (Spring, 1995, Showcase Dealer Exclusive.

1191. Royal Purple 3200 N4 two-piece tumble-up set (Spring, 1998, Showcase Dealer Exclusive).

These Rosalene and Blue Burmese items are Fenton limited editions (if applicable, numerical limits are given in parentheses).

1192. 5228 NX Violets on Rosalene 7" doll, 1999.
1193. 6330 UQ Periwinkle on Blue Burmese 5½" basket, 1999 (1950).
1194. 6548 UQ Periwinkle on Blue Burmese 11" vase, 1999 (1950).
1195. 8100 UQ Periwinkle on Blue Burmese 7" guest set, 1999 (1500).
1196. 5203 NX Violets on Rosalene 4" Praying Children, 1999.
1197. 7059 WA Rosebuds on Rosalene 6" vase, 1998.
1198. 4105 NX Violets on Rosalene 5" w. music box ("My Heart Will Go On"), 1999.
1199. 5270 WA Rosebuds on Rosalene 6½" Natalie Ballerina, 1998.
1200. 5271 NX Violets on Rosalene 4½" Butterfly, 1999.
1201. 7000 WA Rosebuds on Rosalene 6½" perfume bottle, 1998.
1202. 7009 WA Rosebuds on Rosalene 4½" w., two-piece puff box, 1998.
1203. 2785 NX Violets on Rosalene 5" Heart perfume bottle, 1999.

These Red Carnival pieces are from a 1991 Fenton catalog.

1204. 9262 RN 6" Rose bell.
1205. 1995 RN 6" Daisy and Button slipper.
1206. 5151 RN 3½" Sitting Bear.
1207. 9480 RN 8" Chessie candy box.
1208. 4801 RN four-piece Diamond Lace epergne set.
1209. 5730 RN 7" Rose basket.
1210. 1990 RN 4" Daisy and Button boot.
1211. 8654 RN 8¼" Sunburst vase.
1212. 2557 RN 6" Beaded Melon vase.
1213. 8256 RN Mitre and Circle swung vase (8½" to 13" tall, average is 10½").
1214. 8335 RN 7¼" open edge basket.

These Red Carnival items are from a 1992 Fenton catalog.

1215. 5750 RN 9" Rose vase.
1216. 9065 RN 5½" Sable Arche bell.
1217. 5150 RN 6½" Atlantis vase.
1218. 4655 RN 7½" Daffodil vase.
1219. 8233 RN 9" h. Orange Tree and Cherry basket.
1220. 8230 RN 8⅜" w. two-handled bon bon.
1221. 5171 RN 4½" Butterfly on stand.
1222. 9185 RN 8¾" Panelled Daisy candy with cover.
1223. 6573 RN 5½" Peacock and Dahlia basket.
1224. 9120 RN 5¾" Fine Cut and Block comport.

These Red Carnival (RN) and Red Carnival with handpainted Buttercups and Berries (R1) items are from a 1995 Fenton catalog.

1225. 6576 RN 4" Apple tree tumbler.
1226. 6575 RN 8¾" Apple Tree pitcher.
1227. 2924 R1 8½" Holly basket.
1228. 4605 R1 20" Basketweave lamp.
1229. 2857 RN 7¼" Wild Rose vase.
1230. 2927 RN 6" w. Wild Rose rose bowl.
1231. 2926 RN 4½" nutdish.
1232. 2931 RN 5" slipper.
1233. 1936 RN 8" Daisy and Button basket.
1234. 5109 RN 4½" Polar Bear.
1235. 2980 RN 4¼" 2 pc. Pear box.
1236. 6761 R1 7" Paisley bell.
1237. 2970 RN 8½" candy with cover (Mike Fenton signature).
1238. 9499 RN 5" w. Fenton oval logo.
1239. 8405 R1 5¾" fairy light.

1240. 5205 P2 Clown sets (matched and numbered; limited to 970 sets).

1240

These Plum Carnival items are from Fenton's 1997 General Catalog.

1241. PX Diamond Lace four-piece epergne set (samples only; not in the line).

1242. 8769 PX 10" Thistle vase.

1243. 5163 P2 4" Bird.

1244. 6869 PX 9½" pitcher.

1245. 6705 PX 20" Paisley lamp.

1246. 9458 PX 8" Swan vase.

1247. 5165 P2 3¾" Cat.

1248. 5731 PX 7½" Hummingbird basket.

1249. 5305 PX 5" perfume with stopper.

1250. 1535 PX 9½" Paneled Diamond basket.

1251. 9560 PX 6½" Templebells bell.

1252. 6780 PX 7" candy with cover.

These Plum Carnival items are from Fenton's 1998 General Catalog.

1254. 7676 PX 5½" Viking candleholder.
1255. 7653 PX 7½" Daffodil vase.
1256. 7677 PX 13½" l. Viking bowl.
1257. 9014 PX 6½" Aztec jug.
1258. 2035 PX 6" Ruffles basket.
1259. 2970 PX 8½" box with cover.
1260. 9252 AX 6½" Rose vase.
1261. 6838 PX 8" three-toed basket.
1262. 9357 AX 4½" vase.
1263. 5207 AX Bear set (matched and numbered; limited to 1250 sets).
1264. 5292 PX 5½" Rooster.
1265. 6866 AX 7" Medallion bell.
1266. 7640 PX 5½" square box.

1253. 8999 AX 18" Student lamp with prisms.

These Spruce Carnival items are from Fenton's 1999 General Catalog.

1267. 5969 US 8" basket.
1268. 9066 US 6¼" Whitton bell.
1269. 7693 US 6" Melon vase.
1270. 5000 US three-piece Cat set (matched and numbered; limited to 1950 sets).
1271. F9307 US 20" Student lamp with prisms (also sold as 9307 US 20" Student lamp without prisms).

1272. 9188 SI 7¼" tobacco jar.
1273. 5214 SI 3" Scottie dog.
1274. 6869 SI 8½" pitcher.
1275. 5153 SI 3½" hand vase.

1276. 5930 SI 7" basket.
1277. 5177 SI 11" Alley cat.
1278. 2779 SI 8½" Lion basket.

These items were made for (or sold through) the Fenton Gift Shop.

1279. 5150 PL "Peachalene" Atlantis vase (Collector's Sale, 1990).

1280. Z9480 GE Sea Green Satin Chessie box (February Sale, 1998).

1281. Z9188 BR Burmese tobacco jar (February Sale, 1997).

1282. S9188 NC Cobalt Blue iridescent Tobacco Jar (Collector's Sale, 1996).

1283. GS133 HP handpainted Burmese three-piece cat set, matched and numbered (February Sale, 2000).

1284. GS094 HP handpainted Burmese three-piece bear set, matched and numbered (February Sale, 1999).

1285. 8228 RJ Rosalene iridized Hearts and Flowers bowl with crimped edge (February Sale, 1992).

1286. DS288 UB Blue Burmese Coin Dot basket (February Sale, 1999).

1287. GS007 BR Burmese spiral optic Hobnail basket, Bill Fenton signature (February Sale, 1996).

1288. DS289 UB Blue Burmese spiral optic basket (February Sale, 1999).

These Fenton items were sold through Cracker Barrel Restaurant Country Stores. The Asters and Butterflies decoration was developed for 1998 and was used on different items in 1999. The statue of Cracker Barrel's Uncle Herschel was presented to Fenton in 1999 "in appreciation of your friendship and support over the past 30 years."

1289. 9185 OQ Violet Iridescent Panelled Daisy candy box; made in 1999 with CRACKER BARREL OLD COUNTRY STORE 30th ANNIVERSARY on the underside of the base.

1290. 7429 5J 6" comport (Mike Fenton signature, 1999).

1291. 5228 5J doll (Shelley Fenton signature, 1998).

1292. 7370 5J 6" pitcher (Tom Fenton signature, 1999).

1293. 2777 5J 8" basket (Bill Fenton signature, 1998).

1294. 5165 5J 3¾" Cat (Don Fenton signature, 1998).

1295. 6864 5J 6" bell (George Fenton signature, 1998).

1296. 5151 5J 3½" Bear Cub (Lynn Fenton signature, 1999).

1297. 5290 5J 5" Slipper (Scott Fenton signature, 1999).

Made as Special Orders for the Martha Stewart organization, these pieces were sold through the "Martha By Mail" catalog (some are marked MBM on the underside).

1298. DS315 SU lunch plate, 1999.
1299. DS211 SU tumbler, 1998.
1300. DS313 SU 5" bowl, 1999.
1301. DS191 SU medium flower pot, 1997.
1302. DS190 SU small flower pot, 1997.
1303. DS192 SU large flower pot, 1997.
1304. K5182 SU Hen on Nest, 1999.
1305. DS209 SU soap box set, 1998.
1306. K5116 SU Leaf plate, 2000.
1307. 7381 MI Milk Glass footed candy dish, 1998.
1308. K5188 SU Hen plate, 1999.
1309. DS233 SU mini butterfly set, 1998.

As indicated, these Fenton Special Orders pieces were made for a variety of customers.

- **1310.** K1457 T3 Coin Dot Topaz Opalescent vase with Cobalt ring (Rosso, 1998).
- **1311.** K3834 T3 Topaz Opalescent Hobnail basket with Cobalt handle (Rosso, 1997).
- **1312.** D5176 T3 Fern Optic topaz opalescent tulip vase with Cobalt crest (Rosso, 1997).
- **1313.** K8437 T3 Topaz Opalescent Lily of the Valley basket with Cobalt handle (Rosso, 1997).
- **1314.** DS292 T3 Straight Rib Topaz Opalescent vase with Cobalt Crest (Rosso, 1999).
- **1315.** K3183 H8 "Circle of Love" crimped Tulip vase (Joyce's Collectibles, 1998).
- **1316.** G0360 HP handpainted Poinsettias bell (Wheeling Park Commission, 1996).
- **1317.** DS316 HP handpainted French Opalescent bell with Cobalt ring (Longaberger, 1999).
- **1318.** K5134 TO Topaz opalescent snail (Rosso, 1998).
- **1319.** K5168 TO Topaz Opalescent Owl (Rosso, 1998).
- **1320.** K5412 TO Topaz Opalescent Raccoon (Rosso, 1999).
- **1321.** K5166 TO Topaz Opalescent Frog (Rosso, 1998).
- **1322.** K5149 TO Topaz Opalescent Love Bug (Rosso, 1999).
- **1323.** K5215 TO Topaz Opalescent Squirrel (Rosso, 1999).
- **1324.** K7488 H8 "Circle of Love" Blue Burmese ginger jar (Joyce's Collectibles, 1998).
- **1325.** DS122 H8 "Circle of Love" Burmese pitcher (Joyce's Collectibles, 1997).
- **1326.** Burmese Farmyard cuspidor, made from Jewelled Heart mould and Farmyard plunger (Singleton Bailey, 1991).
- **1327.** F177 BE Burmese lamp, Aladdin Industrial Inc., 1997.

These pieces were made as Special Orders for various customers.

1328. DS077 PL Plum drapery vase (Metropolitan Museum of Art, 1998).

1329. M8802 FN Himalayan Mountain Scene sandcarved on Favrene oval vase (Compaq Computer Company, 1999, Frank M. Fenton signature).

1330. D5065 HP handpainted petal pink doll bell (Mary C. Walrath's Southern Belle Collection, No. 2, 1994).

1331. DS090 PX Plum Iridized Poppy vase (Singleton Bailey, 1997).

1332. Cobalt blue iridized Grape and Cable vase (Northwood Art Glass, 1999).

1333. S5474 KN Cobalt blue Dolphin candlestick (Sandwich Historical Society, 1996.

1334. FS038 PL Plum Lovebird vase (Holophane, 1996).

1335. DS197 RN Ruby Satin iridescent Christmas compote (David Richardson, 1997).

1336. Cobalt Blue mortar and pestle (made for West Virginia University's Department of Pharmacy).

1337. K5138 and K5139 PO Plum opalescent Kissing Boy and Girl (Carolyn's Collectibles, 1999).

1338. 4697 SZ MTV logo for awards and presentations, 1991.

1339. FS035 KN Cobalt Blue Mayflower salt dip (Sandwich Historical Society, 1998).

1340. K7463 cobalt blue bell, "Celebrating Our Heritage West Virginia 1799-1999" (Wood County Courthouse scene on reverse).

1341. K1774 Twilight Blue bell, "New Williamstown Bridge 1992".

1342. K7566 Ruby bell ,"First United Methodist Church Parkersburg, West Virginia 200th Anniversary."

1343. 08127 6P Football (crystal sprayed blue) with wood base, made for the first home game at the new Erickson All-Sports Facility in Parkersburg, WV, September 24, 1999.

1344. FS035 LL Misty Blue Opalescent Mayflower salt dip (Sandwich Historical Society, 1998).

1345. DS016 TL Celeste Blue Stretch fan vase (Metropolitan Museum of Art, 1993).

These items were made for QVC.

1346. C5177 SY Stiegel Green iridized Alley Cat, 1994.
1347. CV127 OD 8½" Mulberry vase with floral decoration (Today's Special Value, March 1996).
1348. 3148 CR Cranberry Opalescent pitcher (scheduled for QVC, but not completed due to production problems; these were sold through the Fenton Gift Shop in 1991).
1349. CV098 AZ iridized French Opalescent basket with Spruce Green ring and handle and handpainted azaleas, 1995.
1350. C3801 DN Dusty Rose iridized mini-epergne, 1993
1351. C5532 BZ Azure Blue iridized Butterfly bonbon, 1992.
1352. C9388 RN Ruby iridized candy box and cover, 1991.
1353. CV129 KO Cobalt Blue Opalescent 6" Melon pitcher (George Fenton signature), 1996.
1354. CV120 7B French Opalescent cruet with green stopper and handle and pink and green vining floral decoration (Frank M. Fenton signature), 1997.
1355. CV172 H2 Topaz Opalescent hat basket with floral decoration, 1997.
1356. Cobalt Blue iridized toothpick or votive candle holder (sold with an identical item in Dusty Rose iridized as CV103 AS), 1995.
1357. CV190 Q9 Misty Blue perfume bottle with plum edge and heart stopper and Vining Floral decoration, 1997.

These Burmese Diamond Optic pieces with handpainted rose decoration were sold on QVC during the 1990s.

1358. CV278 RB Arches basket, 1999.
1359. C6450 RB pinch vase, 1995.
1360. CV180 RB guest set, 1997.
1361. CV142 RB three-piece fairy light, 1996.
1362. CV185 RB vase, 1997.

1363. CV120 RB cruet with stopper, 1996.
1364. CV262 RB blown egg, 1999.
1365. C1724 RB rose bowl, 1999.
1366. C1700 RB two-piece fairy light, 1995.

These Burmese Diamond Optic pieces with handpainted rose decoration were sold on QVC during the 1990s.

1367. CV280 RB vase (Bill Fenton signature), 1999.
1368. CV233 RB Ginger Jar, 1998.
1369. CV266 RB vase, 1999.
1370. CV163 RB 4" vase, 1997.
1371. CV001 RB 7" pinch vase, 1996.
1372. CV228 RB urn vase, 1998.
1373. CV241 RB perfume bottle with stopper, 1998.
1374. CV204 RB basket (Don Fenton signature), 1998.
1375. C1132 RB 7" pitcher (Don Fenton signature), 1996.

The Heirloom Collection is an on-going series for QVC. Strictly limited and numbered, these pieces embody elements from a specific design period. Numerical limits are given in parentheses.

1376. CV191 XY Stylized flowers and Chinese willows on a Sea Green pastel vase with Don Fenton signature, 1997 (500).

1377. C2932 Z2 Floral on Rose Overlay basket with Frank M. Fenton signature, 1997 (250).

1378. CV206 NZ Greco-Roman decoration with gold high lights on Cranberry amphora vase with George Fenton signature, 1998 (400).

1379. C7480 N4 Floral decoration and gold highlights on Royal Purple box and cover with George Fenton signature, 1997 (350).

1380. C1649 NG Tudor rose handpainted on Gold Overlay Feather vase, 1999 (800).

1381. C7603 WV Gold floral Baroque motif on Favrene box, 1998 (500).

1382. CV268 BV Italian Renaissance decoration on Cranberry bottle with Nancy Fenton signature, 1999 (1000).

1383. C2743 2L Sandcarved and decorated dark Plum Satin vase, 1998 (500).

These Diamond Jubilee Collection items were sold on QVC during 1998, which was Bill Fenton's 75th year.

1384. C6839 BC Wisteria Stretch basket with dark Plum edge and handpainted Wisteria flowers (October).

1385. CV212 AJ Champagne Opalescent Iridized Satin Drapery basket with Aquamarine edge and handle (March).

1386. CV203 2A Spruce Green Overlay decorated pitcher, accompanied by biographical booklet shown (January).

1387. C1500 Q9 Misty Blue Opalescent guest set with Plum handle and handpainted Pansies decoration (August).

1388. CV221 CC Cranberry Heavy Drape pitcher with ribbed handle (April).

1389. C1554 6J Cobalt Blue 9" Hexagonal vase with Spruce Green edge and handpainted Morning Glories (November).

1390. C7424 U1 Royal Purple rose bowl with handpainted floral decoration (June).

141

These New Century Collection items were sold on QVC during 1999. Each piece featured "skilled glass artisans and the elements that fuel their artistry."

1391. CV257 IV Iridized French opalescent square vase with special spruce green core and handpainted decoration (Blowers--Discovery; Bill Fenton signature).

1392. CV283 BU Spruce Green Opalescent basket with Plum ring and handle and handpainted Peruvian lily decoration (Fenton Family--Vision; 12 family signatures).

1393. CV196 HF Burmese bell with handpainted embossed grapes (Pressers--Tradition; Bill Fenton signature).

1394. CV275 FJ Turquoise pitcher with handpainted peonies and butterfly pattern and gold accents (Decorators--Imagination).

1395. C5301YF Decorated white satin perfume bottle with iridescent stopper (Mouldmakers--Craftmanship).

1396. CV259 KG Cobalt opalescent basket with hand painted white vining flowers (Handlers--Innovation).

1397. CV295 QY Rosalene spiral tulip vase with hand painted decoration (Finishers--Quality; Bill Fenton signature).

These limited editions are Glass Messenger Subscriber Exclusives or Family Signing Event pieces, as indicated.

1398. 1533 JN Roselle on Cranberry basket, Glass Messenger Subscriber Exclusive, 1996 (George Fenton signature).

1399. 7255 UZ handpainted Morning Glory on Burmese Tulip vase, Glass Messenger Subscriber Exclusive, 1998. (Frank M. Fenton signature).

1400. 6831 ZM Dancing Windflowers on Lotus Mist Burmese basket, Glass Messenger Subscriber Exclusive, 2000 (Tom Fenton signature).

1401. 9475 R6 French Rose on Rosalene Melon vase, Glass Messenger Subscriber Exclusive, 1997. (Bill Fenton signature).

1402. 2731 RJ Rosalene Lamb's Tongue basket, Family Signing Events, 1993.

1403. 2786 KO Cobalt Opalescent Snowflake basket, Family Signing Events, 1995.

1404. 7633 LW Champagne Satin basket with Sea Mist Ring, Family Signing Events, 1997.

1405. 4637 IP Plum Opalescent Button Arches basket, Family Signing Events, 1997.

1406. 2778 IP Plum Opalescent Strawberry basket, Family Signing Events, 1994.

1407. 3056 UH Royal Purple Swirl vase, Family Signing Events, 1998.

1408. 7464 7B Burmese pitcher, Family Signing Events, 1993.

1409. 7793 UY Blue Burmese Daffodil vase, Family Signing Events, 1999.

1410. 4026 VQ Blue Harmony vase, Glass Messenger Subscriber Exclusive, 1999 (Don Fenton signature).

These items were made by Fenton for various glass collector clubs, as indicated.

1411. DS162 B3 Ruby Stretch two-handled Dolphin comport (Stretch Glass Society, 1994).

1412-1413. Holiday Green Carnival glass whimsey Apple Tree tumbler and pitcher (National Fenton Glass Society, 1992-3).

1414. DS325 HP decorated Blue Burmese hurricane light (Fenton Art Glass Collectors of America, 1999).

1415. Handpainted iridescent pitcher (International Carnival Glass Ass'n, 1991).

1416. FS004 IT Plum Opalescent Carnival glass Frolicking Bears tumbler (International Carnival Glass Ass'n, 1997).

1417. Green Peacock and Dahlia plate (Carnival Glass Society, UK, 1997).

1418. Whimsey basket, made from DS232 HP plate (Woodsland World Wide Carnival Glass Ass'n, 1999).

1419. FS003 RN Ruby Satin Carnival glass Good Luck plate (Heart of America Carnival Glass Ass'n, 1993).

1420. K9126 TS Topaz Opalescent Poppy rose bowl (San Diego Carnival Glass Collectors Club & Southern California Carnival Glass Club, 1999).

1421-1422. S5277 MN Mandarin Red and K5277 GE Sea Green Satin Happy Cats (Fenton Art Glass Collectors of America, 1996).

1423. Red Carnival glass Strawberry basket (American Carnival Glass Ass'n, 1991).

1424. Sage Mist 5197 Happiness Bird (National Fenton Glass Society, 1991).

1425. FS061 0F Plum Stretch Dolphin sandwich tray (Stretch Glass Society, 1998).

1426. 0553 PX Plum Carnival glass Guardian Angel (Pacific Northwest Fenton Ass'n, 1996).

1427-1429. DS283 PO Plum Opalescent mini vase, tri-crimp; DS286 PO mini fan vase; and DS284 PO mini tulip vase (National Fenton Glass Society, 1999).

DESCRIPTIONS OF COVERS

Front Cover

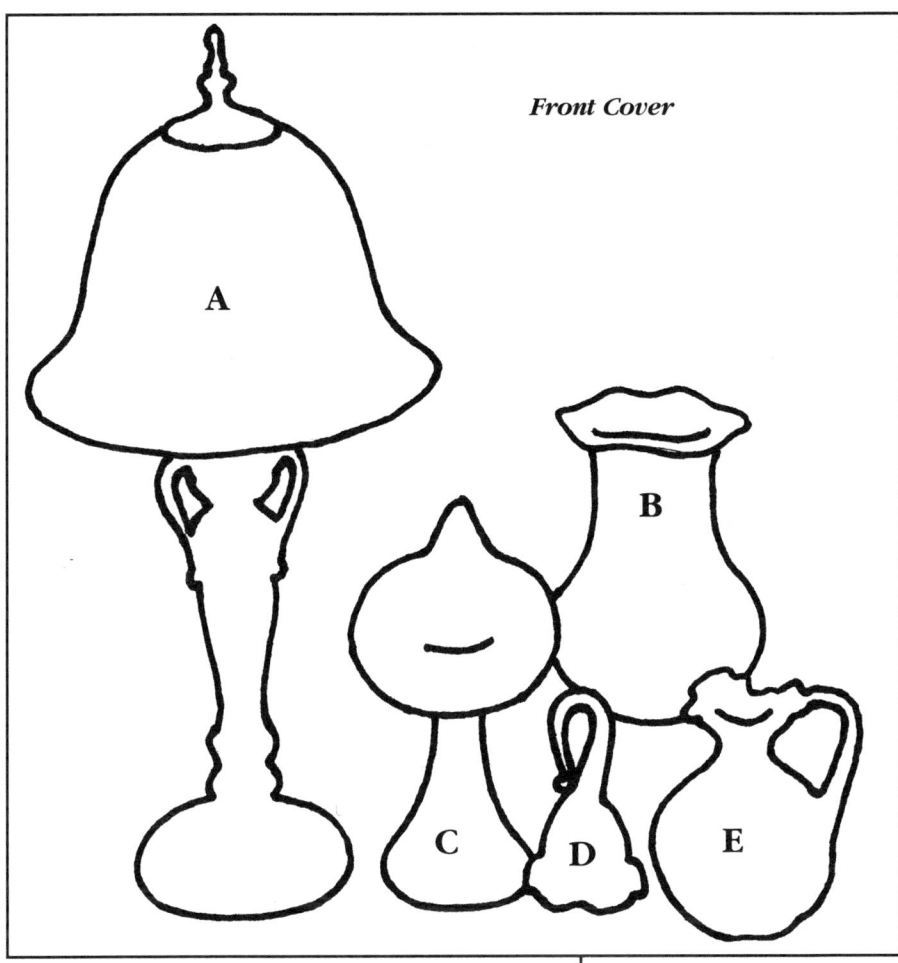

A. 6250 DR Tulips 26" reverse painted crystal satin lamp, with decoration designed by Frances Burton. Connoisseur Collection, 1999 (limited to 750).

B. 5359 WP Leaves and Vines 9" vase, created by David Fetty with decoration designed by Martha Reynolds. Connoisseur Collection, 1998 (limited to 950).

C. 7255 UZ Morning Glories on Burmese 11" tulip vase, with decoration designed by Frances Burton. Glass Messenger Exclusive, 1998 (Frank M. Fenton signature; limited to sales through December 31, 1998).

D. 3271 N4 Royal Purple 6½" blown bell with Colonial Scroll decoration designed by Frances Burton (Don Fenton signature; limited to sales through April 30, 1998).

E. 3275 DM 6½" pitcher with Mary Gregory–style decoration designed by Martha Reynolds, 1998 (limited to 1950).

F. 8812 G1 Favrene 10½" vase with fruit decoration designed by Martha Reynolds. Connoisseur Collection, 1991 (limited to 850).

G. 8817 DJ French Opalescent 8" vase with After the Rain decoration designed by Robin Spindler. Connoisseur Collection, 1998 (12 Fenton family members' signatures; limited to 2250).

H. 1581 BW Rubina Verde 5¼" Melon Box with decoration designed by Martha Reynolds. Historic Collection, 1997 (limited to 1750).

I. 5299 I2 8" Olde World Santa, mould designed by Jon Saffell and decoration designed by Martha Reynolds, 1997 (limited to 3750).

J. 7255 GG Sea Green Satin 11" tulip vase with Floral Interlude decoration designed by Martha Reynolds, Family Signature Series (George W. Fenton and Nancy Fenton signatures; limited to sales through December 31, 1998).

Back Cover

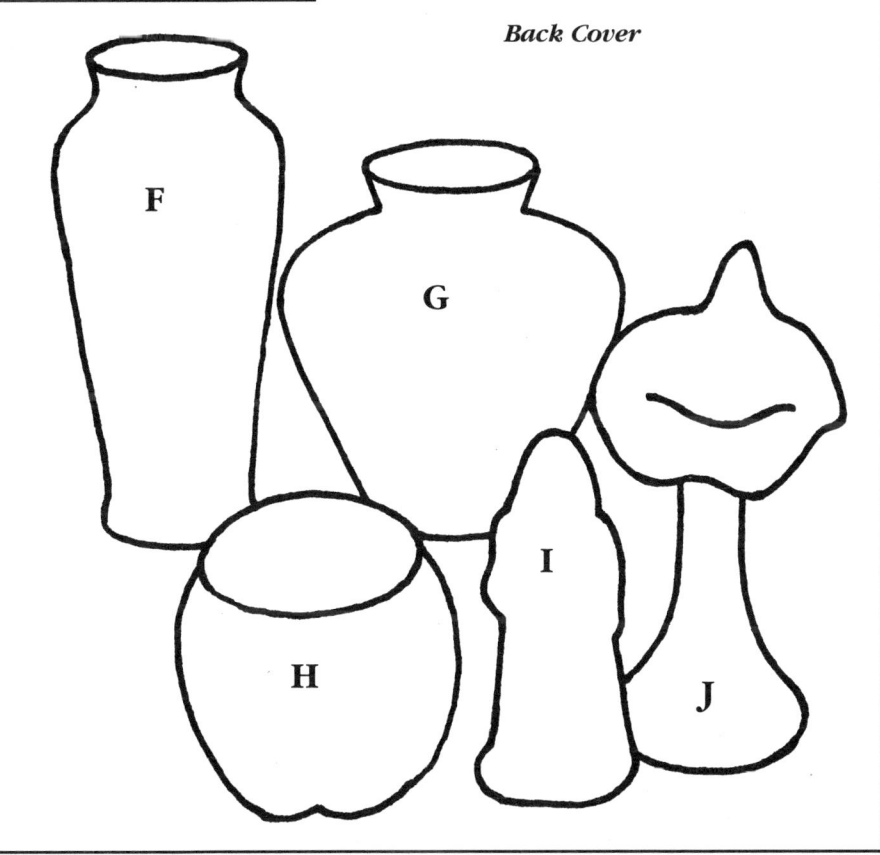

(continued from page 30)

For example, animal covered boxes and figurines were frequently featured in the Easter catalog supplement pages. In 1991 (see p. 40), Fenton made such articles in Shell Pink (PE), iridized Jade Opaline (EZ) and handpainted White Pearlized (PM). In 1992, similar items were available in Jade Pearl (EZ) and Pink Pearl (HZ), as were some articles with handpainted decorations (see p. 41). Ocean Blue (OB) was available in 1993 (see p. 49), along with Rose Pearl (DN) and handpainted Iridized Opal (BT). Both Sea Mist Slag (2A) and Plum Slag (8A) were made in 1994 (see p. 53).

As one might expect, Fenton baskets were also featured for Easter nearly every year. Groups of mini–baskets were offered in both 1992 and 1993 and from time to time thereafter, and an assortment of larger baskets appeared in the 1993 Easter supplement. In both 1994 and 1995, "crested" Easter baskets in the Hobnail pattern were an integral part of the Fenton line.

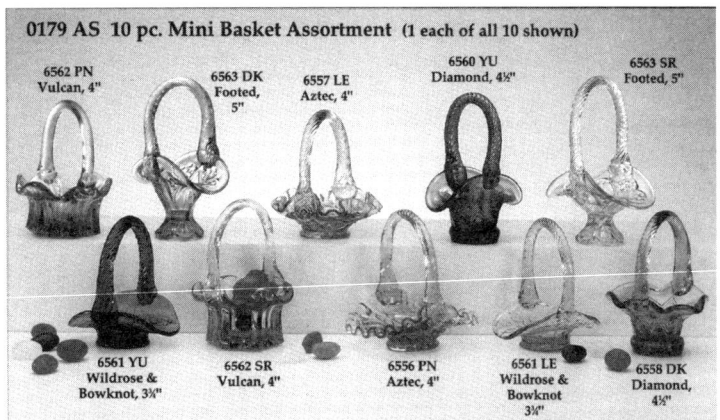

Mini–baskets were made for Easter in 1992.

Opaline (TG) and Champagne Opaline (PM) baskets in the Wildflower and Strawberry patterns appeared in 1996. The year 1997 saw a group of baskets in various sizes in Misty Blue Iridescent (LK) and Champagne Iridescent (PY), along with an assortment of animal figurines (see Figs. 590–601).

The 1998 Easter baskets were headlined by a decorated Topaz Opalescent basket (2039 SF) from the Family Signature Series. The Fenton supplement for Spring 1999 (see p. 69) showed a wide variety of items which one associates with Easter, ranging from baskets in various sizes to animal figurines, covered dishes and other novel items.

The Fenton line often contained items which reflected traditional Christmas themes. For instance, Fenton's vibrant Ruby color was offered for Christmases throughout the 1990s, and two green hues (Holiday Green, 1990–1994, and Spruce Green, 1995–1999) split the decade between them. The shapes offered in Ruby, Holiday Green, and Spruce Green were changed from year to year. As an added attraction, some Spruce Green items were decorated in 1996–97 with a Magnolia and Berry pattern designed by Kim Plauché.

Birds of Winter ornaments from the 1990 General Catalog.

In 1990, the Fenton Birds of Winter limited editions were in their final year, and a group of four Christmas tree ornaments was produced to recall each of the birds which had been featured in the Birds of Winter series. Also in 1990, five animal figurines were decorated in red and white attire; these were called Happy Santas (see p. 30 of *Fenton Glass: The 1980s Decade*). The year 1991 saw sets of Angel Ornaments and Angel bells as well as Angels and Madonnas and a grouping called Baby's First Christmas.

The first Fenton Christmas Tree (5535) was on the front page of the 1992 Christmas supplement. This 6½" tree, which was created by designer Cathy See, was initially available in ruby, green with iced branches, or iridized crystal; each was accented with a tiny gold bird (chickadee) on one of the branches.

A year later, two smaller trees, 5556 (4½") and 5557 (3"), were available in Holiday Green or Ruby as well as a new color called Golden Glow (all were decorated with ice on the branches, but the gold bird was available only on the largest size). These were grouped under the phrase "American Christmas Tree," as was a Christmas tree–shaped ornament (see Fig. 618), complete with a jingle bell and a gold hanger so it could go on a real Christmas tree!

The American Christmas Tree assortment for 1994 featured four colors (Crystal Satin, Golden Glow, Green and Ruby), and each was available either plain or with applied ice. The iced trees in all

FENTON
1995 Easter Collection

Crested Easter Baskets

What a combination! Hobnail baskets with the colors of Spring. Skillfully applied "rings and handles." For the basket collector or just to add the feeling of spring to someone's home.

0457 AS
9 Pc. Crested Baskets Assortment
(Includes 3 shapes in 3 colors)

The handler deftly applies a ribbon of molten glass for the handle.

A colored edge of molten glass is spun on each piece.

3830 IM 10 1/2"
3830 IH 10 1/2"
3830 IQ 10 1/2"
1160 IH 8 1/2"
1160 IM 8 1/2"
1159 IM 6"
1160 IQ 8 1/2"
1159 IH 6"
1159 IQ 6"

In 1995, Fenton French Opalescent Hobnail baskets were available with three different crest and handle colors–Dusty Rose (IH), Cobalt Blue (IQ), and Sea Mist Green (IM). The handler shown is Ron Bayles, who retired in the year 2000 after more than 43 years at Fenton.

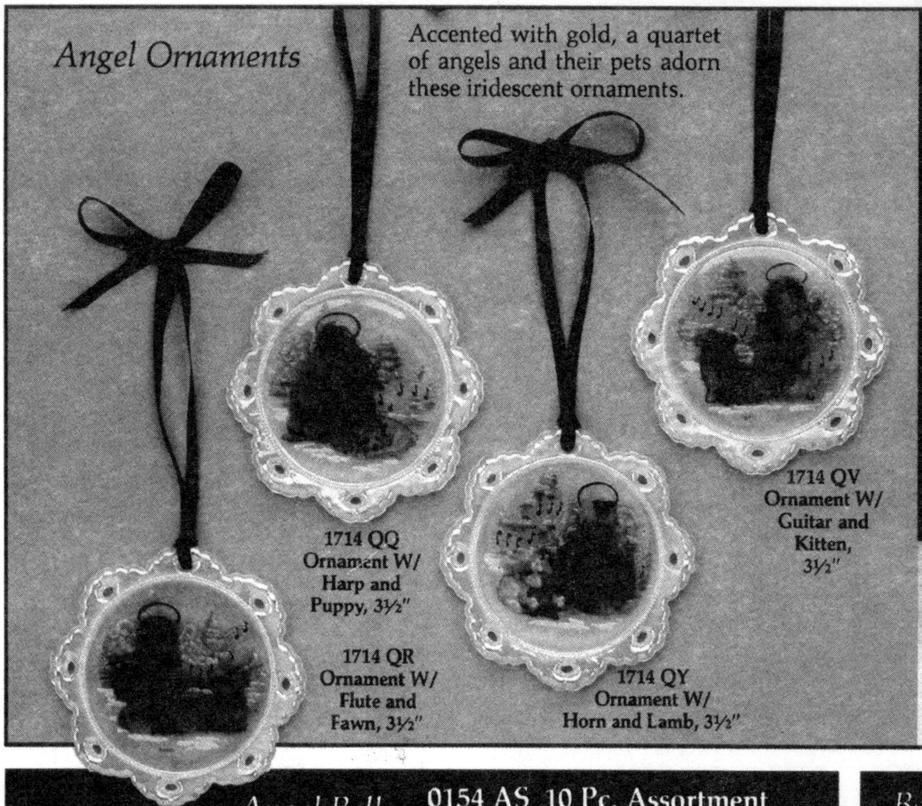

Angel Ornaments

Accented with gold, a quartet of angels and their pets adorn these iridescent ornaments.

0153 AS 24 Pc. Assortment w/display unit. (6 each of 4 designs)

- 1714 QQ Ornament W/ Harp and Puppy, 3½"
- 1714 QR Ornament W/ Flute and Fawn, 3½"
- 1714 QY Ornament W/ Horn and Lamb, 3½"
- 1714 QV Ornament W/ Guitar and Kitten, 3½"

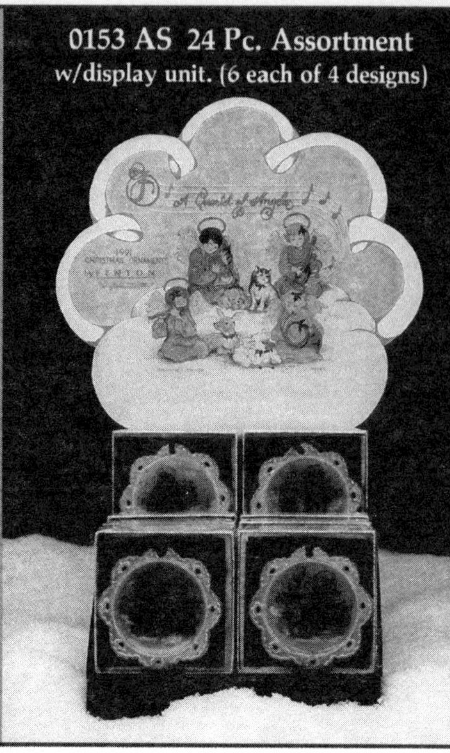

Angel Bells

0154 AS 10 Pc. Assortment (2 each of 4 designs plus 1 each of 2 musicals)

- 7669 QQ Musical Bell, 6½"
- 7669 QV Musical Bell, 6½"
- 7668 QR Flute and Fawn, 6½"
- 7668 QQ Harp and Puppy, 6½"
- 7668 QY Horn and Lamb, 6½"
- 7668 QV Guitar and Kitten, 6½"

Baby's First Christmas

Our cheery little teddy is all decked out to meet Santa. Designed by Martha Reynolds to celebrate that important first Christmas.

- 7662 JW Bell 4½"
- 4610 JW Bootie 4"
- 1714 JW Ornament, Open Edge 3½"

Angels and Madonnas

A multitude of little angels in favorite Christmas colors. The fine detailing in the figurines and Madonna votive lights is part of the Fenton glass tradition.

- 5256 SM Madonna Candlelight
- 5256 WI Madonna Candlelight
- 5114 GH Angel, Girl 5"
- 5113 GH Angel, Boy 5"
- 5113 CV Angel, Boy 5"
- 5114 CV Angel, Girl 5"
- 5113 RU Angel, Boy 5"
- 5114 RU Angel, Girl 5"
- 5114 CY Angel, Girl 5"
- 5113 CY Angel, Boy 5"
- 5113 SM Angel, Boy 5"
- 5114 SM Angel, Girl 5"

These items were shown in the Fenton 1991 Christmas Catalog Supplement.

Cathy See

A designer at Fenton from the beginning of 1991 to 1993, Cathy See made quite an impact on the Fenton line. She created drawings or sculptures for such holiday products as the American Christmas Tree and the Radiant Angel, and she designed the 9½" Feather vase (2756), which was made in many different color treatments during the 1990s decade (see Fig. 256).

See was also responsible for the Guardian Angel (5533) and the first Secret Slipper. Introduced in 1994, the Guardian Angel, with a different birthstone for each month, became a popular birthday gift item. The Fenton catalog characterized the Guardian Angel "for a child, a friend or a loved one in your family ... to protect and guide through life as God's messenger."

Heavenly Angels group from 1993.

three sizes featured a Gold Angel as a tree topper. In 1995–96, the Rose Pearl/Dusty Rose color replaced Golden Glow, and a small gold partridge was tucked into the branches of each tree (see p. 71 for some of the Christmas Trees discussed here). These colors continued through 1997, when a gold cardinal was used to accent the trees. In 1998, Misty Blue Iridescent replaced Rose Pearl/Dusty Rose, and a 22k goldplated squirrel took its place in the branches. The colors stayed the same for 1999, but a 22k goldplated bow was now the featured addition. Incidentally, the largest trees (5535) were available with musical bases or with lighted musical bases at various times.

A group of "Heavenly Angels" was available for much of the 1990s decade. In 1996, Both the 5114 6"Angel and the 5542 7½" Angel were available in decorated opal called Iced Berry (IJ), as well as three color treatments whose key feature was finely ground glass called "ice" which added texture and sparkle to the wings.

The Snowberry decoration (SB) on iridescent satin crystal appeared in Fenton's 1992 Christmas Catalog Supplement.

During the 1990s decade, several decorations (see p. 71) were developed especially for Christmas: Snowberry (SB), 1992; Gilded Star Flowers (HV), 1993; Golden Pine Cones (VC), 1994–95; Poinsettia Glow (P7), 1996–97; Twining Berries (JX), 1998–99; and Woodland Frost (1999). Golden Pine Cones, Poinsettia Glow, and Twining Berries were done on satin–finished Ivory glass, and each of them featured handpainted gold.

The Woodland Frost decoration (see Fig. 634), which was created by Robin Spindler, featured a realistic depiction of pine trees amidst falling snow with a red cardinal on the ground. This motif was a big hit for Christmas 1999, and items were added to the Fenton Christmas line for the year 2000.

Fenton Giftware

For many years, Fenton glass has been popular as a gift item. During the late 1980s, The Fenton Birthstone Bear emerged as the company's leading gift item, and it ranked highly on the lists of "best sellers" from the entire Fenton line for quite some time. During the 1990s decade, other birthday–related articles were created, along with some items especially for particular occasions, such as a child's birthday or a gift for a man.

The Birthstone Bears were joined by the Calendar Cats in the 1994 General Catalog. Made in iridescent Milk Glass, these featured a birthstone necklace and a tag with a personality poem (May reads: "Hi, I'm your May cat, dependable and strong. I can always be counted on to keep my things in order. May cats are there when you need them").

The Guardian Angel was yet another birthstone item. Designed by Cathy See, these were intended for "a child, a friend or a loved one in your family." The head of the crystal Guardian Angel was satin–finished. The birthstone ranks changed again when the Boutonniere Buddies appeared in the 1998 Fenton General Catalog. Each Mouse (5248) was made of satin–finished opal glass, accented with handpainted decoration and finished with an Austrian–made birthstone boutonniere in color.

In 1991, the Fenton Unicorn (5253) appeared in the June catalog supplement. Swarovski colored crystals (amethyst, emerald, topaz, sapphire, aquamarine and ruby) on individual necklaces completed this Fenton Captured Dreams grouping. The display unit associated the respective colors with these "New Age" wishes: love, cheer, strength, joy, peace, and energy. The Unicorn was shown in four transparent colors in the 1993 General Catalog.

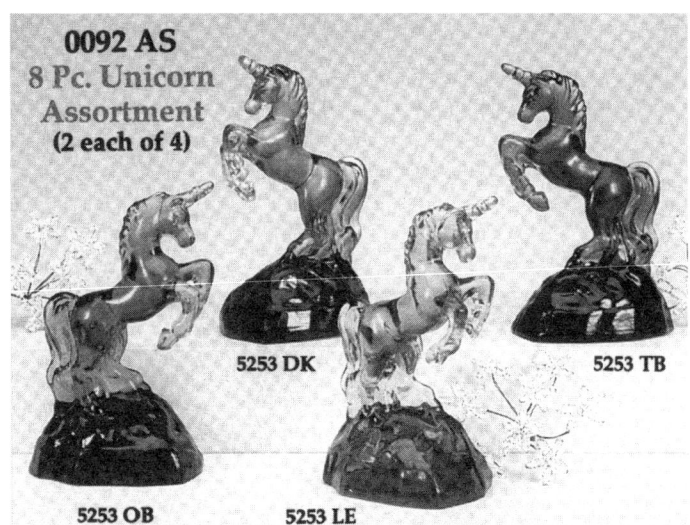

The 5253 unicorn was available in Dusty Rose (DK), Ocean Blue (OB), Sea Mist Green (LE), and Twilight Blue (TB) in the 1993 Fenton General Catalog.

The Guardian Angel made its debut in the Fenton line in 1994.

The 2931 Secret Slipper was available in eight different colors in 1995.

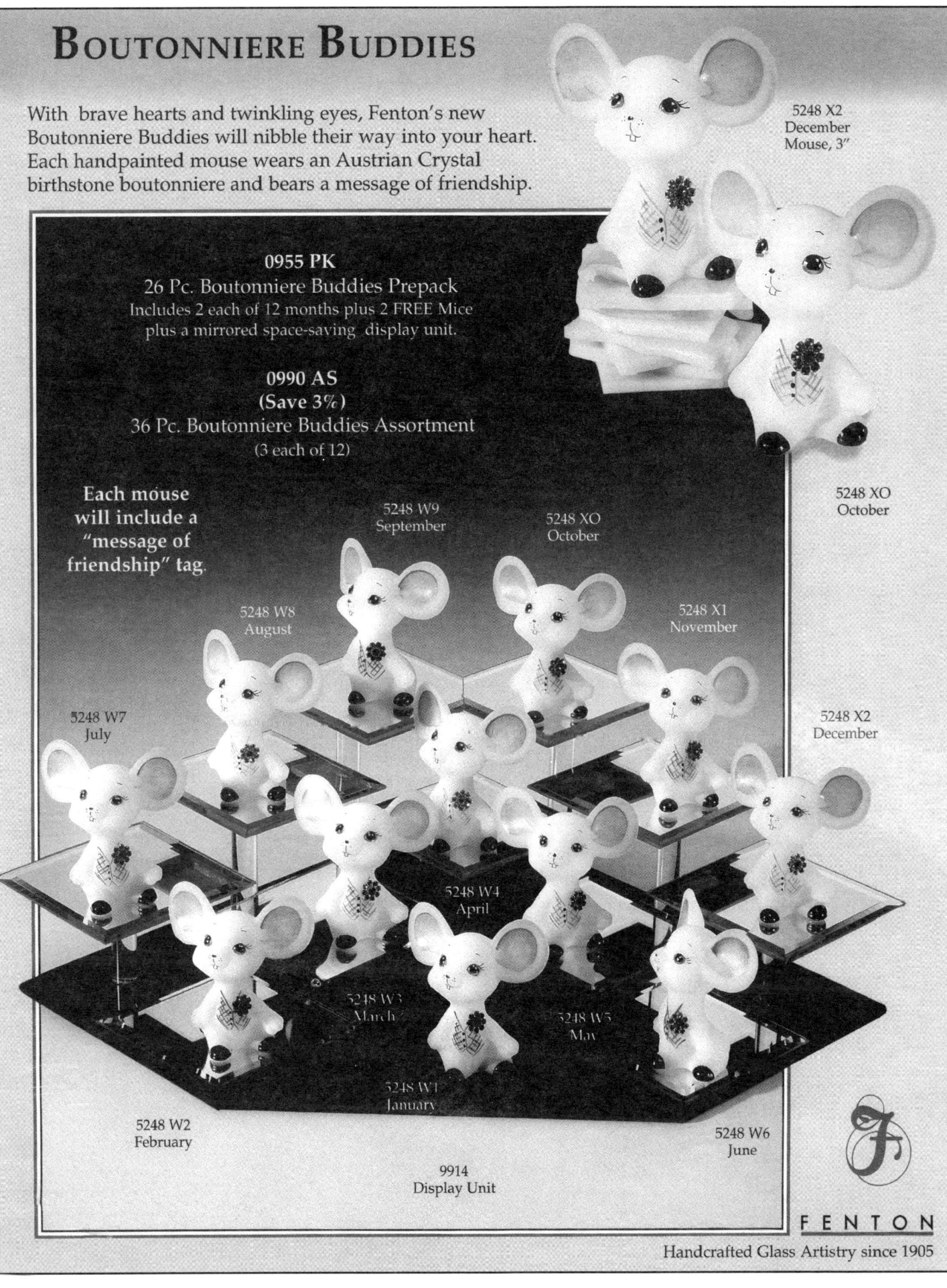

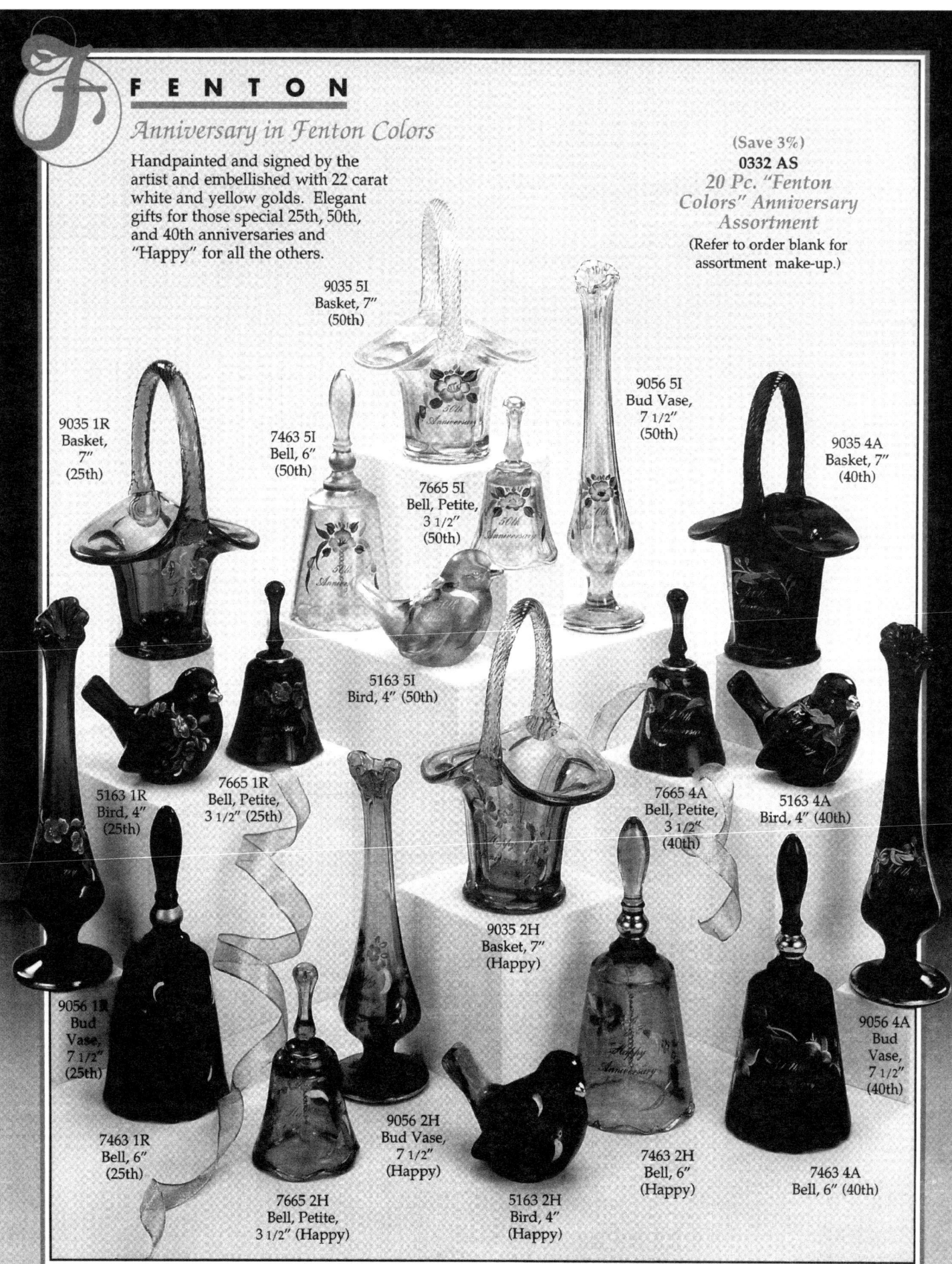

Fenton anniversary items from the 1995 General Catalog.

Various glass shoes had been made by Fenton for some time, but a new grouping, called "The Secret Slipper" appeared in the 1995 General Catalog. Nancy Fenton researched the Medieval legends about knights returning from the crusades with decorated shoes which were somehow imbued with secret powers. The mould for the Paisley slipper (2931) was designed by Cathy See. This assortment continued through 1998–99 with a different slipper, the 9295 Rose slipper which had been designed by Jon Saffell.

Fenton bells are popular in both the gift and collectible areas, and the company has offered many different bells over the years (for a selection of bells from the Fenton line during the 1990s, see p. 77). Some of these were brought into sharper focus for Fenton dealers when the "Bell Medley," an assortment of handpainted bells in various colors, was first offered in 1993. The Bell Medley remained in place throughout the 1990s decade, but the glass colors changed as new colors came into the Fenton line and others were discontinued and new decorative treatments were developed each year.

Fenton offered various decorated swans (5161), bells (7463), and musical bells (7669) as wedding anniversary gifts in the early 1990s. Some of these were intended for various years (such as 1st, 5th, 25th, 50th). In 1994, this idea was expanded when four items (9035 basket; 5163 bird; and two different bells, 7463 and 7665) were offered in four different colors. The Twilight Blue items were decorated with silver (25th), while the Ruby was for the 40th and the Gold for the 50th. The Dusty Rose items read simply "Happy Anniversary." A bud vase (9056) was added in 1995. The grouping changed later when a clock (8600) and a slipper (9591) were added. In 1999, the bud vase and clock were no longer available, and the group was scaled back somewhat.

Introduced in 1997, the Romance Collection was particularly suitable for a wedding or anniversary gift, but the items could certainly be used for other occasions. The iridized ivory glass was speckled with gold paint and decorated with handpainted white roses (see figs. 516–521). In 1998 and 1999, respectively, the Romance Collection included decorated items in French Opalescent.

The Medallion Collection was introduced in 1996 (see p. 64), and it continued in 1997 with some changes and a key addition. This collection was intended primarily as giftware suitable for a man's gift. The various figurines were made of dark colors (black, Cobalt, Plum, and Sea Mist Green), and each was handpainted with metallic colors especially suited for dark glass and accented with bright 22k gold.

The handsome wooden bases for the Medallion Collection pieces had a band of gold, and the underside of the bases displayed the Fenton Medallion Collection Seal. In 1997, a Family Signature Series piece, the black Reverse Melon 8" vase (7565 X5), was added to the Medallion Collection (see Fig. 1007).

Special paints were needed for the Medallion Collection items.

Several items which debuted in 1998 were also intended as gifts for men. Robin Spindler designed both the bass fishing motif (JW) and the golfing scene (JU). These were done on both a clock and a lamp (see Figs. 702–704).

Last, but not least, are the Fenton baby gifts from the 1990s decade. These five items (Angel, Baby Shoe, Bear, Kitten and Rocking Horse) were illustrated in the 1998 General Catalog. Each was available with blue or pink decoration. The Praying Boy and Girl were added in 1999, as was the Ball Cap (see Figs. 705–716)

Chapter Thirty-Three
HISTORIC COLLECTION COLORS

In the 1990s, the Fenton groupings in this area both evolved and grew considerably. Fenton regards these collections as challenges, and there is a strong commitment to create difficult glass formulas and to master or relearn various glassmaking techniques on the part of the company's workers.

During the first half of the decade, these collections, typically consisting of two different colors, were introduced in June of the year. But, by the mid–1990s, they were occupying prominent positions on the first few pages of the Fenton general catalogs released in January. Additionally, hand-painted decorations became increasingly important in this offering as the decade moved along. By the end of the 1990s decade, the Historic Collection limited edition colors (one limited by time and the other by number) were firmly established as key Fenton products.

During the first half of the 1980s, Fenton made relatively small quantities of glass in antique–style colors for the Levay Distributing Company, which was operated by Gary Levi. These included Carnival glass colors, stretch effects, and opalescent colors as well as slag and opaque Chocolate (see *Fenton Glass: The 1980s Decade*, pp. 69–75). The distributor relationship with Levay came to an end in 1985, although Gary Levi continued to work with Fenton on a consultant basis for several years.

Fenton determined that its customers would continue to be interested in these revivals of historic glass color treatments. To this end, Green Opalescent items were made by Fenton in 1985, as were pieces in a slag effect called Ruby Marble. By 1988, such Fenton offerings were dubbed "Collector's Extravaganza," and single–page color sales sheets were included with Fenton catalog mailings. The Persian Blue Opalescent grouping (offered June–December 1989) was particularly popular, so the idea of offering historic glass color treatments was even more firmly established at the outset of the 1990s.

The Collector's Extravaganza theme was continued in both 1990 and 1991. Sapphire Blue Opalescent was offered from March to November 1990. Two colors–Stiegel Blue Opalescent and Light Amethyst Carnival–were available in 1991 (Light Amethyst Carnival was available during the last six months of 1991).

As the 1990s decade progressed, there were some important changes. Historic Collection pieces began to be offered earlier in the year, and new pieces were sometimes added at mid–year, providing customers with additional items for their collections. Moreover, items with handpainted decorations came to be featured in some color groupings. In her role as Director of Design, Nancy Fenton was particularly interested in recreating glass colors from the past that could work well with current home decorating styles.

In 1995, five Burmese items were limited to specific quantities. This approach–announcing a specific numerical limit–became a feature of the Historic Collections for the rest of the decade, wherein one color was produced throughout the year as needed to fill orders while the other was limited by number. Collectors wanted these special Historic Collection colors to be made in groupings of items rather than

Fenton Historic Collection Colors, 1990–1999

1990	Sapphire Blue Opalescent
1991	Stiegel Blue Opalescent
1991	Light Amethyst Carnival
1992	Gold Pearl and Star Flowers on Gold Pearl
1992–93	Persian Pearl
1993	Rose Magnolia Hobnail
1994	Stiegel Green Stretch
1995	Celeste Blue Stretch
1995	Burmese (numbered)
1996	Opaline and Blush Rose on Opaline
1996	Mulberry (numbered)
1997	Topaz Opalescent and Hydrangeas on Topaz Opalescent
1997	Rubina Verde (numbered)
1998	Sea Green Satin
1998	Royal Purple (numbered)
1999	Violet Satin
1999	Gold Amberina (numbered)

as single pieces in a grouping such as the Connoisseur Collection.

Billed as "Authentic Reproductions from Antique Moulds," the Sapphire Blue Opalescent assortment in 1990 consisted of both blown items (see Figs. 742–747) and pressed pieces (see Figs. 748–754). The latter included several pieces in Fenton's Lily of the Valley pattern, which was designed by Tony Rosena and first introduced in 1978. The large Hearts and Flowers bowl was made from a Fenton mould inspired by an old Northwood pattern.

1990 Sapphire Blue Opalescent (BX)

1825 BX	10" Bowl with Bride's Basket in Antique Silver
1800 BX	Fern 23½" Gone With the Wind lamp
1801 BX	Fern 21" lamp with prisms
1802 BX	Fern seven–piece water set
1826 BX	Fern 10" bowl
1830 BX	Fern 5½" basket
1832 BX	Fern 7" basket
1853 BX	Fern 10" tulip vase
1860 BX	Fern 7½" cruet with stopper
8229 BX	Hearts and Flowers 10" bowl
8265 BX	Lily of the Valley 6" bell
8437 BX	Lily of the Valley 6" oval basket
8453 BX	Lily of the Valley 5½" rose bowl
8458 BX	Lily of the Valley 10" bud vase
8489 BX	Lily of the Valley 7" candy with cover
9651 BX	Regency 3½" vase
9700 BX	four–piece miniature table set
9799 BX	Fenton rectangular logo
4801 BX	Diamond and Lace four–piece epergne set

Collections for the rest of the decade, wherein one color was produced throughout the year as needed to fill orders while the other was limited by number. Collectors wanted these special Historic Collection colors to be made in groupings of items rather than

The blown items in Sapphire Blue Opalescent were called Fern, but many collectors refer to this pattern as "daisy and fern." The pattern, which originated with Harry Northwood in the 1890s, comes from a spot mould with the daisy and fern motif.

Sharp–eyed collectors can differentiate the Fenton pattern from a similar one marketed by the L. G. Wright Glass Company for many years. The Fenton daisy has 9 petals (a large Fenton lamp shade will have 12), while the Wright daisy has 10, 11 or 12 petals. Furthermore, the petals on the Fenton daisy are gently curved while those on the L. G. Wright piece are straight.

Some of the items in the Stiegel Blue Opalescent grouping for 1991 were made with moulds formerly used by other companies, such as McKee or the Westmoreland Glass Co. (Paneled Grape, Peacock and others). The opalescent color was light blue with a pastel quality, and Fenton sales materials indicated that "Stiegel" was a term used by Fenton about 1938 for the color, although the color had been made since 1908. Many glassmaking firms use the term "Stiegel" to recall colors made by Henry William Stiegel during the eighteenth century in America.

1991 Stiegel Blue Opalescent (BO)

4601 BO	Paneled Grape 14 pc. punch bowl set
4603 BO	Innovation 15" h. lamp
4612 BO	Saw Tooth covered comport
4613 BO	single crimp basket
4614 BO	five–piece mini water set
4616 BO	mini tumbler
4627 BO	Open Edge Ring and Petal 10¼" bowl
4632 BO	Wildflowers 7" h. basket
4633 BO	Paneled Grape 6" h. basket
4642 BO	Paneled Grape punch cup
4650 BO	Paneled Grape five–piece water set
4653 BO	Paneled Grape 9" Tulip vase
4658 BO	Paneled Grape tumbler
4667 BO	Paneled Grape covered butter
4671 BO	Open Edge Ring and Petal 11¼" cake plate
4672 BO	Open Edge Ring and Petal candlesticks
4673 BO	Peacock cream and sugar
4693 BO	Colonial 6½" footed comport
9560 BO	Temple bells 6¾" bell
(these are handpainted with a grape pattern)	
4605 JU	Basketweave 20" h. lamp
4651 JU	Colonial 10" h. bud vase
4602 JU	Diamond 12½" h. urn with cover

Several Stiegel Blue Opalescent items–the Diamond urn with cover (4602 JU), the Colonial bud vase (4651 JU), and a blown lamp (4605 JU) featured a handpainted grape decoration. These were the first decorated Historic Collection pieces, but there were many others later in the 1990s.

A few of the items from the Light Amethyst Carnival grouping in 1991 (Paneled Grape punch set and Innovation lamp) were also part of the Stiegel Blue Opalescent offering. Several others were made with moulds Fenton had purchased from McKee or the United States Glass Co., and Westmoreland moulds were being used under a royalty agreement. The 4609 DT Fruit five–piece water set proved difficult to produce, so it was replaced by a Paneled Grape (4650 DT) five–piece water set.

1991 Light Amethyst Carnival (DT)

4601 DT	Paneled Grape 14 pc. punch bowl set
4603 DT	Innovation 15" lamp
4609 DT	Fruit five-piece water set**
4611 DT	Paneled Grape with Good Luck interior 12" plate
4617 DT	Innovation 7" three-toed basket
4618 DT	10" l. oval bowl
4619 DT	Good Luck bowl
4642 DT	Paneled Grape punch cup
4643 DT	Innovation three-toed cuspidor
4644 DT	Diamond and Panel toothpick
4645 DT	Fruit tumbler
4646 DT	Innovation basket with looped handle
4679 DT	Eagle covered box
5254 DT	5½" Owl figurine
8680 DT	Regency butter with cover
9065 DT	Sables Arche 6" Bell
9799 DT	Fenton rectangular logo

**Replaced by 4650 DT Paneled Grape five-piece water set

1992 Gold Pearl (GP)

3313 GP	21" Student lamp with prisms
3335 GP	basket with looped handle
3355 GP	6" hand vase
3863 GP	Hobnail cruet with stopper
3908 GP	Hobnail five-piece water set
3949 GP	Hobnail tumbler
4600 GP	Swan box with cover
4801 GP	Diamond Lace four-piece epergne
5252 GP	7" Owl

1992 Star Flowers on Gold Pearl (GF)

5481 GF	9" h. basket
5526 GF	4" candlesticks
5480 GF	12" swung vase
9667 GF	Aurora 7" bell
5479 GF	6" cupped vase
5483 GF	10½" cupped basket
5482 GF	9½" cupped bowl

1992 Persian Pearl (XV)

1801 XV	Fern 21" lamp with prisms
1870 XV	Fern five-piece water set
1875 XV	Fern pitcher
1876 XV	Fern tumbler
2056 XV	5" Curtain vase
2725 XV	Button and Arch 7" basket
2726 XV	Button and Arch creamer
2727 XV	Button and Arch miniature tumbler
2728 XV	4" Button and Arch basket
2730 XV	five-piece Button and Arch miniature water set
3077 XV	Spiral 11" basket
3567 XV	Spanish Lace 6" bell
3674 XV	Hobnail 6" candlesticks
3701 XV	Hobnail four-piece epergne
3784 XV	Hobnail footed candy box
3938 XV	Hobnail 12" bowl
4601 XV	Paneled Grape 14 pc. punch bowl set
4642 XV	Paneled Grape punch cup
9799 XV	Fenton rectangular logo

1993 Persian Pearl (XV)

2754 XV	Swan bowl
3801 XV	Hobnail mini epergne
5127 XV	Swan
5172 XV	Swan candlesticks
8454 XV	Drapery bowl
9101 XV	24" Poppy Gone with the Wind lamp
9435 XV	Drapery basket

Fenton sales materials had this note about the light amethyst hue: "This is the first time this beautiful light amethyst has been made since the early years of the company."

The vibrant yellow color of Gold Pearl for 1992 was produced from a batch containing the cerium and titanium compounds as well as bone ash (calcium phosphate) for the opalescent effect. When the items are reheated, the "pearly white edges" develop. A spray of metallic salts creates the iridescence. There were many problems in making this color because the cerium in the batch made the glass quite brittle. Two items in particular, the Swan covered box (4600 GP) and the Owl figurine (5252 GP), were extraordinarily difficult to produce, and few of these were shipped to dealer accounts. These would be a real "find" for any collector today!

Several of the Gold Pearl items were historic Fenton Hobnail moulds, and the Diamond Lace epergne had appeared in Sapphire Blue Opalescent in 1990. The handpainted Star Flowers on Gold Pearl is a delicate motif, and the burgundy flowers contrast nicely with the yellow glass.

The Persian Pearl grouping was introduced in mid-1992, and most of the pieces (along with seven additional items) were also available through May 30, 1993. The Persian Pearl color is a soft green opalescent, and the light iridescent finish continues the direction Fenton had established with Stiegel Blue Opalescent and Gold Pearl, although none of the Persian Pearl pieces were decorated.

(text carnivued on page 160)

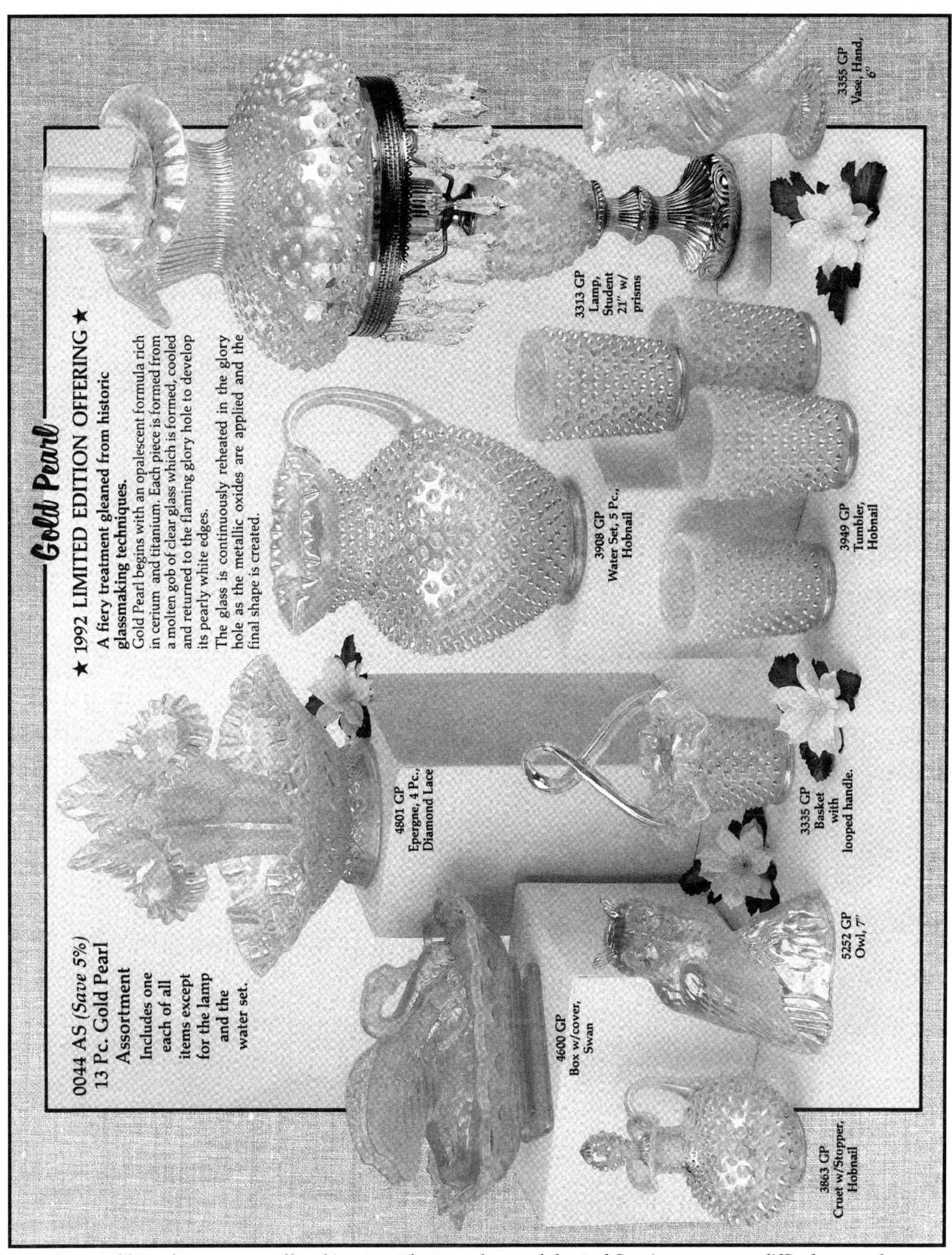

These Gold Pearl items were offered in 1992. The Swan box and the Owl figurine were very difficult to produce.

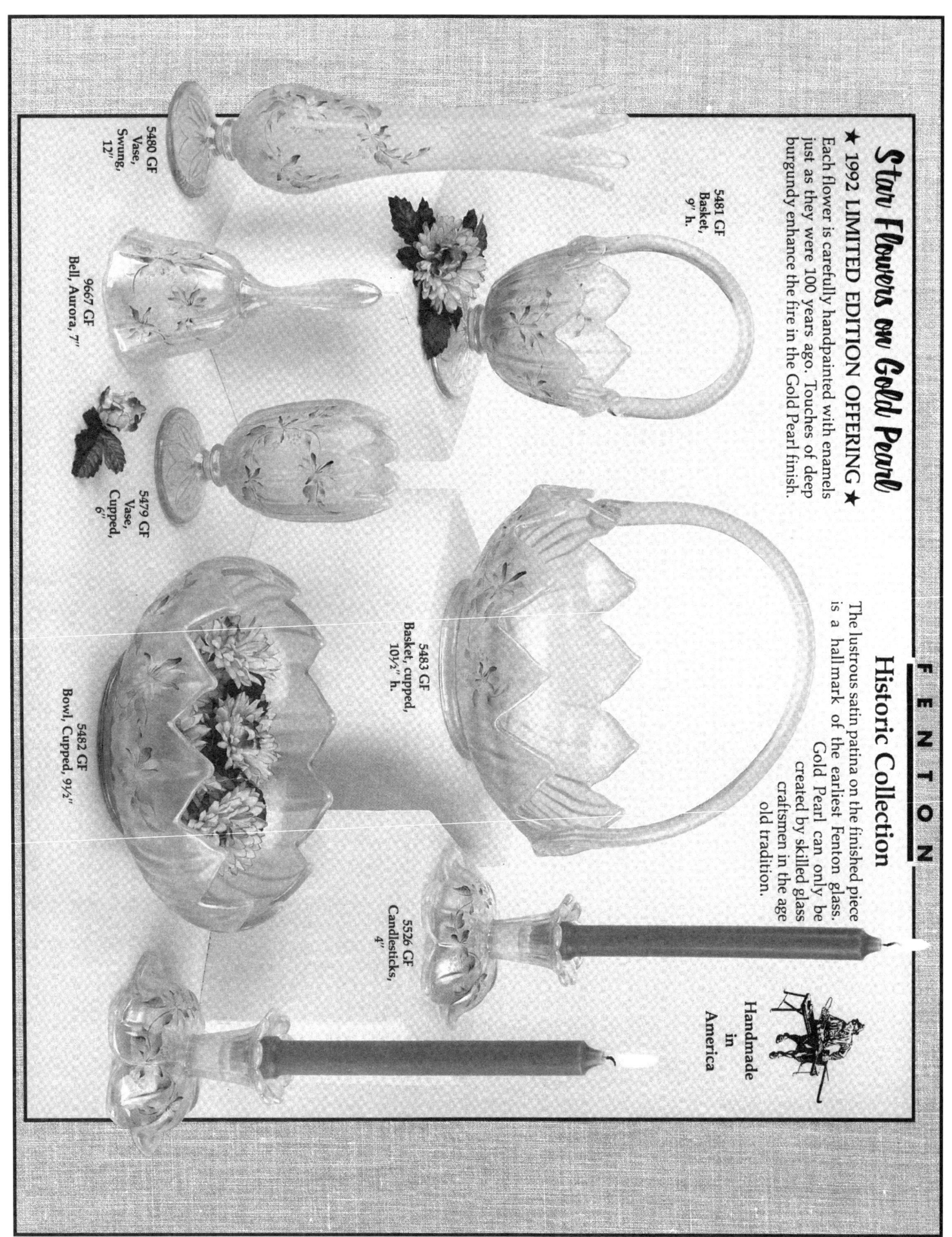

The handpainted Star Flowers motif on these pieces of Gold Pearl features a light burgundy color that is quite attractive.

These Persian Pearl items were shown in Fenton sales materials from mid–1992.

1993 Rose Magnolia in Hobnail (RV)

3313 RV	21" student lamp with prisms
3356 RV	7½" tulip
3645 RV	5½" bell
3701 RV	10" epergne
3712 RV	14 pc. punch bowl set
3764 RV	54 oz. pitcher
3834 RV	4½" basket
3854 RV	4½" vase
3863 RV	6½" cruet with stopper
3908 RV	five–piece water set
3949 RV	9 oz. tumbler
9799 RV	Fenton rectangular logo

In 1993, Rose Magnolia Hobnail continued Fenton's introduction of soft opalescent colors, but Rose Magnolia was not an iridescent hue similar to the "pearl" groups of previous years. Nonetheless, Rose Magnolia is a very appealing color, and it was Fenton's first opalescent rose tone. Rose Magnolia is dichroic, i. e., the color appears to change with different lighting conditions, especially under fluorescent light. Except for the rectangular Fenton logo sign (9799 RV), all the items in the Rose Magnolia grouping were in Fenton's historic Hobnail pattern.

In January 1994, Fenton announced that its Historic Collection color, Stiegel Green Stretch, would be available through November of that year. The Stiegel Green color originated in the 1930s, and Fenton's stretch treatment went back to the 1920s. In keeping with Fenton's original stretch glass, the items in this offering were relatively plain rather than intricately patterned. Fenton sales materials explained the treatment with these words: "Stretch glass is produced by spraying with metallic salts and carefully reheating to a satin finish. Most pieces are then flared or crimped in some way causing the iridescent skin to stretch."

The Stiegel Green Stretch offering was augmented by additional items in mid–1994, including five with a floral decoration called "Wind Flowers," which was designed by Martha Reynolds.

Called simply "90th Anniversary Collection," an impressive grouping of Celeste Blue Stretch pieces kicked off Fenton's 90th year in business during 1995 and added to the company's repertoire of glass colors. These pieces demanded considerable skill to produce, for each was twice reheated and sprayed with metallic salts to achieve the desired effects when finished.

The Celeste Blue hue had been a Fenton staple in the 1920s, and some of the shapes in this grouping were made from vintage moulds first used at that time. The 2990 KA centerpiece with nymph, for example, consisted of the earlier No. 846 bowl

1994 Stiegel Green Stretch (SS)

2759 SS	3½" rose bowl
2773 SS	Open Edge 8" bowl
2799 SS	Lion box
4602 SS	13" Urn with cover
4802 SS	Diamond Lace two–piece epergne
5526 SS	4" candlesticks
5551 SS	9" footed basket
5552 SS	12" bowl
5553 SS	Jack in the Pulpit 7" vase
5554 SS	5½" comport
5555 SS	7" footed basket
5559 SS	8" handkerchief vase
5560 SS	five–piece water set
5561 SS	goblet
5562 SS	jug (pitcher)
7601 SS	13" five–piece epergne set
9667 SS	Aurora 7" bell
9799 SS	Fenton rectangular logo

1994 Stiegel Green Stretch with Wind Flowers (ST)

2759 ST	3½" rose bowl
4381 ST	Lamb's Tongue candy with cover
5259 ST	5" Sparrow
5559 ST	8" handkerchief vase
9667 ST	Aurora 7" bell

1995 Celeste Blue Stretch (KA)

1134 KA	5¼" comport
2911 KA	3" candlesticks
2990 KA	four–piece centerpiece with nymph
7601 KA	13" five–piece epergne set
9001 KA	five–piece Lincoln Inn water set
9049 KA	Lincoln Inn tumbler
9488 KA	10½" candy box with cover
9499 KA	Fenton oval logo

1995 Coralene Floral on Celeste Blue Stretch (JE)

1136 JE	6" fan vase
1142 JE	7" footed basket
9667 JE	Aurora 7" bell
2767 JE	4½" vase
1137 JE	4¼" top hat
1140 JE	7¼" vase with cobalt blue base
1135 JE	Diamond 9½" basket (also Family Signature Series)

These items are marked 90TH in addition to the Fenton logo.

These Celeste Blue Stretch items were on page one of the Fenton 1995 General Catalog.

cupped into a rose bowl shape to hold the flower frog and No. 1645 nymph; the five–footed base was first made by Fenton in black glass during the early 1930s.

Decorating designer Martha Reynolds created a handpainted motif called Coralene Floral for some of the pieces in the Celeste Blue Stretch offering. The texture is achieved with finely ground glass called "ice." The ice used on these pieces was especially designed to create the coralene style of the late nineteenth century.

To further mark Fenton's nine decades in business, the company created a a special collection of five Burmese items. On the front page of the June 1995 catalog supplement, the five Burmese items were dubbed the "1995 90th Anniversary Historical Collection." Incidentally, the Fenton Connoisseur Collection for 1995, also five items, was the smallest of the decade.

1995 90th Anniversary Collection, decorated Burmese items
(numerical limits given in parentheses)

2932 UL	8" Butterfly basket (790)
2955 UL	Hummingbird vase (790)
2968 UN	10" Cherry Blossom pitcher (790)
7502 UQ	Daybreak 33" pillar lamp (300)
2909 UK	Vintage Border bowl with black base (790)

For the first time, Fenton items in an Historic Collection were offered as numbered limited editions. Each Burmese piece was elaborately decorated, and no two pieces were alike! Frances Burton was responsible for the Daybreak lamp, and Martha Reynolds designed the decorations for the other four items. The lamp was limited to 300 pieces, and a limit of 790 was placed on all the others.

The Opaline grouping in 1996 consisted of both pressed and blown pieces in blue opalescent glass with a diamond effect. Each of the six blown diamond optic pieces presented in the January 1996 general catalog had a handpainted decoration called Blush Rose, which was designed by Martha Reynolds. The pressed pieces featured the Diamond Lace pattern, designed by Frank L. Fenton and first made in the late 1940s. Jon Saffell adapted the pattern in his design for a miniature two–piece epergne.

In June 1996, four items were added to the Opaline offering. Three of them–a basket, a bell, and a two–piece tumble–up set–were decorated with Blush Rose. The fourth item was a pressed Cactus pattern cruet, an early twentieth–century Greentown item which had been replicated in new Fenton moulds in 1959. The bottom of this cruet was "cut shut," a glassmaking technique popular in the early

1996 Blush Rose on Opaline (TE)

1146 TE	7" pinch vase
1147 TE	8" basket
1180 TE	two–piece tumble–up set
1705 TE	24" lamp
1795 TE	11" Feather vase
4568 TE	6½" bell
5367 TE	6½" pitcher
7701 TE	7" cruet with stopper
5537 TE	8½" vase
	(also Family Signature Series)

1996 Opaline (TG)

3463 TG	Cactus 6½" cruet with stopper
4806 TG	4½" mini epergne
4808 TG	Diamond Lace 10" epergne
4833 TG	Fenton logo
4835 TG	9½" Diamond Lace basket
4854 TG	Diamond Lace 6½" comport
9499 TG	Fenton oval logo

twentieth century. A team of Fenton's skilled glassworkers, including finisher Paul ("Bubby") Burdette, worked on the cruet production, but the process was time consuming, and shipping all the orders was difficult.

Rounding out Fenton's Historic Collection for 1996 was Mulberry. This color dated back to 1942, when it was available for about six months; it was made again in 1989–91 with a lighter blue than that used in 1996. Mulberry must be made as blown ware, and the procedure involves covering a gold ruby core with azure blue glass. The result, in the words of Fenton's sales materials, is "cased glass which fades from a deep burgundy to rich blue. The rich Mulberry color is glass craftsmanship at its finest."

1996 Mulberry
(numerical limits in parentheses)

Evening Blossom with Ladybug

1671 MD	7½" pitcher (1250)
5581 MD	21" Lamp (500)

Hummingbird and Wild Rose

1531 MS	8" basket (1250)
1689 MS	9½" vase (1250)
2750 MS	8" vase (1250)

Five blown items with handpainted decorations were offered as a numbered limited edition. The lamp was limited to 500, and the other four pieces carried a limit of 1250 each. Robin Spindler created a decorating design called Evening Blossom with a distinctive ladybug, and Martha Reynolds was responsible for the Hummingbird and Wild Rose motif.

1997 Topaz Opalescent (TS)

9750 TS	ten–piece punch bowl set
9048 TS	punch cup
8248 TS	Scroll and Eye nut dish
9295 TS	Rose 6" slipper
2851 TS	Wildrose vase (8½" to 10")
1158 TS	Hobnail 8½" basket
5150 TS	Atlantis 6½" vase
9499 TS	Fenton oval logo
7601 TS	five–piece 11½" epergne
9665 TS	Beauty 6½" bell
2919 TS	Paneled Grape 5½" basket

1997 Hydrangeas on Topaz Opalescent (TP)

9550 TP	8" fan vase (also Family Signature Series)
2000 TP	20" lamp with prisms
2048 TP	9½" vase
2072 TP	6½" pitcher
2033 TP	8" basket
2040 TP	three–piece fairy light (also Family Signature Series)

Topaz Opalescent with Hydrangeas 2000 TP 20" lamp (usually sold with prisms) and 2048 TP 9½" vase; and Topaz Opalescent 7601 TS five–piece epergne.

Older "vaseline glass" was becoming increasingly popular with collectors in the mid–1990s, and Fenton's Topaz Opalescent grouping spoke to that market. Introduced in the 1997 general catalog, these items revived a 1920s color with a satin finish and added a distinctive decoration of hydrangeas to some items.

The articles first available in Topaz Opalescent ranged from a large punch bowl with cups to a large epergne and an attractive lamp with prisms (a hard item to find today!). A drapery optic was used in all of the blown items. The colorful hydrangea blooms and leaves combined for a very colorful look in this collection. Three new items were added in mid–year, including a decorated fan vase with the signature of Tom Fenton.

The mid–year Fenton catalog supplement for 1997 introduced Rubina Verde, a numbered limited edition grouping of six blown items (the lamp was limited to 650, and the limit for all other items was 1750). The color was the same as a short–lived, three–piece decorated group called "Thistle" in the Fenton line during 1994. The Rubina Verde was produced using similar techniques to Mulberry, but Rubina Verde called for the magenta color to be kept in the top one–third of the item and not allowed to flow downward when the piece was blown to its final shape.

1997 Rubina Verde (BW), dragonfly and flower decoration
(numerical limits in parentheses)

1507 BW	24" lamp (650)
1581 BW	Melon 5¼" box (1750)
3066 BW	6" pitcher (1750)
7139 BW	Melon 7½" basket (1750)
7458 BW	Melon 11" vase (1750)
7565 BW	Reverse Melon 8" vase (1750)

Sales materials mentioned that Rubina Verde was made at Hobbs–Brockunier in Wheeling during the 1880s and noted that Fenton's version combined gold ruby glass with Sea Mist Green. The decoration, featuring a dragonfly hovering near a white flower, was created by Martha Reynolds.

Sea Green Satin, a light opaque green with a satin iridescent finish, was limited to orders placed during 1998. Fourteen pieces were introduced for

January, 1998, and five more were added at mid–year. The basic color, first produced in sixteenth century China to imitate celadon porcelain, was similar to Fenton's Green Pastel, which was made in 1955. Sea Green Satin has a smooth, pearl–like quality, and the color harmonizes well with other Fenton hues such as rose, blue, and green.

1998 Sea Green Satin (GE)

2731 GE	Lamb's Tongue basket
5167 GE	2½" sunfish
5290 GE	6" Cat slipper
5301 GE	oval perfume
6840 GE	6½" w. bon bon with cover
7768 GE	6½" bell
8251 GE	Mandarin vase
8252 GE	Empress vase
8450 GE	Lily handkerchief vase (6" to 8")
9071 GE	8½" candlesticks
9080 GE	4" square box
9458 GE	8" Swan vase
9499 GE	Fenton oval logo

1998 Floral Interlude on Sea Green Satin (GG)

5165 GG	3¾" Cat
5197 GG	6" Happiness Bird
5430 GG	Lily 8" basket
6854 GG	Aurora 7" vase
7511 GG	24" Gone with the Wind lamp
7768 GG	6½" bell
7255 GG	11" tulip vase (also Family Signature Series)

Martha Reynolds developed a handpainted motif called Floral Interlude for some of the items in Sea Green Satin. The most spectacular item was the 11" tall tulip vase (7255 GG), for the handpainted flower was adapted to the shape of each individual vase. This piece was honored as "Decorative Collectible of the Year" by the National Association of Limited Edition Dealers (NALED). On behalf of the company and all of its talented decorators, Don Fenton accepted this award in June, 1999, at the International Collectible Exposition in Rosemont, Illinois. The Floral Interlude tulip vase was the best–selling piece of the Family Signature Series in the 1990s.

Described as "a color prized by the elite during the Phoenician and Roman Empire," Royal Purple was Fenton's numbered limited edition Historic Collection color for 1998. The color had its start in a Fenton piece developed for the Connoisseur Collection in 1995 (see fig. 960), and the decoration

1998 Royal Purple with Colonial Scroll decoration (N4)

(numerical limits in parentheses)

1617 N4	8" basket (2950)
1509 N4	20" student lamp (1450)
1689 N4	9½" vase (2950)
3265 N4	6½" pitcher (2950)
1610 N4	7½" 3 pc fairy light (2950)
3290 N4	6½" round perfume (2950)
6470 UF	6½" vase (2950)
3271 N4	6½" blown bell (also Family Signature Series)

was first used on a QVC Heirloom Collection piece in 1997 (see Fig. 1379).

Royal Purple is a cased glass, made by covering the bud of gold ruby glass on a blowpipe with cobalt blue glass. All pieces must be made as blown ware. Decorating designer Frances Burton created a decoration called Colonial Scroll. Her inspiration was a plaster ceiling medallion in the drawing room of a South Carolina plantation called Drayton Hall. The use of 22k gold in the Colonial Scroll decoration makes Royal Purple a truly rich art glass.

Most Royal Purple items were limited to 2250 pieces (the lamp's limit was 1450), and an interesting blown bell with applied handle could be ordered only through April 30, 1998 (this piece has Don Fenton's signature). The two–piece tumble–up (which has Bill Fenton's signature) could be purchased only through Fenton Showcase Dealers. A vase (6470 UF), produced from a mould designed by glass artist Dan Dailey, was added to the Royal Purple group during the second half of 1998; this piece has another color code (UF), because the decoration is somewhat different from Colonial Scroll..

Violet Satin, which was limited to orders placed during 1999, was based on Fenton's Orchid transparent glass from 1927. The Fenton team added a rich luster of satin iridescence to create a color that was both historic and in keeping with trends in home decorating. The handpainted floral developed by Kim Plauché uses the icy greens which are commonly paired with violet in home decor.

Fenton's numbered limited Historic Collection color for 1999 was called Gold Amberina. The items closely resemble a mid–1880s glass color called Amberina, which was patented by Joseph Locke at the New England Glass Company.

Locke's Amberina glass depended upon batch ingredients including lead, however, while Fenton's Gold Amberina was made by casing a bud of gold ruby glass with amber (the method is similar to that used for Mulberry, Rubina Verde, or Royal Purple).

1999 Violet Satin (XK)

2963 XK	Jack–in–the–Pulpit 7" vase
4559 XK	Lance 8" vase
4650 XK	five–piece Paneled Grape water set
4658 XK	Paneled Grape water glass
5290 XK	6" Cat slipper
5320 XK	7½" perfume
7601 XK	13" five–piece epergne
9499 XK	Fenton oval logo
9560 XK	Templebells 6½" bell

1999 Violet Satin with handpainted floral (XP)

1602 XP	24" Gone with Wind lamp
2777 XP	7" basket
4106 XP	Heart trinket box
5065 XP	5" Cat
5151 XP	3½" bear
5405 XP	5" fairy light
7255 XP	11" tulip vase
7568	6" Legacy bell
7484 XP	5" covered box (also Family Signature Series)

1999 Gold Amberina (AV)
(numerical limits in parentheses)

1211 AV	9½" pitcher (2500)
1533 AV	hexagonal 11" basket (2500)
3047 AV	6½" vase (2500)
3075 AV	7" cruet (2500)
3240 AV	11" vase (2500)
6150 AV	24" lamp (950)

The techniques used in gathering and in blowing the glass to shape allow the rich ruby hue to remain concentrated in the topmost areas of the item and fade smoothly into the amber portions below.

Just six different items were offered in Gold Amberina; the limit on each was 2500, except for the lamp (950). All were decorated with 22k gold and a handpainted motif created by Robin Spindler which featured ferns and open seedpods. Both Fenton dealers and collectors were quite enthusiastic about the Gold Amberina color, and the tall pitcher with French curl handle and the cruet were particular favorites. Unfortunately, Gold Amberina was difficult to produce, and the lamp was particularly troublesome to make.

For the year 2000, Fenton developed two Historic Collection colors, Lotus Mist Burmese and Willow Green Opalescent. The new Burmese color (called simply "green Burmese" by collectors) was welcomed enthusiastically by Fenton glass buffs, and the numbered limited edition pieces were selling well during the first six months of the year. The stories behind these two colors, however, will have to wait for the next Fenton book!

Chapter Thirty–Four
CONNOISSEUR COLLECTION

The first Connoisseur Collection made its debut in mid–1983, and Fenton's announcement promised "a very special offering for those who love glass and desire the unique." In the 1990s, Fenton continued to develop the Connoisseur Series as a showcase for its very best glassmaking efforts.

The Fenton Connoisseur Collection has always strived for the unique, embracing a wide range of interesting hot metal effects and cold metal treatments–from cased glass, iridized glass or heat–sensitive glass to handpainted decorations or elaborate sandcarving. During the 1990s, Fenton's approach was sharpened, as Nancy Fenton explains: "We began to research the finest decorated art glass from the Golden Age of Glass. We concentrated on specific art forms developed in early art glass."

Frances Burton and Martha Reynolds designed many handpainted decorations for the 1990s Connoisseur Collection pieces. Designers Robin Spindler and Kim Plauché contributed their talents during the latter half of the decade, and some pieces were made using new moulds which had been designed by Jon Saffell, who first came to Fenton in 1993.

Between 1991 and 1999, Fenton offered 64 Connoisseur Collection pieces. Of these, 11 were produced from Favrene and 18 were made with Burmese glass (ten Burmese items comprised the "85th Anniversary Offering" in 1990, too). Four Connoisseur items were made in Rosalene and four in Wild Rose.

Retail prices for Connoisseur Collection items ranged from $30 for a Rosalene piece without decoration to $750 for a large reverse painted lamp. Most Connoisseur items were in the $95–195 range, and all were packaged in individual gift boxes accompanied by certificates of authenticity.

With the exception of 1990, Connoisseur Collection pieces were offered as numbered, limited editions. The Fenton catalog supplements give the numerical limits, but collectors should note that the quantities actually made and sold were often lower than the stated limits. This occurs because an article sometimes proved especially difficult to produce because of problems encountered in Hot Metal.

See the following certificate. The left illustration is the front of the certificate; the right is the backside.

FENTON

The Connoisseur Collection

The Connoisseur Collection demonstrates Fenton's commitment to a vanishing art form. Artistic treatments developed during the 19th century "Golden Age of Glass" have been recreated by the proud crafts men and women at Fenton. Careful research into the styles and methods of Bohemian, English and American art glass inspired each creation.

Many of the glass formulas used in this collection are produced nowhere else in the world. Each is then decorated using techniques such as sandcarving, raised paste enameling or intricate detailing with 22k gold. The Fenton family and over 500 employees wish you many years of enjoyment from this unique work of art.

The Connoisseur Collection 1997

Tranquility Vase

This vase was made from French Opalescent glass which has been struck all over to a soft translucence. Robin Spindler has used a mould designed by Jon Saffell in 1996 to capture a pastoral scene viewed through arches of 22 karat gold. Limited to 1500 pieces.

9866 FX

Authenticated By *George W Fenton*
George W. Fenton, President

FENTON
1905-1997
HANDMADE IN U.S.A.

Connoisseur Collection certificate from 1997.

In 1990, an "85th Anniversary Offering," celebrating a milestone in Fenton's history, took the place of the Connoisseur Collection. All ten items were made in Burmese glass, and various hand-painted motifs were developed by Fenton decorating designers. The yellow in Burmese glass comes from depleted uranium in the batch ingredients. The pink blush is due to pure gold in the batch; when the piece is carefully reheated, the pink color is developed.

Unlike the other Connoisseur Collection offerings during the 1990s decade, these Burmese items for the 85th Anniversary Offering in 1990 were not limited by number; instead, they were restricted to sales between May and November, 1990. Each has this wording, "Fenton–85th Anniversary" as well as the artist's signature and the year "1990."

Petite Floral was created by Linda Everson; her decoration was used on a two–piece epergne (7702 QJ) and a cruet (7701 QJ). Everson was also responsible for Raspberry Burmese, which appeared on three items: a 7" basket (7731 QH); a 21" student lamp (7412 QH), and a seven–piece water set (7700 QH). Frances Burton adapted Trees Scene, a Louise Piper design originally called Scenic Decorated, for a vase (7792 QD) and a basket (7732 QD). Dianna Barbour adapted Piper's Rose Burmese for two vases (7791 RB and 7790 RB) and a 20" lamp (9308 RB).

The 1991 Fenton Connoisseur Collection consisted of eight items, divided among several of the company's most innovative and popular glass colors. Fenton's vivid iridescent Favrene glass, made with pure silver, is reminiscent of Louis Comfort Tiffany's Blue Favrile and Frederick Carder's Blue Aurene.

Two Favrene vases (8812 FQ and 8812 G1) were made with the same mould, and Frances Burton and Martha Reynolds developed the respective decorations. These were difficult to make, and Fenton's production was short of the projected 850 limit on each piece. The Favrene three–piece Ogee candy box (9394 FN) featured a metallic look to its decorated base, and the undecorated box and cover showed the full splendor of Favrene.

The decorations used a year earlier on Burmese glass were again available in 1991, but in just one item each. Frances Burton's Paisley lamp (6701 RB) featured Rose Burmese on its font and shade, and an attractive crimped vase (7252 QH) was offered in Linda Everson's Raspberry Burmese.

Three items in Rosalene rounded out the 1991 Connoisseur Collection. The Empress basket (4647 MD) and the Paisley bell (6761 UZ) displayed different floral motifs.

The Fish paperweight (5193 RE) was not decorated. Like Fenton's Burmese, Rosalene contains pure gold and is a heat–sensitive glass which acquires its distinctive pink color when the glass is reheated.

The 1992 Connoisseur Collection was introduced in Fenton's June catalog supplement with these words: "Artistic treatments developed during the 19th century Golden Age of Glass have been recreated by the proud craftsmen and women at Fenton. Careful research into the styles and methods of Bohemian, English, and American art glass inspired each creation."

Cranberry glass returned to the Connoisseur grouping after an absence of several years in a dramatic 9" pitcher (1211 RW) with a mid–1880s Bohemian–style decoration designed by Martha Reynolds. This ewer–shaped pitcher has an especially interesting applied handle with a French curl at its lower point.

Sandcarving also returned to the Connoisseur Collection with Frances Burton's Seascape vase (8817 QZ). The blown custard glass used for this piece was iridized with special metallic salts and reheated to create a gold lustre. Custard glass was originally called "Ivory" when it first appeared in America during the 1890s.

One of Frank M. Fenton's favorite pieces, the Wave Crest covered box, was decorated with an unusual marbelized lustre and handpainted floral in a design developed by Frances Burton (6080 RH). This combination recreated the look of C.F. Monroe's "Kelva" line from the early twentieth century.

The lustre on the cover is purposely shaded to diminish toward the center (where a floral decoration appears), but some collectors mistakenly thought the marbelized color was "evaporating" and would someday be gone! This rumor had a life of its own for a time, but Fenton collectors may rest assured that the marbelized lustre is there to stay–permanently!

The 1684 RP Rosalene vase displays the delicate pink of this Fenton color in vertical stripes. Martha Reynolds' decoration, "Twining Floral," adds an antique touch.

Two Connoisseur items for 1992 were offered in Burmese glass. A 6½" tulip vase (5541 QH) continued the raspberries decoration for a third year, and a 4½" pitcher (5531 QP) depicted another berry motif.

FENTON

1993 Connoisseur Collection

Fenton's 1993 Connoisseur Collection recreates styles and techniques from the "Golden Age of Glass". Inspired by the famous glass designers of the 19th Century – L.C. Tiffany, Handel and Pairpont – this collection demonstrates Fenton's skill in the production of rare glass.

A. Made of Ruby Stretch glass, this bowl is made with Ruby glass that has been sprayed with metallic salts while hot. It is then reheated and the edges turned back to stretch the metallic finish on the surface. The beautiful authentic gold scrollwork was designed by Martha Reynolds.

D. 7661 P4 Vase, 9", "Leaves of Gold" (950)

A. 2747 RX Bowl, Rolled Rim (1250)

B. 1710 R5 Perfume w/stopper, (1250) "Rose Trellis"

C. 8805 X3 Vase, "Victorian Roses" (950)

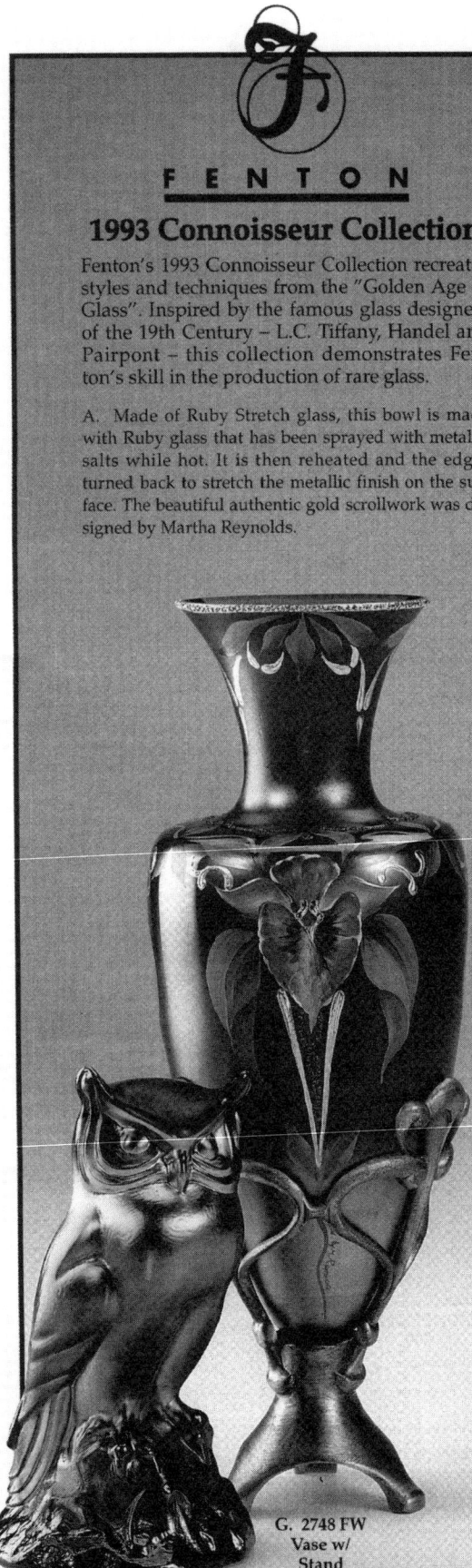

B. This perfume bottle is made of Rosalene glass which contains pure gold. "Rose Trellis" was designed by Frances Burton and is highlighted with genuine gold.

C. Made of Persian Blue Opalescent, this vase is carefully cooled and reheated before blowing to develop the delicate translucent color. "Victorian Roses" was designed by Martha Reynolds and features an amethyst lustre collar.

D. This vase is made of Plum glass which has been sprayed with metallic salts while still hot. "Leaves of Gold" was designed by Martha Reynolds to be sandcarved deeply into the surface of the glass. It is carved in repeated steps to achieve the shading on the berries and leaves.

E. This Reverse Painted Shade is from an original Handel mould and the painting technique is true to the method used by Handel. Multiple painting and firing steps are required to create "Spring Woods", designed by Frances Burton.

E. 2780 CX Lamp, "Spring Woods" (500) 2/store

G. 2748 FW Vase w/ Stand (850) 2/store

F. 5258 FN Owl, 6" (1500)

Favrene Glass

F. & G. The treatment used on these two pieces is called Favrene which was first developed as Blue Favrile by L.C. Tiffany. This glass contains cobalt and silver and is sensitive to the slightest variations in heating. (F) This collection marks the first use of the owl mold. (G) The decorated Favrene vase, an amphora in a decorative brass stand, was designed by Martha Reynolds and features genuine gold highlights.

The Connoisseur Collection appeared on the front page of Fenton's June, 1993, catalog supplement.

In 1993, the Connoisseur Collection consisted of nine items in a wide variety of glass colors, shapes and decorative treatments. Two pieces were shown in Fenton's Favrene, as a new Owl figurine (5258 FN) and a decorated amphora vase (2748 FW) in a metal stand were offered. Martha Reynolds designed the decoration for the amphora vase. The design for the metal stand was based on a silverware pattern found by Nancy Fenton. A firm in New England, B & J Metal, worked out the details to get the proper fit for the amphora vase.

Frances Burton developed a handpainted rose motif to complement a Rosalene glass perfume bottle with a diamond optic treatment and a heart–shaped stopper (1710 R5).

A rich gold decoration, designed by Martha Reynolds, contrasts strongly with the iridescent ruby glass with stretch finish in a rolled rim bowl (2747 RX). Martha Reynolds also designed two other items–the Victorian Roses vase (8805 X3) in Persian Blue Opalescent and the sandcarved Leaves of Gold vase (7661 P4) in Plum glass.

Perhaps the most spectacular item in the 1993 Connoisseur Collection was Spring Woods (2780 CX), a reverse painted lamp designed by Frances Burton. The shade was made from an original Handel mould, and Burton's decoration was faithful to the methods developed by Handel many years ago. Over the next half–dozen years, Burton continued to create interesting lamps using these methods.

The 1994 Connoisseur Collection was composed of seven items, including two pieces in Favrene, a 7" vase (2743 JP) and a clock (8691 JV). The decorations for these were created by Martha Reynolds and Frances Burton, respectively. Reynolds' decoration featured matte gold lattice work and coralene flowers, while Burton's used raised gold and enamels to create surface texture.

The popular Burmese glass was represented by a tall pitcher (2729 JI) featuring a raised lattice decoration and heavily sculpted roses designed by Frances Burton. Fenton's Plum Opalescent color in pressed glass, which was in the line in the Hobnail pattern during 1959–62, made its first appearance in the Connoisseur Collection in a vase (2744 JK) with diamond optic interior and scrollwork decoration developed by Martha Reynolds.

A new glass color was created by casing gold ruby with amber glass. The beautiful result, called Gold Amberina, was featured in a tall vase (3161 JQ) decorated with an elaborate floral motif designed by Martha Reynolds which used highly glazed enamels to complement the shiny amberina surface. Several years later, Fenton offered Gold Amberina as one of its Historical Collection colors.

Richard Delaney, who had been instrumental in Fenton's development of sandcarving technology in the 1980s, teamed with Martha Reynolds to develop the design for a large cranberry cameo bowl (7727 JC) with an intricate floral pattern. The interior layer of gold ruby glass was meticulously sandcarved to reveal the layer of French opalescent glass.

Frances Burton contributed yet another innovatively decorated lamp (5580 JB) in the 1994 Connoisseur Collection. Her realistic depiction of a hummingbird in flight was achieved by handpainting both the inside and the outside of a delicate, bell–shaped shade made of opaque glass. The handpainting and firing required three steps over several days.

The five–piece 1995 Connoisseur Collection was the smallest of the 1990s decade, because Fenton simultaneously offered five decorated Burmese glass items as its 90th Anniversary Historical Collection (see p. 84). Favrene glass was well–represented by a three–piece ginger jar (2950 VN) with Martha Reynolds' matte enamel floral decoration.

Favrene three–piece ginger jar (2950 VN) and Royal Purple amphora vase with metal stand (2947 US) from the 1995 Connoisseur Collection.

Reynolds also designed the decorations for several other items in the 1995 Connoisseur Collection. Her delicate rose floral was created for a Wild Rose vase (7691 WF); the Wild Rose color was first in the Fenton line in the early 1960s. The color presents a real challenge for the glassworkers, who must reheat the piece just right to create the pink hue.

Realistic cherries with gold and ivory highlights contrasted nicely with Fenton's new Royal Purple color in an amphora vase with metal stand (2947 US).

The Victorian–style pitcher (2796 AM) also has a delicate floral motif with roses, but the glass technology inherent in this piece must also be noted. Gold ruby is cased with milk glass and subsequently layered with celeste blue. A crystal ring and a graceful ribbed handle are applied, and an iridescent finish completes this extraordinary triple–cased piece.

Collector interest in Fenton's reverse painted lamps was further stimulated by Frances Burton's Butterfly and Floral lamp (5486 VU). The shade was made using an original Handel mould, and the decoration is remarkably three–dimensional when the lamp is lighted.

The 1996 Connoisseur Collection consisted of seven pieces, including three decorated items in Burmese glass. Inspired by her enjoyment of fishing and the outdoors, Robin Spindler created the Trout vase (9866 TR) while Frances Burton developed a water floral motif with a realistic dragonfly for a pitcher (2960 WQ). The pitcher and vase moulds were new to the Fenton line, having been designed by Jon Saffell, who came to Fenton after more than twenty–five years at Fostoria in Moundsville, West Virginia.

3254 QJ Burmese Queen's Bird vase (Connoisseur Collection, 1996).

9855 EV Favrene vase with cut–back decoration (Connoisseur Collection, 1996).

6584 CD Mandarin Red decorated box with metal lid (Connoisseur Collection, 1996).

Martha Reynolds created the decoration for the Burmese Queen's Bird vase (3254 QJ). Reynolds also designed a detailed berry motif for an 11" vase (2782 DD) in Wild Rose glass as well as a cut–back sand-carved floral pattern for a Favrene vase (9855 EV), which was made from a new mould designed by Jon Saffell.

The decoration for the 2782 DD Wild Rose vase incorporated a raised paste technique to add great texture and detail to the berries; the mould for this piece was designed by Cathy See.

For her initial contribution to the Fenton Connoisseur Collection, designer Kim Plauché created a gold filled chrysanthemum pattern to coordinate with the brass lid on a Mandarin Red box (8684 CD), which was made from an original Handel mould. The heat–sensitive Mandarin Red color dates back to the 1930s, when Fenton first produced it.

Frances Burton's Poppies lamp (6805 EA) continues the reverse painting techniques of her creations for previous years. This lamp is quite tall, measuring 33" to the top of its finial, and the shade is 17" wide. Elaborate hardware recaptures the authentic look of a Handel lamp from the early 1900s.

The 1997 Connoisseur Collection, which was composed of seven items, contained both well–established favorites (Burmese, Favrene, Wild Rose and a reverse painted lamp) and some new directions. For the first time, a Connoisseur piece was offered with Fenton family signatures.

The Summer 1997 issue of the Glass Messenger introduced the Connoisseur Collection with these words: "Martha, Frances, Robin and Kim eagerly anticipate designing the Connoisseur Collection. They bring out wonderful ideas they've saved throughout the year and lovingly transfer them to glass. Each design emerges as a personal work of art."

Opalescent glass was featured in two vases. Martha Reynolds' detailed floral (2965 UD) complements the Opaline glass, which had been featured by Fenton as an Historical Color in 1996. Robin Spindler's Tranquility vase depicted an English countryside viewed through a gold archway. The 22k gold was applied using special techniques and required a second firing. The Tranquility vase won an "Award of Excellence" from *Collector Editions* magazine.

The Burmese pieces for the 1997 Connoisseur Collection were an 11½" tall basket (7632 BQ) with Robin Spindler's Fenced Garden motif, and the Trillium vase (2961 BY), which featured her beautifully detailed floral decoration.

The basket used crushed glass (called "ice") for added sparkle, and the 22k gold border is reminiscent of the tall wrought iron fences which enclose park gardens.

The Trillium vase, made from a mould first used by Fenton in the early 1930s, was inscribed with the signatures of all 11 Fenton family members who were associated with the company at the time.

The sandcarved Favrene Daisy vase (8807 FR) was designed by Martha Reynolds in an art nouveau style. The mould for this vase was purchased from the Imperial Glass Corp. in the mid–1980s. Martha's decoration added 22k gold to a sandcarved curling floral motif, and a polished brass mount and cap provided a perfect final touch. Some of these pieces were finally delivered to Fenton dealers in 1998 because the brass parts were improperly sized by the supplier and had to be re–done.

Kim Plauché developed a handpainted tea rose pattern for the Wild Rose pitcher (8966 ZJ), which also featured an applied twisted rib handle in crystal glass. The mould was first used in the 1940s for Fenton's Coin Dot opalescent.

The Scenic Floral reverse painted lamp (7939 BJ) was designed by Frances Burton. The sheer colors and impressionistic background of her motif were achieved by careful steps involving painting, wiping and multiple firings. The blank 18" shade was purchased by Fenton from Davis–Lynch, a longtime manufacturer of quality lighting goods whose glass plant is located in Star City, West Virginia.

An unusual vase created with off–hand techniques and four pieces of Burmese glass were the highlights of the 1998 Connoisseur Collection. The off–hand Leaves and Vines vase (5359 WP) combined the talents of Dave Fetty, Hot Metal supervisor, and decorating designer Martha Reynolds (both Dave's and Martha's signatures are on this piece). The green and purple threads contrasted nicely with milk glass, and Martha Reynolds developed a coordinating handpainted design for the top area of the vase.

8966 ZJ Wild Rose pitcher with rose decoration (Connoisseur Collection, 1997).

Dave Fetty

A skilled glassworker, Dave Fetty retired in 1999 after more than 40 years in the glass industry. Dave came to Fenton in 1965 after learning the trade in Milton, West Virginia, at the Blenko Glass Co., where he began as a carrying–in boy when he was 19. Dave's mentor at Blenko was glassworker "Shorty" Finley, who taught Dave many of the skills needed to make glass off–hand (without moulds).

In the mid–1970s, Dave worked with glass artisan Robert Barber, helping to design and create some of Fenton's first limited edition pieces. In 1998, Dave taught a "pulled feather" technique to other glassworkers, and he supervised them as they produced this vase (5359 WP) for the 1998 Connoisseur Collection.

Even after his "official" retirement, Dave has continued to contribute to Fenton. During 2000, he worked closely with the glassworkers who produced a "hanging hearts" vase for the Connoisseur Collection.

Glassworker Jim Ralston watches as Dave Fetty works on the threading technique for the Leaves and Vines vase in the 1998 Connoisseur Collection.

5359 WP Leaves and Vines 9" vase (Connoisseur Collection, 1998).

Kim Plauché created two distinctive motifs for Burmese items in the 1998 Connoisseur Collection. The Papillon vase (7557 UW) featured a vivid butterfly in the Art Nouveau style, and her Blackberry Bouquet basket (7139 NP) depicted ripe blackberries and a realistic bumblebee.

Martha Reynolds was responsible for the Jacobean Floral lamp (4505 WD), and Robin Spindler's Bountiful Harvest pitcher (2998 YZ) is a realistic still life accented by gilded wheat. The Bountiful Harvest pitcher was a finalist for the National Association of Limited Editions Dealers' "Decorative Collectible of the Year" award.

Robin Spindler also continued to work with techniques for decorating with gold on French Opalescent glass. Her "After the Rain" vase (8817 DJ) won a Discovery Award from the Society of Glass and Ceramic Decorators. This piece included the signatures of 12 Fenton family members and was the first to include the signature of Scott K. Fenton, who joined the company in January, 1998.

A Spruce Green base and plain hardware contrasted nicely with Frances Burton's reverse painted lamp for 1998. Called Trysting Place (6802 SV), the lamp's shade depicts a gazebo in a secluded garden.

The Seasons vase in sandcarved Favrene glass (9259 FN) was made from a mould purchased by Fenton from the Holophane Glass Company in the mid–1960s. Martha Reynolds added graceful trees to the original design of American sculptor Carl Schmitz. Inspired by 14th century Spanish art, Reynolds also created the Spanish–style Alhambra vase (4604 BZ), which was made from Wild Rose glass.

The final Connoisseur Collection of the 1990s was composed of eight items, including one in Favrene and four in Burmese. The Favrene piece was a small ginger jar (7488 FH) decorated with a stylized orchid and 22k gold accents developed by Kim Plauché.

The Burmese items included two new moulds designed by Jon Saffell. The 13" tall vase (6359 WS) is decorated with Martha Reynolds' poppies motif in the Arts and Crafts style, and the matte and polished golds pods are especially noteworthy.

The basket (6831 U5) has a distinctive six–point lily crimp and is decorated with Robin Spindler's realistic bluebird on windblown pampas grass. The Golden Gourds ewer (1862 VV) was created with a mould used years ago to make bottles. Martha Reynolds decoration design is an accurate still life.

The final item in Burmese, Robin Spindler's Memories lamp (6200 HW), depicts hibiscus flowers framed by intricate scrollwork. These flowers were particular favorites of Robin's husband Buck, who passed away in February, 1999.

The Tulips lamp (6250 DR), designed by Frances Burton, is painted inside and out, and the sand textured finish creates a three dimensional appearance when the lamp is lighted. Three blue butterflies highlight this piece.

One of Nancy Fenton's favorite decorative styles is the realistic florals of the Charleton line sold by Abels–Wasserberg in the early 1940s. Fenton, which did not have a decorating department at the time, sold glass blanks to the Abels–Wasserberg firm, which had a staff of decorators in New York City. Working with some Charleton pieces from Nancy's collection, Kim Plauché designed a delicate rose motif to be used on a Peach Crest basket with crystal handle (7139 WC).

Mulberry glass, made by covering gold ruby with azure blue, provided the background for Martha Reynolds' snowy white egret and realistic branches. Jon Saffell designed a metal stand to hold this amphora vase, and Mystical Bird (3090 ZF) completed the Connoisseur Collection for 1999.

At the end of the 1990s decade, the Fenton Connoisseur Collection was firmly established as sought–after Fenton limited edition collectibles. The extraordinary craftsmanship and artistry, coupled with keen collector interest, made the Connoisseur Collection a strong performer in the secondary market.

1990 85th Anniversary Offering
(limited to sales May–November, 1990)

7202 QJ	epergne
7701 QJ	cruet
7731 QH	7" basket
7412 QH	21" student lamp
7700 QH	seven piece water set
7792 QD	9" vase
7732 QD	5½" basket
7791 RB	6½" vase
7790 RB	6" vase
9308 RB	20" lamp

(see p. 97)

1991 Connoisseur Collection

8812 FQ	10½" vase (850)
9394 FN	candy box (1000)
8812 G1	10½" vase (850)
4647 MD	Empress basket (1500)
6701 RB	Paisley 20" Lamp (500)
6761 UZ	Paisley bell (2000)
7252 QH	7½" vase (1500)
5193 RE	Fish paperweight (2000)

(see p. 98)

1992 Connoisseur Collection

8817 QZ	8¼" vase	(750)
1211 RW	pitcher	(950)
5541 QH	tulip vase	(1500)
5531 QP	pitcher	(1500)
6080 RH	covered box	(1250)
1684 RP	vase	(950)

(see p. 99)

1993 Connoisseur Collection

2747 RX	bowl	(1250)
1710 R5	perfume w/stopper	(1250)
8805 X3	vase	(950)
7661 P4	vase	(950)
5258 FN	6" owl	(1500)
2748 FW	vase w/stand	(850)
2780 CX	lamp	(500)

(see p. 100)

1994 Connoisseur Collection

3161 JQ	vase	(750)
2729 JI	pitcher	(750)
7727 JC	bowl	(500)
2744 JK	vase	(750)
2743 JP	vase	(850)
8691 JV	clock	(850)
5580 JB	lamp	(300)

(see p. 101)

1995 Connoisseur Collection

2950 VN	ginger jar	(790)
2796 AM	pitcher	(490)
2947 US	amphora w/metal stand	(890)
5486 VU	lamp	(300)
7691 WF	vase	(890)

(see p. 102)

1996 Connoisseur Collection

2782 DD	vase	(1250)
6805 EA	lamp	(400)
3254 QJ	vase	(1350)
9866 TR	vase	(1450)
2960 WQ	pitcher	(1450)
9855 EV	vase	(1250)
6584 CD	box w/metal lid	(1250)

(see p. 103)

1997 Connoisseur Collection

2961 BY	vase	(1750)
8807 FR	vase	(1350)
7632 BQ	basket	(1750)
7939 BJ	lamp	(550)
9866 FX	vase	(1500)
2965 UD	vase	(1500)
8966 ZJ	pitcher	(1350)

(see p. 104)

1998 Connoisseur Collection

6802 SV	lamp	(750)
8817 DJ	vase	(2250)
5359 WP	vase	(950)
9259 FY	vase	(1350)
4604 BZ	vase	(1500)
4505 WD	lamp	(750)
2998 YZ	pitcher	(2250)
7557 UW	vase	(2500)
7139 NP	basket	(2250)

(see p. 105 & 106)

1999 Connoisseur Collection

6200 HW	lamp	(950)
6359 WS	vase	(2500)
1862 VV	ewer	(2500)
6831 U5	basket	(2950)
7139 YC	basket	(1750)
3090 ZF	amphora w/metal stand	(1250)
7488 FH	ginger jar	(1750)
6250 DR	lamp	(750)

(see p. 107)

Chapter Thirty–Five
FAMILY SIGNATURE SERIES

The Family Signature Series made its debut in January 1993, when the five premier pieces were pictured on the first page of the Fenton General Catalog. The catalog mentioned company founder Frank Leslie Fenton's "artistic and creative" talents and went on to describe the rationale for this new series: "F. L. Fenton's enthusiasm and pride have been carried down through the second and third generations of the Fenton family. The Family Signature Series is comprised of a few select pieces that represent the glass worker's and glass decorator's finest work."

There are quite a few Fenton items from the 1990s which bear the signature of one or more members of the Fenton family. However, collectors should realize that not all of these items are from the Family Signature <u>Series</u>, for the signatures of various family members have been a feature of several other limited editions (such as Showcase Dealer Exclusives, the Glass Messenger Subscriber Exclusive, and some items made for QVC). Family Signature Series items are dated with the year of issue and inscribed with the signature of one or more Fenton family members, as indicated in the discussion below (almost all of the Family Signature Series pieces are shown in color in this book; see pp. 109–112). Family Signature Series items are packaged with certificates of authenticity.

Collectors who enjoy the Family Signature pieces often ask this question: "How does a family member's name come to be associated with an item in the Family Signature Series for a given year?" When the series began in 1993, there were five items and ten family members, so the Fenton family members who had been working most closely with collectors and retailers at that time were featured (Bill, Don, Frank, George, and Shelley).

Between 1994–99, many Fenton family members were active in Family Signing Events at retailers in various parts of the country. They made presentations or attended other functions at one or more of the Fenton collector club conventions, and collectors got to know Mike, Nancy, and Tom a bit better. Lynn Fenton joined the company in 1994, and she soon met dealers and collectors alike at national collectibles shows. Scott Fenton joined Fenton's sales department in early 1998 and did the same. The Family Signature Series evolved to include all of them.

There is a bit of friendly competition among the Fenton family members as they see how the various items in the Family Signature Series are received in the marketplace. For the past several years, the quarterly Glass Messenger has reported some sales figures for Family Signature Series pieces.

Both second generation Fenton family members–Frank M. Fenton and Bill Fenton–were represented in the first offering in 1993, as were three third generation Fenton family members–George Fenton, Don Fenton, and Shelley Fenton. In subsequent years during the 1990s, the number of Family Signature Series items varied from six to eight.

As with all pieces in the Family Signature Series during the 1990s, the five initial pieces in 1993 were produced in color treatments which were then present in the regular Fenton line. For example, a Red Carnival vase (2752 RN) carried the signature of Frank M. Fenton, and a 9" vase with the Cottage decoration (7661 Z8) had Shelley Fenton's signature.

Starting with 1994, the Family Signature Series was expanded somewhat by adding something new at mid–year. Six items (to be sold through April 29) were introduced in the 1994 General Catalog, and two more were shown in the Fenton Limited Edition Collectibles supplement in June, 1994.

These pieces from the Family Signature Series were available during the second half of 1994: 2887 ST Stiegel Green Stretch basket with hand-painted Wind Flowers (Bill Fenton signature) and 1568 CW Pansies on Cranberry pitcher (Frank M. Fenton signature).

The 1995 Family Signature Series, which contained seven items, included a handpainted Trellis basket. This was the first item to have the signature of Lynn Fenton, who joined the company in 1994. Also shown was the Thistle pitcher (1566 FS), which had the signature of Don Fenton. Five Signature Series items were shown in the January catalog, and two appeared in the June 1995 supplement.

FENTON

1995 Family Signature Series

The Family Signature Series is comprised of a few select pieces that represent the glass worker's and glass decorator's finest work. Dated 1995 and numbered, these pieces will be inscribed for a limited time * with the signature of a member of the Fenton family who helps carry on the tradition begun in 1905.

Handmade in the U.S.A.

Inscribed with the signature of two Second Generation Family Members-
Bill Fenton, Chairman of the Board and Past President
and
Frank M. Fenton, Past Chairman and President

*All pieces are limited to sales through April 30, 1995.

Mike Fenton
Third Generation
Purchasing Manager and Safety Director

2970 RN

1649 KG

Shelley Fenton
Third Generation
Graphics Manager, Sales and Marketing

Don Fenton
Third Generation
Vice President, Sales

1135 JE

1566 FS

Lynn Fenton
Fourth Generation
Sales & Marketing Specialist

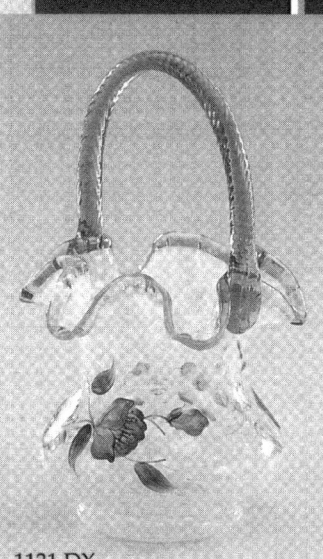
1131 DX

Five items comprised the 1996 Family Signature Series at the outset of the year, and two more were added in mid–year. As with other mid–year items in the Family Signature Series, these were sold through late November of the year. The Meadow Beauty Feather vase (1563 PD), which had the signature of Nancy Fenton, was the year's best seller of the Family Signature Series with sales of over 3200. At least 2000 of each of the other items were produced.

The 1997 Family Signature Series consisted of six items. Five were introduced in the January General Catalog, and the sixth item, a 13" Spruce Green covered urn with handpainted Magnolia and Berry decoration (George Fenton signature), appeared in the mid–year Fenton Christmas Supplement. The Sweetbriar on Plum Overlay basket with Lynn Fenton's signature (4648 P9) has a particularly interesting spiral handle made with rods of milk glass applied to the Plum color. The production technique was developed by a "handle team" composed of designer Jon Saffell, mouldmaker Jerry Stevens, product development assistant Sarah Smith, mould holder Don Riddle, toolmaker Byron Butts, and skilled glassworker Bob Buchanan.

2040 TP Hydrangeas on Topaz Opalescent three–piece fairy light, 1997 (Frank M. Fenton signature).

In 1998, the Family Signature Series appeared on page two of the Fenton General Catalog. Five items were shown there, and the Twining Berries sleigh (Mike Fenton signature) was in the 1998 Christmas Supplement. Sea Green Satin and Royal Purple were Fenton's Historic Collection colors for 1998, and the Family Signature series items in these colors were quite popular among collectors. The Royal Purple blown bell (Don Fenton signature) topped 3000 in sales. The Sea Green Satin 11" tulip vase with Martha Reynolds' Floral Interlude decoration (Nancy and George Fenton signatures) sold over 4800 and was recognized as "Decorative Collectible of the Year" by the National Association of Limited Edition Dealers (NALED). This was the best–selling Family Signature Series piece of the 1990s decade.

The 1999 grouping included the first Family Signature Series item (4566 CG handpainted Morning Mist pitcher) to have the signature of Scott K. Fenton, who had joined the company's sales department in early 1998. Among the other items in 1999 were a decorated Rosalene basket (Lynn Fenton signature) and a vase in Tranquility (Bill and Don Fenton signatures).

Fenton collectors look forward to the annual release of new pieces in the Family Signature Series. Fenton family members enjoy the process of choosing the pieces as they plan for the Fenton regular line, and they anticipate the element of competition that is brought by each new Family Signature Series group.

5440 LS Irises on Misty Blue pitcher, 1997 (Don Fenton signature).

FAMILY SIGNATURE SERIES, 1993–1999

(* indicates two signatures on an item)

Bill Fenton
1993 6730 PJ.................... handpainted Lilacs 8½" Paisley basket
1994 1559 CW... Pansies on Cranberry 9½" vase
1994 2787 ST..................... handpainted Stiegel Green Stretch 8" basket
1995 1135 JE...... Coralene Floral on Celeste Blue Stretch 9½" Diamond basket*
1999 1689 LN................. 9½" Tranquility vase*

Don Fenton
1993 1786 PV.....Vintage 10" Diamond Melon vase
1994 7380 AW...........................Autumn Leaves on Black 9½" candy
1995 1566 FS............handpainted Thistle 9" pitcher
1995 1554 S9 handpainted Spruce Green 9" vase
1996 3065 KT...........................Mountain Berry on Gold Overlay 6½" pitcher
1997 5440 LS......Irises on Misty Blue 7½" pitcher
1998 3271 N4...........................Colonial Scroll on Royal Purple 6½" blown bell
1999 1689 LN................. 9½" Tranquility vase*

Frank M. Fenton
1993 2757 RN....................... ..Red Carnival 9" Alpine Thistle vase
1994 1568 CW...................Pansies on Cranberry 6½" pitcher
1994 1217 AO...............Autumn Gold Opalescent 11" basket
1995 1135 JE......Coralene Floral on Celeste Blue Stretch 9½" Diamond basket*
1997 2040 TP...Hydrangeas on Topaz Opalescent 7½" three–piece fairy light

George Fenton
1993 1640 C1.............................handpainted Cranberry 11" Rib vase
1994 1216 EH...............Fuschia 10" Spiral vase
1995 1567 CW......... Pansies on Cranberry 7" vase
1996 5357 TE...Blush Rose on Opaline 8½" vase
1997 4602 SE.....................Magnolia and Berry on Spruce 13" urn
1998 7255 GG.....................Floral Interlude on Sea Green Satin 11" Tulip vase*
1999 7484 XP............Violet Satin 5" covered box

Lynn Fenton
1995 1131 DX....................handpainted Trellis 8½" Diamond Optic basket
1996 3065 DP.............Asters on Rose Overlay 6½" pitcher
1997 4648 P9.........Sweetbriar on Plum Overlay 9" basket
1998 8691 LS...............Irises on Misty Blue Satin 4½" clock
1999 6833 HH.....handpainted Rosalene 8" basket

Mike Fenton
1995 2970 RN.............................Red Carnival 8½" candy with cover
1996 4759 SE.....................Magnolia and Berry on Spruce 10" vase
1997 7565 X5.....................Medallion Collection 8" Reverse Melon vase
1998 4695 JX............Twining Berries 7½" sleigh

Nancy Fenton
1996 1563 PD... Meadow Beauty 11" Feather vase
1998 7255 GG.....................Floral Interlude on Sea Green Satin 11" Tulip vase*

Scott Fenton
1999 4566 CG...............Morning Mist 6" pitcher

Shelley Fenton
1993 7661 Z8.............................Cottage vase
1994 2738 PJ......... handpainted Lilacs 7½" basket
1995 1649 KG.............Golden Flax on Cobalt 9½" Feather vase
1996 5585 PF...............Pansies 5½" covered box
1997 4751 PI.............................Field Flowers on Champagne Satin 6" vase
1998 2039 SF......handpainted Topaz 10½" basket (this basket was made with either a fine crimp or a double crimp)
1999 3070 AZ.............. Martha's Rose 8½" vase

Tom Fenton
1994 2779 RN............................. Red Carnival 8½" Lion/Leaf basket
1996 3127 NG............................ Starflowers on Cranberry Pearl 7½" basket
1997 9550 TP................. Hydrangeas on Topaz Opalescent 8" fan vase
1998 4830 DX.................. Trellis 9½" hat basket
1999 9333 JX........ Twining Berries 7" covered box

Chapter Thirty–Six
EASTER and CHRISTMAS LIMITED EDITIONS

During the 1990s decade, Fenton limited editions were among the company's most popular products, and Easter and Christmas limited editions occupied prominent places in Fenton sales materials. Because the term "limited" is used in a variety of senses by various manufacturers, it may be useful to see how Fenton approaches this. For Fenton, "limited" is an umbrella term which applies to several different kinds of production. Some Fenton limited editions are strictly limited "by number" while others are limited "by time."

When an item is limited to a specific quantity, the number is announced in print when the items appear in a Fenton catalog or supplement. For example, various items in the Birds of Winter Series made from 1987 to 1990 were limited to specific quantities, as were many other limited editions made during the 1990s.

Fenton's numbered limited editions are individually numbered in the Decorating Services Department at Fenton Art Glass. For items limited to a specific quantity, the number looks like this: 435/2500. Because the pieces are assigned numbers from 1 to 2500 in sequence, the first number (435) is used only once. The second number (2500) appears on every piece so that collectors will know the precise numerical limit for their item.

Another type of numbered limited edition is not restricted to a predetermined quantity. Production schedules are adjusted to fill orders placed by Fenton customers within a certain time period. The numbered limited editions which are limited "by time" are assigned numbers in sequence beginning with "1" and proceeding to whatever number is dictated by the quantity of pieces ordered by a certain time (or when the item is discontinued for some reason such as production difficulties).

The employees who do the numbering on these pieces maintain careful records to ensure that the numbers are assigned correctly. Occasionally, an item is broken during packing or in shipment, and the records will note that a replacement has been numbered.

When an item is limited "by time," it means that Fenton will fill orders for the item which have been placed by its dealers before a specific date which is announced in print in Fenton sales materials. These items are typically not individually numbered. They may, however, be dated with the year of production (e. g., blown eggs for Easter).

Easter Limited Editions

Within the wide variety of Fenton items from the 1990s which were associated with Easter, there are some interesting limited editions. Collectors should also realize that there are many items offered in Fenton's Easter or Christmas sales materials which, strictly speaking, are not limited editions. Some of these were discussed earlier in Chapter 32, The Fenton Line.

During the 1990s decade, Fenton's emphasis on Easter evolved from a separate focus on Easter with its own sales materials to combining Valentine's Day and Easter items in a catalog supplement and, later, merging both occasions into a more lengthy catalog supplement for "Spring."

The first Easter limited editions of the decade were two blown eggs (the 4½" 5031 WD and a somewhat smaller 3½" 5030 QB), which were shown in the "Easter 1991" sales materials. The eggs were described this way: "These magnificent hand-blown eggs have had the full treatment. Iridized with a Mother of Pearl finish to accent the pink, blue, green and lavender tones of Easter. They are then skillfully handpainted and accented with 22k gold paint for an exquisitely expensive look. Each egg is then signed by the artist and dated 1991 on the bottom."

As described below, other blown eggs were made during the next five years (see Figs. 1037–1048 for all of the blown eggs for the 1990s decade). Longtime Fenton glassblower Bob Hays was responsible for production of the blown eggs. Although they were not a formal series, these handpainted eggs are dated with the year and signed by the artist.

Two blown eggs with a light iridescent treatment were offered for Easter 1992. Both had ware number 5031, but one had a floral decoration with a hummingbird (5031 Q2) while the other had a floral decoration and gold bands (5031 Q3). The Fenton Catalog Supplement promised that these would "delight every egg collector" because they were "eggsactly what they've been looking for!" For 1993, the blown eggs (both 5031) were offered in two colors, Plum (5031 WE) and Ocean Blue (5031 WJ), with handpainted decorations. These were limited to sales through April 11, 1993.

For 1994, the two blown eggs, 5031 FU and 5031 FV, had handpainted decorations designed, respectively, by Martha Reynolds and Frances Burton. These were limited to sales through April 1, 1994. In 1995, there were also two blown eggs, 5031 YX and 5031 YW (limited to sales through April 16, 1995). The blown eggs were last made in 1996. A French Opalescent egg (1642 JO) was decorated with a butterfly motif, and a Cranberry egg (1642 JM) featured a bluebird.

The 1995 Easter sales materials also showed a limited edition fairy light (8405 YZ, limited to sales through April 16, 1995) and the 5188 YZ Covered

Hen Egg Plate, which was limited to 950 (see Figs. 1035–1036). The decoration for these was designed by Martha Reynolds. The Covered Hen Egg Plate was also produced in 1997 with a different decoration as a limited edition of 950 (see Fig. 1146).

In 1995 and 1996, Fenton issued catalog supplements which embraced both Valentine's Day and Easter. By 1997, the emphasis on Valentine's Day and Easter as separate occasions was clearly shifting toward collectibles introduced as a "Spring" offering. These included Cranberry Opalescent Heart Optic and Mary Gregory, as well as the emerging Folk Art Collection (see Chapter 37 for discussions of these and other limited editions).

In 1998, the only limited edition associated with Easter in the catalog supplement was a Family Signature Series basket (see Fig. 1002), which had first appeared in the General Catalog in January. The 1999 catalog supplement featured limited edition collectibles for "Early Spring" and "Late Spring," but none was associated with Easter as they had been in the early years of the 1990s decade. These limited editions are discussed in Chapter 37 of this book.

Collectible Eggs

Fenton's Collectible Eggs spanned almost the entire 1990s decade. They were not included in the Fenton Easter supplements, but, because of the natural association of eggs with Easter, many collectors have viewed them as Easter collectibles (see Figs. 1074–1089 for various eggs from this series).

The premier collection of seven pressed eggs was introduced on a separate sales sheet in mid–1991, launching an on–going series that has continued into the year 2000. Fenton decorators were more than equal to the challenge of developing innovative decorative treatments for the Collectible Eggs, which were made in a wide variety of colors with many different handpainted decorations.

Between 1991 and 1994, four sets of Collectible Eggs were made with the moulds for the 5140 "egg on stand," which was formerly associated with many different colors and decorations during the 1970s and 1980s. In the Collectible Eggs Series, the smooth, plain stand was decorated with a shiny 22k gold finish. The eggs for 1991 were limited to 1500 each. In 1992, the limit for each of the seven new eggs was 2500. There were eight eggs in 1993; seven were limited to 2500, but the eighth, a "Special Egg" (5140 ZN) in a sandcarved Black Carnival glass treatment, was available in an edition of 1500. There were seven eggs in the 1994 offering, and each was limited to 2500.

The 1995 Collectible Eggs were the first from a new mould which was designed by Jon Saffell. The 5145 egg is called "leaf base" because of the stylized motif on the base. At about 4" tall, the 5145 egg is larger than the 5140 egg. There were seven eggs in

These are the 1993 Collectible Eggs, which were limited to 2500 each; an additional "Special Egg" with sandcarved decoration was limited to 1500.

These line drawings show the different bases on the Fenton Collectible Eggs; left to right: plain base (1991–94); leaf base (1995–97); and sculpted base (1998–99).

1995, and each was limited to 2500. The 1996 and 1997 groupings also contained seven eggs apiece, and these were limited to 2500.

In 1998, yet another new egg mould was introduced. Also designed by Jon Saffell, this was called the "sculpted base" and carried the 5146 designation. These seven eggs were limited to 3000 each. The 1999 Collectible Eggs assortment consisted of eight eggs, and each was limited to 3000.

Christmas Limited Editions

Christmas is a special time, and Fenton has marked this occasion with a number of regular line and limited edition items. These range from individual items to articles in a series which runs for several years.

The Birds of Winter series ran from 1987 to 1990. Produced in conjunction with the Marietta–based magazine *Bird Watcher's Digest*, the series spotlighted a different bird each year: Cardinal in the Churchyard (BC) in 1987; A Chickadee Ballet (BD), 1988; Downy Woodpecker–Chisled Song (BL), 1989; and A Bluebird in Snowfall (NB), 1990. Items from the 1989 and 1990 limited edition offerings are pictured in *Fenton Glass: The 1980s Decade* (p. 145).

The year 1990 marked the start of a new series. Billed as "limited edition" collectibles, the Christmas at Home series consisted of five items each year between 1990 and 1993 (see Figs. 1058–1061). Four items were the same each year (7300 fairy light; 7418 8" plate; 7668 bell; and 8600 clock). The 7204 16" hammered colonial lamp was offered in 1990, 1991, and 1993. The 9380 20" lamp was offered only in 1992 (incidentally, an incorrect lamp was pictured in Fenton's 1991 Christmas catalog supplement, but a correction was made in both the catalog and the price list).

In 1992, several other Christmas limited editions were shown in Fenton's catalog supplement. Two numbered eggs (each limited to 2500) were available: the 5140 SD was made in ruby glass and decorated with a manger scene; the 5140 SU was made in opaque white glass and decorated with a red poinsettia. The 7669 ZX musical bell (limited to 950) was made in opaque white and decorated with an elaborate floral motif which combined elements from the Flowers of Christmas items in the regular line (see Fig. 1070). The 7463 ZW Winter Twilight bell (limited to 2500) featured platinum highlighted with glass ice on blue glass.

Christmas at Home Series
Designed by Frances Burton
(limits in parentheses)

1990 Sleigh Ride
7204 HD 16" lamp (1000)
7300 HD fairy light (3500)
7418 HD 8" plate (3500)
7668 HD bell (3500)
8600 HD clock (1500)

1991 Christmas Eve
7204 HJ 16" lamp (1000)
7300 HJ fairy light (3500)
7418 HJ 8" plate (3500)
7668 HJ bell (3500)
8600 HJ clock (1500)

1992 Family Traditions
7300 HQ fairy light (3500)
7418 HQ 8" plate (3500)
7668 HQ bell (3500)
8600 HQ clock (1500)
9380 HQ 20" lamp (1000)

1993 Family Holiday
7204 HT 16" lamp (1000)
7300 HT fairy light (3500)
7418 HT 8" plate (3500)
7668 HT bell (3500)
8600 HT clock (1500)

"Christmas Eve" was the second of the four–part Christmas at Home series, which ran from 1990–1993.

"Family Traditions" was the third of the four–part Christmas at Home series, which ran from 1990–1993.

"Sleigh Ride" was the first of the four–part Christmas at Home series, which ran from 1990–1993.

The Poinsettia (5140 SU) and Manger Scene (5140 SD) eggs were for Christmas 1992. The Angel (5140 SW) and Woods (5140 SV) eggs were for Christmas 1993. Each of these was limited to 2500.

"Family Holiday" was the fourth of the four–part Christmas at Home series, which ran from 1990–1993.

Limited edition Christmas items, as indicated: (A) 7465 GQ green musical bell, 1993, limited to 2500; (B) 7465 VK ruby musical bell, 1994, limited to 1000; (C) 7463 TV bell, 1993, limited to 2500; (D) 5145 VK egg, 1994, limited to 1500; (E) 5145 VG egg, 1994, limited to 1500; (F) 7463 VP bell, 1994, limited to 1000; (G) 7464 VG bell, 1994, limited to 1000; and (H) 7463 SD ruby bell, 1993, limited to 2500.

Martha Reynolds created five limited edition items for Christmas in 1993. There were three 7463 bells with different decorations and two eggs, each of which was limited to 2500 pieces. One egg (5140 SW) depicted an angel with a trumpet, while the other (5140 SV) had a woodland scene.

A new Christmas grouping, the Christmas Star Series, began in 1994 and continued through 1997 (see Figs. 1054–1057). This series used a different glass color each year, but all the items in a given year were made in the same color and decorated with the same scene. There were five items each year, and four of them (5145 egg; 7300 fairy light; 7418 8" plate; and 7463 bell) were the same from year to year. The 7204 lamp was part of the series in 1994 and 1996, while the 2940 lamp was in the series during 1995 and 1997.

Christmas Star Series
Designed by Frances Burton
(limits in parentheses)

1994 Silent Night
Blue Satin glass
5145 VS egg on stand (1500)
7204 VS 16" lamp (500)
7300 VS fairy light (1500)
7418 VS 8" plate (1500)
7463 VS bell (2500)

1995 Our Home is Blessed
Green Satin glass
2940 VT 21" student lamp (500)
5145 VT egg on stand (1500)
7300 VT fairy light (1500)
7418 VT 8" plate (1500)
7463 VT bell (2500)

1996 Star of Wonder
Gold satin glass
7204 SN 16" lamp (750)
5145 SN egg on stand (1750)
7300 SN fairy light (1750)
7418 SN 8" plate (1750)
7463 SN bell (2500)

1997 The Way Home
Ruby Satin glass
2940 RX 20" lamp (750)
5145 RX egg on stand (1750)
7300 RX fairy light (1750)
7418 RX 8" plate (1750)
7463 RX bell (2500)

Martha Reynolds created five limited edition items for Christmas in 1994. There were two 7463 bells with different decorations and a 7465 musical bell (each limited to 1000) as well as two 5145 eggs (each limited to 1500).

In 1995, the entire front page of the Christmas catalog supplement was devoted to limited editions. Robin Spindler developed the Heavenly Angel bell (5144 TW), which was limited to 1900. Martha Reynolds was responsible for the Radiant Angel figurine (5542 TA; limited to 900), which came with a Sankyo musical base featuring "Silent Night."

Reynolds also created the designs for three bells and eggs in gold, ivory or ruby glass (all limited to 900) as well as the Golden Pine Cones 2966 V2 pitcher (limited to 900), which featured both matte and shiny gold and was quite a hit with collectors. Incidentally, the year 1995 marked Fenton's 90th year in business, so Don Fenton came up with the idea of having the numbers "9" and "0" appear together in the limits.

The year 1996 brought forth several new Christmas limited editions. There were decorated bells and decorated eggs in gold, green and ruby glass; these were called Holly Berries (see Fig. 1072), Golden Partridge, and Moonlit Meadow, respectively, and each was limited to 1500. Martha Reynolds added 22k gold to the Poinsettia Glow Radiant Angel (5542 QB, limited to 1000), and Robin Spindler developed the decorations for a Nativity fairy light (9401 N7) and bell (9463 N7; see Fig. 1068); these were made with moulds which dated back to the early 1980s (see *Fenton Glass: The 1980s Decade*, p. 94).

Nativity fairy light and bell (1996; limited to 1500 each).

FENTON

The first limited edition design by Robin Spindler captures the delicate freshness of a young angel. Her special trim features matte gold with raised gold enamel beads which must be painted and fired twice. A lovely piece to make Christmas 1995 memorable. Limited to 1900 pieces.

Designer Martha Reynolds has woven tiny poinsettias along the flowing ivory satin gown and highlighted her wings with sparkling crystal. The 18 note Sankyo musical plays "Silent Night" beneath this elegant handmade angel. Limited to 900 pieces.

0828 AS

Radiant Angel on Musical Base
5542 TA
Angel on Musical Base, 9 3/4"
(900)

Heavenly Angel
5144 TW
Angel, Bell, 5 3/4" (1900)

Christmas Limited Editions

5145 TP - Egg, Gold, 3 1/2" (900)

7463 TP
Bell, Gold, 6 1/2" (900)

Three exquisite new designs created by Martha Reynolds. Each is hand-painted, signed and numbered. Limited to 900 pieces each and 2 per store.

7667 TQ
Bell, Ruby, 5 1/2"
(900)

5145 TQ
Egg, Ruby, 3 1/2"
(900)

2967 TH
Bell, Ivory, 6 1/2"
(900)

5145 TH
Egg, Ivory, 3 1/2" (900)

Handmade in the U.S.A. since 1905

Christmas Star Series Second Edition "Our Home is Blessed"
Designed by Frances Burton. Each Limited Piece is Signed by the Artist, Numbered and Dated.

7418 VT
Plate, 8"
(1500)

7668 VT
Bell, 6 1/2"
(2500)

2940 VT
Lamp, Student, 21"
(500)

5145 VT
Egg, 3 1/2" (1500)

7300 VT
Fairy Light, 4 1/2" (1500)

Christmas Star Series: "Our Home is Blessed"
Frances Burton understands the special love that families share during the Christmas season. Her newest design for the Christmas Star Series radiates the warmth of a loving home. The bow on the mailbox and wreaths by the door say "Welcome" as the Christmas Star bestows its blessing on a happy home.

The Golden Winged Angels assortment was offered in 1996. The egg was limited to 1500, and the other items to 2000 each (left to right: 5144 AV Angel bell; 5145 AC egg; 2967 AC bell; 1714 AC ornament; and 7300 AC fairy light).

Perhaps the most dramatic Christmas limited edition offering for 1996 was the Golden Winged Angels grouping developed by Martha Reynolds. The Angel bell (5144 AV, limited to 2000) was decorated with a floral motif, but each of the other five items has a Renaissance–style angel with gold wings (see Fig. 1069).

In 1997, Robin Spindler created new decorations for the Radiant Angel (5542 HJ) and the Angel bell (5144 BM); these were numbered and limited to sales through November 15, 1997. An Olde World Santa figure (discussed later in this chapter) was also featured in the 1997 Christmas supplement.

Kim Plauché developed the decoration for the Nativity bell (9463 ND) and fairy light (9401 ND), and she also created a Christmas floral motif for a bell, egg, and fairy light in ruby glass. Robin Spindler was responsible for the decorations on bells, eggs, and fairy lights in French Opalescent and Golden Glow. All of these were numbered and limited to sales though November 15, 1997.

The Christmas, 1998, offering extended Fenton's emphasis on collectible bells, eggs and fairy lights. Three new decorations–Lenten Rose (see Fig. 1064), Ornamental Magic (see Fig. 1062), and Woodland Frost–were available (these were numbered and limited to sales though November 15, 1998). Kim Plauché developed the decoration for the Radiant Angel (5542 HQ) and the Angel girl (5144 HN); these were numbered and limited to sales though November 15, 1998.

The year 1998 also marked the outset of a new four–year Christmas series called Birth of a Savior (see Figs. 1049–1053). Each of the five pieces–lamp, bell, egg, fairy light, and plate–is a numbered limited edition. The 1998 items depicted "The Arrival." The 1999 items were called "The Announcement," and those for Christmas 2000 depicted "The Journey." The articles scheduled for 2001 will feature a Nativity scene.

Birth of a Savior Series
Designed by Frances Burton
(limits in parentheses)

1998 The Arrival
Spruce Green Satin
7678 XS 26" lamp (850)
7300 XS fairy light (2500)
5146 XS egg (2500)
7610 XS 9" plate (2500)
7566 XS bell (2500)

1999 The Announcement
Cobalt Satin
3205 KP 11" hurricane candle lamp (1750)
7300 KP fairy light (2500)
5146 KP egg (2500)
7610 KP 9" plate (2500)
7566 KP bell (2500)

2000 The Journey
Spruce Green Satin
7520 QP 11" hurricane candle lamp (1750)
7300 QP fairy light (2500)
5146 QP egg (2500)
7610 QP 9" plate (2500)
7566 QP bell (2500)

2001 (yet to be named)
Cobalt Satin
Pieces and limits to be determined

Fenton designer Jon Saffell created three Santa Claus figures in the late 1990s (see Figs. 1093 and 1100–1101). Not solid figurines, these were hollow items made upside down as pressed glass. Jon's research into historical Santas began in 1995, and his Olde World Santa (5299 I2; limited to 3750), complete with decorating designed by Martha Reynolds, was ready for Christmas 1997. Patriotic Santa (5249 VP; limited to 4750) made his debut in 1998, and the Enchantment Santa (5279 JM; limited to 4750) was on the market in 1999.

After their first year of issue, the first two Santa moulds were used again, and completely different decorations were developed for them (see Figs. 1097–1099). The 5299 mould was used in 1998 for the Northern Lights Santa (5299 VL), an innovative

(text continued on page 188)

Jon Saffell

Glass design demands a knowledge of the working characteristics of a unique molten material as well as the mechanics of glass moulds. Working in clay or plaster, sculptor Jon Saffell creates shapes which both take advantage of the properties of colored glass and anticipate production challenges.

Jon came to Fenton in 1994, and many new Fenton moulds used to create beautiful baskets and vases during the second half of the 1990s decade are the result of his remarkable expertise in designing objects to be made in glass. Those collectors who own a Fenton 3240 vase (see Fig. 689) or a 5065 Cat (see Fig. 654) can attest to the beauty which results from Jon's creative energies.

Several Fenton limited edition Christmas items–such as the Nativity Set and the popular Santa figurines made in 1997–1999–are among the most recent testaments to Jon's talent (see Figs. 1093 and 1097–1105). He has also designed a wide variety of Fenton giftware and lighting ware items.

Jon particularly enjoys children, and Fenton's Praying Children figurines (see Fig. 1196) were modeled after his grandchildren Ashley and Dax. His granddaughter Alyssa was the model for the Fenton 5328 doll figurine, which made its debut in 1999 as a Fenton Showcase Dealer Exclusive (see Fig. 1166).

Jon has been involved with glass design since 1957, when he was first employed at the Fostoria Glass Company in Moundsville, West Virginia. Among the many designs he created there were a lead crystal stemware pattern called Kimberly and a blown bell for Fostoria's American line.

design depicting an outdoor scene on a human figure (complete with a moon on Santa's pack!). The 5299 mould was also used in 1999 for the Bejeweled Santa (5299 JO). The 5249 mould was used for the Golden Age Santa (5249 JN) in 1999.

The Radiant Angel (5542 PU) and the Angel girl bell (5144 PU) were offered in 1999 with a new decoration called "Angels Aglow," which was created by Martha Reynolds (these were numbered and limited to sales through November 15, 1999). The Renaissance Angel Ornament (5542 WU) featured a gold finished metal frame. This piece, limited to sales through November 15, 1999, is dated (see Fig. 1073). The Renaissance Angel might have launched more similar ornaments, but collectors did not think it looked like glass, so this direction was abandoned.

Decorated bells, eggs, and fairy lights continued to be a mainstay of Fenton's limited editions for Christmas in 1999 (see p. 115). Kim Plauché's decoration on gold glass was called Iced Pinecones (see Fig. 1065), and Robin Spindler's Poinsettias were on ruby (see Fig. 1063). Cobalt blue was featured for the first time, and Martha Reynolds' Jolly Snowman motif was quite a hit with collectors (see Fig. 1066–1067). All of these bells, eggs and fairy lights were numbered and limited to sales through November 15, 1999.

The Fenton Nativity Set is a group of twelve figurines that was offered three pieces at a time over the span of four Christmas seasons, 1997–2000 (see Figs. 1102–1105). All of the items were designed by Jon Saffell. The Nativity Set concept was of great interest to the New Product Development Committee, and the specifics were worked out over several years. Jon's clay sculptures were used to make masters of each item in epoxy resin, and Fenton's skilled mouldmakers spent many hours on the details of each figurine.

The three-piece Holy Family (5280 NF) set was available for Christmas 1997, followed by the Three Wise Men (5289 WM) a year later (a 22k goldplated Star backdrop was also available in 1998). Production of these figurines enabled Fenton to learn a great deal about the challenges of forming fine facial details in different kinds of glass. The head on the Joseph figurine was modified considerably after the items for 1997 were produced.

In 1999, the Gloria Angel Set (5050 NA) consisted of an angel figurine and a camel and a donkey. The final three pieces were originally scheduled to be a kneeling shepherd, a lamb and a cow, but the cow was replaced by a standing shepherd who has a metal staff. The Shepherd Set (5055 NS) was released in the year 2000.

Martha Reynolds and Robin Spindler developed decorations for separate pieces in the Nativity Set, and the individual figurines backstamped "First Edition" were sold only in the years of their respective initial releases. In subsequent years, the hand-painted decorations were changed, and these figurines are not backstamped (see Figs. 1107–1109).

At the close of the 1990s decade, Fenton limited editions were an important part of the Fenton line. Among many Fenton collectors, the pieces described in this chapter had become treasured keepsakes associated with special holiday occasions.

Chapter Thirty–Seven
OTHER LIMITED EDITIONS

During the 1990s, Fenton made a wide variety of limited edition items. Many of these–such as Historical Collection colors, the Connoisseur Collection, and the Family Signature Series–are discussed in previous chapters of this book. This chapter is devoted to limited editions produced for such occasions as Valentine's Day and Mother's Day along with other limited editions made during the 1990s by Fenton: Mary Gregory, Folk Art, Designer Bells, Miniatures, Jewelry, Lamp Specials, the Millennium Collection, and some others, such as Showcase Dealer Exclusives and Direct Mail Catalog Exclusives.

As indicated in the previous chapter, "limited" is an umbrella term which applies to several different kinds of Fenton products. Some Fenton limited editions are strictly limited by number while others are limited by time.

Numbered limited editions may be restricted to a specific quantity. The Designer Bell Series, for example, is limited to 2500 of each bell (these will have numbers that look like this: 44/2500). Other numbered limited editions are not so restricted, and orders placed by customers within a certain period will be filled. For instance, the annual Glass Messenger Subscriber Exclusive pieces (see Chapter 41) are assigned numbers in sequence beginning with "1" and proceeding to whatever number is dictated by the quantity of pieces ordered.

When an item is limited "by time," it means that Fenton will fill orders for the item which have been placed by dealers by a specific date which is announced in print in Fenton sales materials. Most of these items are not individually numbered, but they may be dated with the year of production (e. g., Mother's Day items).

From 1990 to 1994, Fenton distributed separate sales materials for its Valentine's Day and Easter items (these were brief 2 or 4 page catalog supplements). Beginning in 1995, the Sentiments Collection catalog supplement embraced both Valentine's Day and Easter items.

Valentine's Day

The first limited editions associated with Valentine's Day began in 1992. Prior to this, the Fenton Sentiments Collection catalogs offered various gift items for this special occasion. The catalog supplement for 1990 showed assortments in Petal Pink (PN) and Pearly Sentiments (PT) along with Christine Victoria items. The 1991 Sentiments Collection included crystal bears with red hearts in various locations (these were called "Red Heart Lovers"). Pink Pearl (HZ) and Pearly Sentiments assortments were offered, and a "Fools in Love" display unit was developed for some clown items.

The limited editions for Valentine's Day 1992 consisted of a decorated bell (7668 XB) and three items in cranberry opalescent glass with a "heart optic" effect. Fenton first made heart optic bottles in French opalescent for several perfume companies in the late 1940s and early 1950s, but the moulds had seen little use since that period.

Nancy Fenton saw a sample piece in heart optic, and everyone soon shared her enthusiasm for this treatment as "an absolutely perfect fit" for Valentine's Day. Fenton offered heart optic items in Cranberry Opalescent from 1992 through 1998 (see Figs. 1110–1120). These were limited to orders placed by a particular date (mid–February in 1992–95, and March 31 in 1996–98). Incidentally, there was also one heart optic item (CV154 CR Melon pitcher) produced for a QVC show in 1997.

Heart Optic by Fenton. On the cover of the February/March 1998 *Glass Collector's Digest*.

Cranberry Opalescent Heart Optic

1992
6568 CR 4" vase
6580 CR perfume with oval stopper
6567 CR 6" basket

1993
2732 CR Caprice 7" basket
2740 CR trinket box
2749 CR 5½" Melon vase

1994
2755 CR 5½" ribbed vase
2760 CR perfume with heart stopper
2736 CR 7" basket

1995
2774 CR 5½" Melon pitcher
2745 CR 8" Melon basket

1996
2903 CR 3-pc. fairy light
7122 CR 8" Melon basket
7100 CR 5" Melon perfume

1997
2169 CR 6½" pitcher,
4950 CR 4" puff box
4965 CR 7' hat basket

1998
4905 CR 5" fairy light
4990 CR 4½" covered box
4955 CR 5" vase

Mary Gregory

This popular Fenton collectible of the 1990s began modestly enough with an egg (5140 E7) that was part of the first offering of Collectible Eggs in 1991. The classic Mary Gregory style (white enamel profiles of children) originated in the early nineteenth century when Bohemian decorators attempted to replicate expensive carved cameo glass.

In 1992, four Mary Gregory bells were available, but these were not limited edition items. The 1993 Sentiments Collection catalog, however, showed a ruby bell (7463 RQ) with a Mary Gregory decoration created by Martha Reynolds (these were limited to sales by February 14, 1993).

Glass collectors liked the Mary Gregory style and requested more pieces. Fenton responded in 1994, and items were offered throughout the 1990s decade and into the year 2000 (see Figs. 1121–1132). The sales period was lengthened to October 31 for the years 1994–95, when all the items were made of pressed ruby glass. The theme for 1994 was "Loves Me, Loves Me Not," and the items depicted a young woman plucking petals from a daisy. The theme for 1995 was "Butterfly Delight," and the four pressed ruby pieces were decorated with a scene depicting a young woman with a butterfly alighting on her outstretched hand.

The Mary Gregory pieces for 1996–99 were numbered limited editions. These were blown items made in cranberry glass, and the decorations were more elaborate. Nancy Fenton and Frank M. Fenton had met authors Robert and Deborah Truitt several years earlier, and they discussed Mary Gregory–style decorations with them. Soon thereafter, Nancy Fenton and Martha Reynolds sought to make Fenton's Mary Gregory pieces top quality. Working with various paints, Reynolds developed techniques to create considerable depth and detail, The paint fired like "liquid china" and remained both opaque and slightly raised from the surface. This made intricate details (such as buttons and ruffles) important features in the Mary Gregory offerings.

Although it was not part of the 1999 Mary Gregory group, a Collectible Egg (5146 A7, limited to 3000) in pressed ruby was available with a Mary Gregory–style decoration (see Fig. 1088).

Mary Gregory

1994 ruby glass
"He Loves Me, He Loves Me Not"
8319 RY 9" plate with stand
7463 RY 6" bell
8673 RY 7½" oval basket
(sales through 10/31/94)

1995 ruby glass
"Butterfly Delight"
7463 RG 6½" bell
8319 RG plate with stand
8637 RG 7½" oval basket
5145 RG 4" egg on stand
(sales through 10/31/95)

1996 cranberry glass
(limits in parentheses)
1532 RK 6½" Swan bell (200)
1554 RP 9" Daydreaming vase (1500)

1997 cranberry glass
(limits in parentheses)
1593 DQ Girl Swinging basket (1500)
1500 DI Breezy Day guest set (1500)
1505 DW Meadow Flowers fairy light (1500)

1998 cranberry glass
(limits in parentheses)
2906 RK Swans perfume (1950)
1533 DI Breezy Day 11½" basket (1950)
3275 DM Girl 6–12" pitcher (1950)

1999 cranberry glass
(limits in parentheses)
3201 RK Swans lamp (1250)
3248 R8 Boy Fishing 5" vase (1250)
1613 R8 Boy Fishing 8" basket (2250)
1671 RD Girl/Butterfly pitcher (2250)

Mother's Day

During the 1970s and 1980s, Fenton made a number of Mother's Day items, and this emphasis continued into the 1990s decade.

The 1990 General Catalog showed Linda Everson's swan motif on the 7418 SN plate and a bell (7668 SN or 7669 SN for the musical version). These were designed for Mother's Day 1990 and are dated with the year and signed by the artist). In 1991, the plate and bell, along with a clock (8600 NB), were offered with a decoration called "Mother's Watchful Eye."

Items for Mother's Day 1993.

These Mother's Watchful Eye items were made for Mother's Day in 1991: 9600 MS clock; 7418 MS 8" plate; and 7668 MS bell.

These Let's Play with Mom items were made for Mother's Day in 1992: 9600 X5 clock; 7418 X5 8" plate; and 7668 X5 bell.

Items for Mother's Day 1994.

Mother and Child pendant (1999).

For 1992, Martha Reynolds created the "Let's Play with Mom" decoration for a bell, clock and plate. Reynolds also developed a "touching scene of a mother deer and her fawn" for 1993 and "Loving Puppy" for 1994.

The next item designated specifically for Mother's Day occurred in 1999. A "Mother & Child" pendant (5399 L9) in Misty Blue was available (limited to sales through April 30, 1999). Jon Saffell sculpted the bas–relief, and Margarita de Santis, a free–lance jewelry designer who lives in Rhode Island, created the mounting and chain.

Folk Art

These beautifully decorated items (see p. 120), which have become popular with collectors, were developed during the last half of the 1990s decade. Some of these items were also made in various treatments and offered as Easter gifts.

Three Folk Art animal boxes (4680 Rooster, 4683 Bunny, and 5186 Hen on Nest) appeared in the 1996 Fenton General Catalog, and they were also shown in the 1996 Sentiments Collection catalog supplement. Strictly speaking, these were not limited editions for 1996, but the decorative treatments were not used again.

The three animal boxes were given new decorative treatments designed by Robin Spindler in 1997, and they were then offered as limited editions. The 4680 NJ Rooster, 4683 NU Bunny, and 5186 NE Hen on Nest were limited to sales through March 31, 1997, as was a Rooster figurine (5292 NO).

The decoration for these four items was changed for the next year, and they were limited to sales through March 31, 1998. The large Standing Rooster (5257 FV) was added to the Folk Art Animals collection in 1998. Made from a mould purchased by Fenton from the Paden City Glass Co. in the early 1950s, the Standing Rooster is impressive, but he is difficult to make!

The company tried to produce the Standing Rooster in iridescent and transparent colors (Pink Pearl and Sea Mist Green; see Figs. 149 and 493) during 1996, but the glass proved quite brittle and success was most elusive! About a year later, soft opal glass worked much better, and the Folk Art Standing Rooster was featured on the cover of *Figurines and Collectibles* magazine in October, 1998.

Robin Spindler created more new decorations for 1999, and a 2¾" Rooster (5265 CB) appeared in the Folk Art Collection for the first time (sales were limited to March 31, 1999, and the 5186 NE Hen on Nest was not in this grouping).

Robin Spindler

While visiting the Fenton Gift Shop years ago, Robin and her mother admired the handpainted glass. "You can paint like that!" exclaimed Robin's mother. Robin replied "No, I can't" at the time, but more than two decades of Robin's work at Fenton now speak for themselves.

Robin has developed a great personal style with lots of whimsey. When you find a Fenton Art Glass collectible signed "J. K. Spindler" (Judith Kay), then you've found Robin!

Born and reared in Morgantown, West Virginia, Robin loves the outdoors, and animals are among her favorite subjects. "I like to capture the spirit in their eyes," she says.

Robin became a Fenton designer in 1994, and she has been employed at Fenton since 1979. She has created decorating designs for many of the pieces in Fenton's Connoisseur Collection. One of Robin's Connoisseur Collection vases (After the Rain, 1998) won a Discovery Award for technical excellence from the Society of Glass and Ceramic Decorators (see Fig. 980).

In 1997, she was recognized for her design work with an Award of Excellence from *Collector Editions* magazine for the Connoisseur Collection vase "Tranquility" (see Fig. 973). A 1998 Connoisseur Collection piece, the Bountiful Harvest Burmese pitcher (see Fig. 984), was a finalist in the Decorative Collectible of the Year competition sponsored by the National Association of Limited Edition Dealers (NALED).

OVER 1000 LISTINGS – SECONDARY MARKET PRICE GUIDE

FIGURINES & COLLECTIBLES

FOR THE CONTEMPORARY COLLECTOR

OCTOBER 1998

FIRST LOOK!
101 EXCITING RELEASES
INCLUDING THE LATEST HALLMARK KEEPSAKE ORNAMENTS

SPECIAL FEATURE
Collecting Folk Art
CELEBRATE THE ART OF THE PEOPLE

PLUS MARIE OSMOND AND L.L. KNICKERBOCKER PRESENT A KODAK MOMENT

$3.99 US $4.99 CAN

Fenton Art Glass
THE FAMILY TRADITION CONTINUES

Designer Series Bells

First introduced in the Fenton General Catalog for 1996, the Designer Series of bells features the work of Fenton's Decorating Designers–Frances Burton, Kim Plauché, Martha Reynolds, and Robin Spindler. The catalog had this to say about them: "Fenton is proud of its team of talented designers. They study design trends and experiment with new materials and techniques as they strive to bring you fresh, exciting products each season. They work closely together, providing tremendous energy to the design process."

Butterflies bell (1145 GF) from 1997.

The Designer Series Bells consisted of four bells per year between 1996 and 1999 (see p. 121). Each designer was responsible for one bell each year, and their individual personalities and design interests are reflected in the decorations they create.

Several Designer Series Bells have merited national honors. Most recently, Martha Reynolds' Iridescent Floral bell for 1999 (7566 HT) was recognized with an Award of Excellence from *Collector Editions* magazine. Reynolds' Butterflies bell (1145 GF) for 1997 also received this same award as did Frances Burton's Blue Burmese bell for 1999.

Frances Burton

Frances Burton loved art long before she first began her training as a Fenton decorator under Louise Piper in 1973. After balancing work with raising a family for a few years, Frances came to Fenton Art Glass full–time in 1984 and progressed quickly from decorator to trainer, designer, head designer and, finally, to department supervisor, the position she has occupied since 1991.

Her decorating designs have graced many items in the Fenton Connoisseur Collection, and Frances was responsible for much innovative work on reverse painting techniques. Her Butterfly and Floral reverse painted lamp (see Fig. 961) in the 1995 Fenton Connoisseur Collection won an Award of Excellence from *Collector Editions* magazine. Two other reverse painted lamps–Poppies (1996 Connoisseur Collection; see Fig. 967) and Trysting Place (1998 Connoisseur Collection; see Fig. 978)–received Discovery Awards from the Society of Glass and Ceramic Decorators.

She developed the elegant Colonial Scroll decoration for Fenton's Royal Purple glass, and the bell (see front cover) from this grouping won an Award of Excellence from *Collector Editions* magazine. Her 1998 Fenton limited edition Christmas plate, "The Arrival" (see Fig. 1052), also received an Award of Excellence. In 1999, Frances shared an Award of Excellence with Martha Reynolds for the Blue Harmony vase (see Fig. 1410), which was the 1999 Glass Messenger Subscriber Exclusive.

In a recent National Association of Limited Edition Dealers (NALED) competition, Frances' Morning Glories on Burmese tulip vase was first runner–up for Decorative Collectible of the Year. This piece (see Fig. 1399) was the Glass Messenger Subscriber Exclusive for 1998.

Frances enjoys growing some of the beautiful flowers she later brings to life on glass. Romance novels and classic movies also capture her interest. She and her husband, Lanny, love to escape to Vermillion on Lake Erie where they fish and share the quiet beauty.

Miniatures

The first Fenton limited edition miniature, a 6800 Hobstar and Feather punch bowl and four cups in iridized Dusty Rose), debuted in the 1996 Sentiments Collection catalog supplement (limited to sales through March 31, 1996). This miniature (see Fig. 1171) was designed by Jon Saffell, who took his inspiration from a large punch set made by the Millersburg Glass Co. around 1909–10. The Hobstar and Feather miniature punch set was offered in Pearlized Sea Mist Green the next year (limited to sales through March 31, 1997; see Fig. 1169).

The 1998 grouping of Fenton limited edition miniatures consisted of three separate sets, each made in Champagne Satin with a Plum glass ring (see Figs. 1167–1168 and 1170). The Diamond Lace pattern mini epergne (4807 PT) recalled a Fenton pattern that was first made in the late 1940s. A five–piece Hobstar and Feather punch set (6801 PT) was also available.

The five–piece Button and Arch water set (1960 PT) was made with moulds acquired in the early 1990s, but the pattern goes back to the 1890s. Applying a ring of molten Plum glass to the top rim of a small pitcher was quite a challenge, but ringers Butch Wright and Dave Vincent were able to perfect this operation. All of these miniatures were limited to sales through March 31, 1998.

Kim Plauché created an English daisy decoration for the French Opalescent set (8901 N9) which was offered in 1999 (see Fig. 1173). This miniature table set–covered butter, creamer, spooner, and covered sugar accompanied by a 10½" tray–was limited to 1500.

Jewelry

Glass jewelry is a relatively recent development for Fenton. The first item, a Trinket Box and Pendant set (9486 PQ, limited to 2500) was introduced in 1997. The silver mounting and chain were created by jewelry designer Margarita de Santis. The trinket box and pendant are made of Champagne Satin glass.

For 1998, two Fenton jewelry sets were made. The first, made of iridescent amethyst glass, consisted of a trinket box, pendant and matching earrings (clip, C998 PX or pierced, P999 PX). These were numbered and limited to sales through March 31, 1998. The Topaz iridescent pendant (9988 AQ) was numbered and limited to sales through November 15, 1998.

Champagne Satin glass was used for a three–piece Butterfly jewelry set (8590 AT). The glass butterfly for the necklace and brooch were sculpted by Jon Saffell, and the settings were designed by Margarita de Santis. The heart–shaped trinket box was handpainted with a butterfly and floral motif (this set was limited to sales through March 31, 1999). As noted earlier in this chapter, a Mother and Child pendant (5399 L9) in Misty Blue was available for Mother's Day, 1999 (limited to sales through April 30, 1999).

For Christmas 1999, Fenton offered a three–piece Snowflake pendant and earrings set (clip, C909 WH or pierced, P909 WH), another collaboration of Jon Saffell and Margarita de Santis. Made of iridescent crystal, the Snowflake pendant and earrings set was limited to sales through November 15, 1999.

Lamp Special Exclusives

For many years, Fenton offered a Fall Lamp Special to its dealer accounts. This consisted of an assortment of lamps from the Fenton line as well as some produced especially for the offering. In 1995–98, Fenton sales materials informed dealers about some limited edition lamps that were available as part of the Fall Lamp Special (see p. 123). The Lamp Special was not offered in 1999 due to demands on Fenton's production capacity.

The lamps discussed below, produced in small quantities, were "limited" in a somewhat different manner from other Fenton limited edition items. Dealers who ordered five lamps from the Fall Lamp Special listing were permitted to purchase two of the limited edition lamps. Those dealers who ordered eight or more lamps from the Fall Lamp Special could purchase four of the limited edition lamps.

The limited edition lamp (5575 FI) for Fall, 1995, was a reverse painted lamp designed by Frances Burton. The limited edition lamp (5575 5X) for Fall, 1996, was in Burmese with an elaborate floral motif (complete with honeybee!), which was designed by Martha Reynolds.

For Fall, 1997, Martha Reynolds created a lamp called Spring Woodlands (9509 XQ). Fenton sales materials described it with these words: "Pretty Bluebirds flit along the edge of an awakening Spring woods. Martha Reynolds has captured the dewy freshness of Spring in her reverse painted lamp for 1997. Look closely to find the Bluebird house tucked into her pretty scene."

A lamp called Wild Rose (9872 XF) was featured for Fall, 1998. Designed by Martha Reynolds, this lamp had a sanded crystal shade. The detailed design consisted of both reverse painting and additional flowers on the outside.

Millennium Collection

As other manufacturers were marketing all sorts of articles to herald the arrival of "new millennium," Fenton offered a three–piece collection (see Figs. 1178–1180) in iridescent gold with a stylized butterfly decoration its June, 1999, catalog supplement. The butterfly symbolized "the anticipation, energy and sense of rebirth" which heralds a new century." The rolled rim 10" bowl (2747 JE) was reminiscent of the 1920s, but a vase designed by Dan Dailey (6470 JE) had a decidedly contemporary look. The final item, a Happiness Bird (5197 JE), was a longtime favorite among Fenton glass collectors. The Millennium Collection was limited to sales through November 15, 1999.

Showcase Dealer Exclusives

Instituted in 1994, the Fenton Showcase Dealer program soon led to some limited edition items which were available only through these dealer outlets. From 1995–99, there were two Showcase Dealer Exclusives per year, as one was released for Spring sales and the other for Fall sales. The items sold in the Spring were limited by time, but the Fall pieces were numbered limited editions (see Figs. 1185–1191 for many of the Showcase Dealer Exclusives).

The Spring 1995 Showcase Dealer Exclusive was a Cranberry Opalescent vase (3558 CR) with the signature of company President George Fenton (see Fig. 1190). The "Buttons and Braids" motif is an historic Fenton opalescent treatment which dates back to the factory's earliest days in Williamstown (c. 1908–10). The item for Fall was the Sea Dreams vase in Burmese (1649 UY). This beautifully decorated piece depicted sea shells and starfish and featured raised coralene made with finely ground glass. The Sea Dreams vase was limited to 790 (see Fig. 1188).

The Spring 1996 Showcase Dealer Exclusive was a Champagne Satin fan vase (9550 DC) with hummingbird decoration designed by Martha Reynolds. This piece has Bill Fenton's signature and was limited to sales through April 30, 1996. Robin Spindler created the Evening Blossom decoration for the Fall 1996 Showcase Dealer Exclusive, a Mulberry covered box (7603 MD). This piece, which was limited to 1250, has the signatures of the 11 Fenton family members who were involved with the company at that time.

The Spring 1997 Showcase Dealer exclusive was a French Opalescent pitcher with Sea Mist Green ring and handle (3185 ER) and an enhanced Meadow Beauty floral decoration designed by Robin

Showcase Dealer Exclusives from 1996.

Spindler (see Fig. 1187). Limited to sales though April 30, 1997, this piece has Bill Fenton's signature. Martha Reynolds created a handpainted wisteria pattern with butterfly and gold accents for the Fall exclusive, a Mulberry vase (1649 MZ) with the signatures of Don, George and Tom Fenton. This vase was limited to 1750 (see Fig. 1189).

Royal Purple was a Fenton Historical Collection color for 1998, and the Spring showcase Dealer Exclusive was a two–piece tumble–up set (3200 N4) with the Colonial Scroll decoration designed by Frances Burton (see Fig. 1191). With Bill Fenton's signature, this was limited to sales through April 30, 1998. A Rubina Verde 9½" vase called Fields of Gold (1559 HC) was available in Fall 1998. Limited to 1950, this piece has the signatures of Bill and Frank Fenton (see Fig. 1186).

For Spring 1999, the Showcase Dealer Exclusive was a Nancy Fenton signature piece in Violet Satin (see Fig. 1166). This "little sister" doll (5328 XP) came from a new mould designed by Jon Saffell, and the decoration was designed by Kim Plauché (these were numbered and limited to sales through April 30, 1999; see Fig. 1166). A Periwinkle on Blue Burmese three–piece fairy light (7501 TA) was the final Showcase Dealer Exclusive of the 1990s decade. Inscribed with the signatures of Bill and Frank Fenton, this piece was limited to 1950 (see Fig. 1185).

Direct Mail Catalog Exclusives

A number of Fenton dealers take advantage of a company sales program begun in the early 1990s through which dealers can order multiple copies of a full–color, reduced–size catalog which shows many items from the regular Fenton line. These catalogs have the store name imprinted on them, and the dealers mail these directly to their retail customers.

Beginning in 1995, these catalogs began to feature limited edition items which were available only through the retailers who used the direct mail catalog program. These items are called "Catalog Exclusives" by the company and retailers alike. The first Catalog Exclusive was a Plum Overlay basket with handpainted decoration (1531 P6). This piece has Bill Fenton's signature.

The Catalog Exclusive for 1996 was a Dusty Rose Overlay basket with floral decoration (3144 QM). This piece has the signature of George Fenton. In 1997, the two Catalog Exclusives were Champagne Satin glass. The handpainted pitcher (2796 XT) pitcher has Lynn Fenton's signature. The other item was the popular butterfly on stand (5171 XU).

The Catalog Exclusives for 1998 were made in French Opalescent Satin and decorated with handpainted fuschias. Bill Fenton's signature is on the vase (2965 WC) and the butterfly (5271 WE), and

Catalog Exclusive for 1996.

The Catalog Exclusives for 1998 were the 2965 WC vase and 5271 WE butterfly (left) and the Catalog Exclusives for 1999 were the 2915 S3 basket and 5065 S3 Cat (right).

these pieces are numbered. The vase was accompanied by a biographical booklet commemorating Bill's 75th year (this same booklet also accompanied the first piece in the Diamond Jubilee Collection sold on QVC in January, 1998).

The Direct Mail Catalog Exclusives for 1999 were Burmese glass. Both the basket (2915 S3) and the Cat (5065 S3) have Bill Fenton's signature and are numbered.

Kim Plauché

Sometimes a person identifies so completely with her occupation that it's difficult to separate who she is from what she does. That's the case with Fenton Art Glass decorating designer Kim Plauché.

Kim sees herself as an artist and a Pisces, and she is particularly interested in scenes which include water. Her decorating design concepts have contributed to the Fenton Collectible Eggs and the Connoisseur Collection as well as many other limited edition items.

Her work on a Favrene Dolphin vase was honored with a Discovery Award from the Society of Glass and Ceramic Decorators. She was responsible for the design of the floral motif which graced Fenton's Violet Satin glass, a 1999 Historic Collection color (see pp. 94–95).

"Most of my art education has been on–the–job experience here at Fenton," she says. "I believe in staying busy with my job, and I like spending time with my family." Kim collects Elvis, Marilyn Monroe and Princess Diana memorabilia.

Kim is also drawn to people. She began working at Fenton Art Glass in 1979 and moved up through many different departments, getting to know the nature of handmade glass and her fellow employees as well.

She enjoys training other decorators when new designs are being added to the Fenton product line. Kim also likes to meet Fenton glass collectors when they come to Williamstown for their conventions, and the banquet evenings are among her favorite memories.

Martha Reynolds

The word "vibrant" is the perfect term to describe both Martha Reynolds and her work. A decorating designer at Fenton Art Glass since 1990, Martha is always experimenting with new materials and styles. Her designs range from the simple and contemporary to the ornate and richly–embellished look of Victorian glass. She is particularly proud of the Trellis decoration (see p. 61), which has been in the Fenton line since 1995, and of the on–going limited edition pieces in the Mary Gregory collection (see Figs. 1121–1132).

Martha has often been honored with design awards since graduating *cum laude* from Shepherd College. In 1993, the Society of Glass and Ceramic Decorators presented her with their prestigious Vandenoever Award for an original design on a Favrene amphora vase.

Many of Martha's designs have appeared in the Fenton Connoisseur Collection. She designed a Cranberry Cameo bowl (see Fig. 954) in 1994, and this piece won a Discovery Award from the Society of Glass and Ceramic Decorators (the award was shared with Richard Delaney). Her Berries on Wild Rose vase (see Fig. 964), which was in the 1996 Connoisseur Collection, also won a Discovery Award, as did the Mulberry Mystical Bird amphora vase (see Fig. 990) from the 1997 Connoisseur Collection.

She has also won Awards of Excellence from *Collector Editions* magazine for her 1997 Butterflies Designer Bell (see Fig. 1157) and her 1999 Designer Bell (see Fig. 1159), as well as the Blue Harmony vase (see Fig. 1410), which was the 1999 Glass Messenger Subscriber Exclusive (this award was shared with Frances Burton).

Martha created the Floral Interlude motif for Fenton's Sea Green Satin glass in 1998 by adapting an original design by Dianna Barbour. The tulip vase (see Fig. 882) from this grouping was chosen as Decorative Collectible of the Year by NALED, the National Association of Limited Edition Dealers.

On weekends, Martha and her husband Gary search for old jewelry and other antiques.

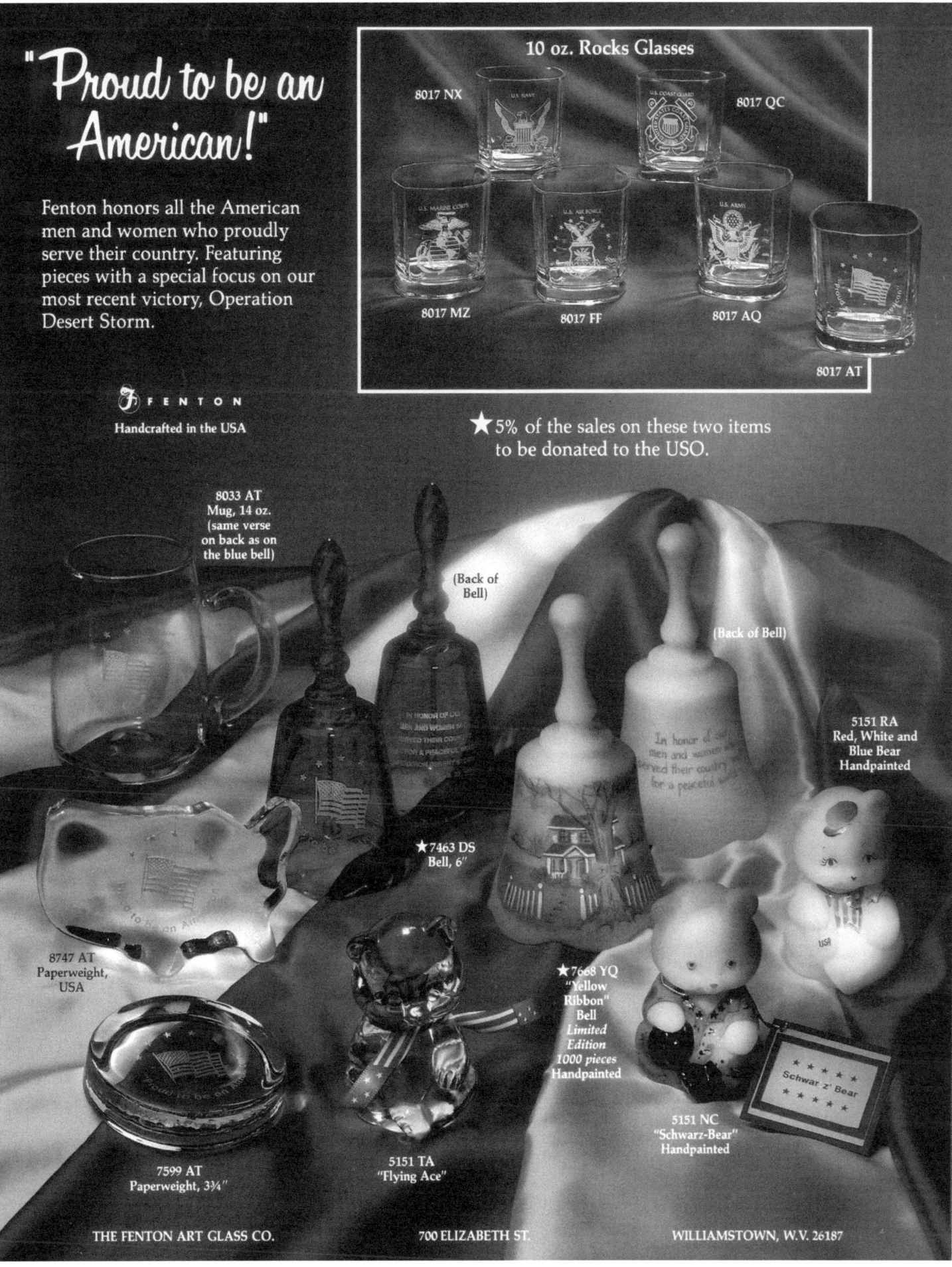

Additional Limited Editions

Some of the Fenton limited editions from the 1990s decade do not fit neatly into the other classifications in this chapter or elsewhere in this book. Many of these were offered in the Valentine's Day or Easter sales materials from Fenton, although they do not relate directly to these occasions.

In late March, 1991, Fenton prepared a single page color sheet with its "Proud to be an American" offering. Some of the items, such as the crystal beverage glasses with sandcarving, were standard Fenton ware sold through PX stores at military sites. The Schwarz–Bear (5151 NC) was a special creation, as was the limited edition Yellow Ribbon bell (7668 YQ). This bell, which was limited to 1000, was a quick sellout (see Fig. 1181).

In 1992, Fenton marked the 500th anniversary of the discovery of America with the Columbus Quincentennial bell (see Figs. 1182–1184). These were available in three iridescent colors–Cobalt Carnival (TZ), Red Carnival (RN), and White Carnival (WI). In separate panels, these bells have a portrait of Christopher Columbus and a sailing ship as well as this wording: "Discovery of America, 1492–1992."

The 1993 Sentiments Collection catalog offered the "Southern Girl" figurine in decorated white opal satin (5141 NI) and Rose Pearl (5141 NX), the latter being an iridescent treatment on the longstanding Fenton Dusty Rose color. Designed by Cathy See, these were limited to sales by February 14, 1993.

The January 1995 general catalog included two limited edition pieces in ivory satin with a decoration called Kristen's Floral that was in the Fenton regular line (see p. 59). The 5228 YB doll figurine came with a musical base. This item and the 2785 YB perfume bottle with heart stopper were each limited to 2500. Both were shown again on the first page of the 1995 Sentiments Collection catalog supplement.

The doll figurine (5228 WB, limited to 2500) was offered in the 1996 Sentiments Collection catalog supplement with a tea rose decoration and beaded border that had been created by Martha Reynolds (see Figs. 1164 and 1172). The same decoration was used for a Beaded Melon vanity set (7199 WB, limited to 1500).

The popular girl figurine was made in decorated Burmese in 1997 (5141 BG, limited 2000). Robin Spindler's floral decoration accented with gold and ice was also used for a Burmese vanity set consisting of a powder box and perfume bottle on a round tray (2905 BG, limit 2000).

The 5270 WA "Natalie" Ballerina figurine (named for Mike Fenton's daughter) in Rosalene was offered in Fenton's Spring, 1998, catalog supplement (see Fig. 1199). These were numbered and limited to sales through March 31, 1998. Three other Rosalene items (7000 WA perfume bottle, 7009 WA puff box, and 7059 WA vase), all decorated with rosebuds developed by Robin Spindler, were also limited to sales through March 31, 1998 (see p. 126).

Two popular collectible colors, Rosalene and Blue Burmese, were featured in Fenton's limited editions for Spring, 1999 (see p. 126). Six Rosalene pieces, all decorated with handpainted violets, were offered, including a heart–shaped music box (4105 NX) and the Praying Children (5203 NX). These were limited to sales through March 31, 1999.

The Blue Burmese color had not been in the Fenton line for about 15 years, so collectors welcomed the Spring, 1999, offering of numbered limited edition items. A guest set (8100 UQ) was limited to 1500, and a basket (6330 UQ) and an 11" vase were limited to 1950. The vase was featured on the front page of the quarterly Glass Messenger for December, 1998, just after the collection was first announced to Fenton dealers.

During the early part of the 1990s decade, Fenton developed a number of innovative limited editions for a wide variety of gift–giving occasions, including Valentine's Day and Mother's Day. During the last half of the decade, Fenton broke new ground with limited editions such as the Designer Bells series, which reflected the talents of Fenton's four decorating designers–Frances Burton, Kim Plauché, Martha Reynolds, and Robin Spindler.

Chapter Thirty-Eight
CARNIVAL GLASS

During the 1990s, Carnival glass was a key component of the Fenton line. Red Carnival glass was produced continuously from 1990 through 1996. More than 80 different Red Carnival glass pieces were made, so collectors may encounter a wide variety of items indeed, including some with handpainted decorations. The years 1997–98 saw Fenton offer Plum Carnival glass, and an assortment of Spruce Carnival glass debuted in 1999 (this color continued into the year 2000). Incidentally, Light Amethyst Carnival glass was offered in 1991 as one of the Historic Collection colors (see pp. 155–156 and Figs. 774–780).

Those familiar with Fenton history will realize the importance of this glass treatment in the factory's earliest days. In late 1907, company founders Frank L. Fenton and his brother John W. Fenton were the first to enter the marketplace with low–priced "iridescent ware." Other manufacturers–such as Dugan, Imperial, and Northwood–soon produced their versions of this product, and the years 1908–1930 found numerous American glass companies making the iridescent glassware that came to be called "Carnival glass" by avid collectors many years thereafter.

In fact, collector enthusiasm for the early Carnival glass stimulated the Imperial Glass Corp. in Bellaire, Ohio, to create their "genuine re–issues" of the old Imperial iridescent ware. These re–issues began in 1962, and, by the mid–1960s, Imperial was making several dozen different items in Carnival glass colors called Rubigold and Peacock, the same terms Imperial had used over a half–century earlier. Those who collected the "old" Carnival glass were leery of these "new" articles at first, but the items were typically marked with an Imperial trademark, and collectors began to acquire these pieces with increasing fervor. Today, an organization called the Collectible Carnival Glass Association unites those who have an interest in this glassware.

Author Rose Presznick approached the Fenton organization in the late 1960s and asked them to produce some Carnival glass for her Carnival glass museum in Lodi, Ohio. Fenton did so, and this project led to much effort and experimentation with techniques for iridizing glass. In 1970, Fenton marketed an assortment of items (as well as the initial plates for two series) in "original formula Carnival glass." Collectors enjoyed these items, all of which were marked with a distinctive Fenton logo.

In the 1980s, Fenton produced Amethyst Carnival and Cobalt Marigold Carnival in its regular line as well as some special Carnival glass colors for the Levay Distributing Co. (see *Fenton Glass: The 1980s Decade* for information on these).

The remainder of this chapter covers Fenton's Carnival glass production during the 1990s decade.

The year 1990 marked the return of the most sought after of Fenton's original iridescent hues–Red Carnival glass. The 1990–91 Fenton catalog pictured a dozen different items and added this explanatory note: "Fenton Red Carnival is made with Ruby glass and iridized with a special metallic salt formula. Occasionally there will be unusual colorations because of the way the ruby strikes and some pieces will have an amberina effect. These variations will be searched out by the collector as being the most rare of the collection" (see *Fenton Glass: The 1980s Decade*, p. 140, for these items).

The same note was carried in the January 1991 catalog supplement, where eleven new Red Carnival glass items were shown (see Figs. 1204–1214). The 1992 Fenton catalog offered ten new pieces in Red Carnival. The Columbus Quincentennial bell was also made in Red Carnival during 1992 (see Fig. 1183).

The Red Carnival grouping for 1993 consisted of twelve items, including the satin finished Alpine Thistle vase (2752 RN), which was among the initial Family Signature Series items sold through April 30, 1993 (see Fig. 1027). This piece was inscribed with signature of Frank M. Fenton, past company President and Chairman of the Board. Another Red Carnival piece (2779 RN; signature of Tom Fenton) was in the Family Signature Series for 1994 (see Fig. 1020). The Red Carnival offering for 1994 was composed of thirteen pieces.

In 1995, Fenton's Red Carnival Apple Tree 6555 RN water set was composed of four tumblers (6576 RN) and a pitcher (6575 RN).

Red Carnival glass (RN) from Fenton's 1993 General Catalog.

From Fenton's 1996 General Catalog.

In conjunction with the 1995 Red Carnival glass grouping (twelve pieces), decoration designer Martha Reynolds created a floral motif called "Buttercups and Berries" which was used on five items (see p. 128).

The Family Signature Series included the 2970 RN covered candy box with the signature of Mike Fenton. The final Red Carnival glass offering of the 1990s decade was in 1996. There were a dozen items, and five were decorated with Frances Burton's Damask Rose motif.

Plum Carnival (see Figs. 1240–1266) was produced during 1997 and 1998, and a new development emerged, namely sets of items which were numbered and matched (each individual item is numbered, and all the articles in a given set have the identical number).

The 1997 Plum Carnival grouping had eleven items, including two handpainted figurines–a Cat (5165 P2) and a Bird (5163 P2). Kim Plauché designed the decoration for these, and she was also responsible for the four–piece Clown sets, which were limited to 970 numbered and matched sets.

The set for 1998 (1250 numbered and matched) consisted of three bears, and the Plum Carnival group had thirteen more items, including four with handpainted decorations.

Spruce Carnival, which debuted in 1999, recalls some of Fenton's earliest products–those which are known as "green Carnival glass" to collectors today. The 1999 offering (see Figs. 1267–1278) of Spruce Green Carnival glass was composed of eleven items plus a numbered and matched set of three cat figurines (5000 US; 1950 numbered and matched). The set and four other items in Spruce Green Carnival were available with handpainted decorations designed by Martha Reynolds.

Spruce Carnival glass continued to be offered in 2000. There were fourteen different items in the assortment, including some pieces made with moulds purchased from the L. G. Wright Glass Co. Seven items were available with a handpainted wild rose decoration created by Martha Reynolds.

In addition to the articles called "Carnival glass" in various catalogs and supplements, Fenton used iridescent treatments on other items made during the 1990s. These include the following: Celeste Blue Stretch, Champagne Satin, Pink Pearl, Rose Pearl, Sea Green Satin, Shell Pink, and Violet Satin. Readers should consult the Index to find specific coverage of these.

1990 Red Carnival (RN)

8625 RN	6½" Puritan comport
5233 RN	4" bear
9384 RN	4" Floral trinket
9059 RN	10½" Grape and Cable bowl
9074 RN	9½" Grape and Cable basket
9752 RN	7¾" Daffodil vase
9295 RN	6" Rose slipper
9240 RN	6¼" Rose basket
8691 RN	4½" alarm clock
9560 RN	6¾" Templebells bell
5241 RN	5" Lion
9666 RN	5" Sandwich pitcher

1991 Red Carnival (RN)

4801 RN	four–piece Diamond Lace epergne set
9262 RN	Rose 6" bell
1995 RN	Daisy and Button 6" slipper
9654 RN	Sunburst 8¼" vase
2557 RN	Beaded Melon 6" vase
8335 RN	Open Edge 7½" basket
5151 RN	3½" sitting Bear
2557 RN	6" Beaded Melon vase
5730 RN	7" Rose basket
9480 RN	Chessie candy box
8256 RN	Mitre and Circle 8½" to 13" vase (average height is 10½")

(see p. 127)

1992 Red Carnival (RN)

5750 RN	Rose 9" vase
9065 RN	Sable Arche 5½" bell
5150 RN	Atlantis 6½" vase
4655 RN	Daffodil 7½" vase
8233 RN	Orange Tree and Cherry 9" basket
8230 RN	Butterfly 8⅜" two–handled bon bon
5171 RN	4½" Butterfly on stand
9185 RN	Paneled Daisy covered candy
6573 RN	Peacock and Dahlia 5½" basket
9120 RN	Fine Cut and Block 5¾" comport

(see p. 127)

1993 Red Carnival (RN)

6703 RN	Paisley 20" lamp with prisms
8489 RN	Lily of the Valley candy with cover
3356 RN	Hobnail 8" tulip vase
2733 RN	Vintage 7½" basket
6564 RN	Elite 8" vase
5142 RN	3½" Raccoon
1940 RN	perfume with stopper
5253 RN	5" Unicorn
2734 RN	Button and Arch 7" basket
9660 RN	Fenton trademark bell
2726 RN	Button and Arch pitcher
2752 RN	Alpine Thistle 9" vase

(Family Signature Series)

1994 Red Carnival (RN)

2792 RN	student lamp with prisms
3161 RN	11" vase
5226 RN	6" Fox
5488 RN	Hearts and Flowers 10½" basket
3762 RN	Hobnail 6 oz. pitcher
9280 RN	5½" candy with cover
9422 RN	Persian Medallion 7" comport
9066 RN	Whitton 6" bell
1167 RN	three–piece fairy light
8253 RN	Vessel of Gems 7" vase
5533 RN	3½" Angel
8429 RN	Water Lily 3" rose bowl
2997 RN	Lion/Leaf 8½" basket

(Family Signature Series)

1995 Red Carnival (RN)

6575 RN	Apple Tree 8¾" pitcher
6576 RN	Apple Tree 4" tumbler
6555 RN	Apple Tree 5 pc water set
2857 RN	Wild Rose 7¼" vase
2927 RN	Wild Rose 6" rose bowl
1936 RN	Daisy and Button 8" basket
2980 RN	4¼" two–piece Pear box
2926 RN	4½" nut dish
2931 RN	5" slipper
9499 RN	Fenton oval logo
2970 RN	8½" candy with cover

(Family Signature Series)

(see p. 128)

"Buttercups and Berries" on Red Carnival (R1)

4605 R1	Basketweave 20" lamp
2924 R1	Holly 8½" basket
6761 R1	Paisley 7" bell
8405 R1	5¾" fairy light
5109 R1	4½" Polar Bear

(see p. 128)

1996 Red Carnival (RN)

5258 RN	6" Owl
7538 RN	Ribbon Tie 8½" basket
9188 RN	Grape and Cable tobacco jar
9529 RN	Verlys 9" bowl
9625 RN	Butterfly 7" bell
5182 RN	6½" hen on nest
1231 RN	Spanish Lace 7½" basket

Damask Rose on Red Carnival (RC)

5351 RC	Melon 8" vase
2936 RC	8" basket
9307 RC	20" student lamp
9590 RC	2½" boot
5220 RC	3" Pig

1997 Plum Carnival (PX)

6705 PX	Paisley 20" lamp
6869 PX	9½" pitcher
8769 PX	Thistle 10" vase
9458 PX	Swan 8" vase
5731 PX	Hummingbird 7½" basket
5305 PX	perfume with stopper
1535 PX	Diamond Panel pitcher
6780 PX	candy with cover

(see p. 129)

Decorated Plum Carnival (P2)

5163 P2	4" Bird
5165 P2	3¾" Cat
5205 P2	four–piece Clown set (970 numbered and matched sets)

(see p. 129)

1998 Plum Carnival (PX)

7676 PX	Viking 5½" candleholders
7653 PX	Daffodil 7½" vase
7677 PX	Viking 13½" bowl
9014 PX	Aztec 6½" jug
2035 PX	Ruffles 6" basket
2970 PX	8½" box with cover
6838 PX	8" three–toed basket
5292 PX	5½" Rooster
7640 PX	5½" square box

(see p. 130)

Decorated Plum Carnival (AX)

8999 AX	18" student lamp with prisms
9252 AX	Rose 6½" vase
9357 AX	4½" vase
6866 AX	Medallion 7" bell
5207 AX	three–piece Bear set (1250 numbered and matched sets)

(see p. 130)

1999 Spruce Carnival (SI)

5930 SI	7" basket
5177 SI	11" Alley Cat
2779 SI	Lion 8½" basket
9188 SI	Grape and Cable tobacco jar
5214 SI	3" Scottie dog
6869 SI	8½" pitcher
5153 SI	3½" hand vase

(see p. 131)

Decorated Spruce Carnival (US)

5000 US	three–piece Cat set (1950 numbered and matched sets)
5659 US	8" basket
9066 US	Whitton 6¼" bell
9037 US	20" student lamp
F9037 US	20" student lamp (with prisms)

(see p. 131)

Chapter Thirty–Nine
SPECIAL PRODUCTS

In the 1980s, Fenton's Special Products department, which had been generally confined to private mould work, came to embrace some new directions such as custom handpainting and sandcarving, college and university–related products, commemorative items, and recognition or incentive awards. Most of these areas continued during the 1990s decade, and, as a result, Fenton produced a wide variety of interesting items, some of which may surprise those readers who associate Fenton with giftware and collectible glass.

This handpainted plate was made for the First Congregational Church in Marietta, Ohio.

Handpainted snowflake ornament, made for a Williamstown High School band fundraising project in 1996.

Sometimes Fenton moulds are used to create glassware which is then handpainted with a special motif requested by the customer (see Figs. 1316–1317, respectively, for bells created for the Wheeling Park Commission and the Longaberger Company). Fenton made special items for both Mary C. Walrath (see Fig. 1330) and for her daughter, the proprietor of Joyce's Collectibles (see Figs. 1315 and 1324–1325).

This handpainted bell was made for the Ohio State Angora Rabbit Club in 1997.

This Fenton clock appeared in the 1993–1994 United States Golf Association mail order catalog.

On other occasions, the customer's own moulds are used in producing glass with colors from the Fenton line (see Fig. 1327 for an Aladdin lamp in

Burmese). The Northwood Art Glass Company, which is operated by David McKinley (great–grandson of Carl Northwood), created a contemporary Grape and Cable design for a vase, and Fenton made the glass using the Northwood firm's new mould (see Fig. 1332), which was made by Island Mould and Machine of Wheeling, WV.

This Christmas ornament was one of many different ornaments made for Memories in Glass of Tulsa, OK, in various colors.

The Fenton Gift Shop often places orders with Fenton's Special Products department. The annual mid–February Gift Shop sales are well–known to seasoned Fenton glass collectors, and a special item (or set of items) has been associated with each February sale. In 1999 and 2000, for example, sets of bears and cats were made in Burmese glass (see p. 132 for these and for some other Fenton Gift Shop Special Order items from the 1990s decade).

The Fenton regular line has been available for quite some time in the Old Country Stores within Crackel Barrel restaurants. In 1998–99, Fenton produced limited edition items (with various Fenton family member's signatures) especially for Cracker Barrel. Robin Spindler created a decoration called Asters and Butterflies for the white satin glass, which was accented with a rose blush. This proved popular, so four more items–again numbered, limited, and with family signatures–were created for 1999. These items are now known as the "Cracker Barrel Old County Store Collector Series" (see Figs. 1290–1297 for all of these pieces).

The year 1999 marked the 30th anniversary of Cracker Barrel's association with Fenton. In recognition of this occasion, the Cracker Barrel organization presented Fenton with a statue of Cracker Barrel's "Uncle Herschel" (see p. 133), and a glass item with a brightly–printed carton was created with an inscription (CRACKER BARREL OLD COUNTRY STORE 30th ANNIVERSARY) on the underside of the base (see Fig. 1289). This Violet Satin covered candy box (9185 OQ) is Fenton's Panelled Daisy pattern, which was inspired by an old United States Glass Company pattern called "Brazil" when it was first made by the Bryce Brothers firm in the 1890s.

For the past several years, Fenton has made articles for the Martha Stewart organization, which publishes the magazine *Martha Stewart Living* and produces a syndicated television show. The Fenton–made items can sometimes be seen in the background on these broadcasts, and they are sold through the "Martha by Mail" catalog. The Martha Stewart organization was particularly interested in opaque green glass similar to the "jadeite" hue which was popular in the Depression era. Fenton has made several items in this color (see p. 134). Some pieces have also been made in opaque white (see Fig. 1307).

During the 1990s, Fenton made a variety of interesting items for Helen and Phil Rosso of Port Vue, PA, and for Singleton Bailey of Loris, SC. Collectors were especially intrigued by Rosso's articles in Topaz Opalescent glass (see p. 135). Some of Bailey's articles were made from old Imperial moulds (see Fig. 1331) while others came from modern moulds which replicated early twentieth century patterns (see Fig. 1326).

This Coinspot pitcher in French Opalescent glass was made for the Metropolitan Museum of Art in 1993.

FENTON
Cracker Barrel Exclusive

Exclusively for Cracker Barrel Stores, Fenton artist Robin Spindler has designed handpainted "Asters and Butterflies" on soft white satin glass with a blush of rose. Limited to 1998 sales, these four pieces will be numbered and inscribed with a Fenton Family member's signature.

HANDPAINTED AND SIGNED BY THE ARTIST

5228 5J Doll, 7"
Inscribed with the signature of Shelley Fenton, Graphics Manager, Key Accounts
$39.50

2777 5J Basket, 8"
Inscribed with the signature of Bill Fenton, Chairman of the Board
$45.00

6864 5J Bell, 6"
Inscribed with the signature of George Fenton, President
$29.50

5165 5J Cat, 3 3/4"
Inscribed with the signature of Don Fenton, Vice-President, Sales, $26.00

Additional items will be considered for 1999.

Experience Fenton . . . Handcrafted Glass Artistry since 1905.

During the 1990s, Fenton made several items in antique–style treatments for the Metropolitan Museum of Art (see Figs. 1328 and 1345). Fenton also made similar items, such as candlesticks and salt dips (see Figs. 1333, 1339 and 1344), for the Sandwich [Massachusetts] Historical Society.

In 1997, David Richardson, owner of The Glass Press and publisher of *Glass Collector's Digest*, brought a vintage 1910 mould to Fenton with the hope that it could be used to make glass once more. The mould, which was discovered in storage at the L. G. Wright Glass Co., was for the Dugan Christmas compote, a much–coveted item among collectors of old Carnival glass.

The Fenton Mould Shop made some repairs to this old mould, and Richardson soon had his Christmas compotes in several colors, including iridescent ruby (both shiny and satin), green opalescent, and topaz opalescent (see Fig. 1335; for the full story, see the October/November, 1997, issue of *Glass Collector's Digest*). During 2000, the Christmas compote was made in cobalt Carnival glass for Richardson.

Fenton's custom sandcarving business, which began about 1983, continued to flourish in the 1990s. Many organizations sought Fenton sandcarved items for various occasions or as special awards. One of the most spectacular was a large vase made for Compaq Computer (see Fig. 1329).

This football with custom sandcarving and silver decoration was made for the high school in Martins Ferry, Ohio, in 1998.

Other custom sandcarved items included bells (see Figs. 1340–1342) and a football–shaped desk accessory which could stand alone or fit snugly into a wooden base (see Fig. 1343).

Many schools, churches, clubs, and other organizations have used Fenton products in their fundraising activities. The Brown County Fair in Georgetown, Ohio, for example, has an ongoing series of limited edition sandcarved bells (500 per year). These Fenton bells feature designs created by the winners of an annual contest. The year 2001 will mark the 150th anniversary of the fair and bring the number of different Fenton bells for this special occasion to an even dozen!

The Parkersburg Lions Club has had Fenton make many different sandcarved bells. Typically, the bell depicts an historic Wood County building, and these are of great interest to those who enjoy local history as well as those who collect Fenton glass. The proceeds from sales of these bells help the Lions with many community projects and their longtime sight conservation ventures.

Editor's note: Fenton always welcomes inquiries from groups interested in custom glass products. Contact: Don Cunningham, Fenton Art Glass Co., 700 Elizabeth St., Williamstown, WV 26187 or use this email address: specialorders@fentonartglass.com

Chapter Forty
FENTON AND QVC

In the 1990s decade, the relationship between the Fenton Art Glass Company and electronic retailer QVC continued to grow (see Chapter 24 of *Fenton Glass: The 1980s Decade*). Fenton glass was featured on QVC at regular intervals throughout each year of the 1990s. As QVC branched out overseas, company President George Fenton appeared with Fenton glass on QVC broadcasts in England and Germany.

The company developed two on-going collections for QVC, the Museum Collection and the Heirloom Collection. The Museum Collection pieces are inspired by items in Fenton Museum displays or archives, and a number of different pieces have been made for QVC. The Heirloom Collection, which is far smaller in size, was created to reflect particular periods in the history of art and design. In addition, two special QVC offerings were created, the Diamond Jubilee Celebration collection (1998) and the New Century Collection (1999).

Typical Museum Collection certificate.

Burmese glass is one of Fenton's most popular and collectible colors, and QVC broadcasts featured Burmese items regularly, including quite a few made with a "diamond optic" effect and decorated with a rose motif (see Figs. 1358–1375). These items are among Bill Fenton's favorite pieces of Fenton glass, and he always enjoys talking about Fenton chemist Charlie Goe and the initial creation of Burmese glass in 1969 for the Fenton line.

When Fenton was first on QVC in 1987–88, some of the items sold were from the regular Fenton line. Both QVC and Fenton soon determined, however, that the Fenton glass treatments (particular combinations of shapes and colors and/or decorations) made for QVC would be exclusive to QVC. Coupled with the typical quantities requested by QVC, this makes Fenton/QVC items collectibles in their own right.

During the 1990s, the company supplied the various Fenton collector clubs with information regarding the items slated for each show. Collectors often communicated and made arrangements to order items for one another when they were not able to see a particular show (or when QVC was not available on their cable provider!). The majority of the Fenton items on QVC in the 1990s were "sold out" within a few minutes. Occasionally, some small quantities of Fenton/QVC items which could not be shipped in time for a scheduled show (and were not reordered by QVC for a subsequent show) were sold through the Fenton Gift Shop.

This biographical booklet accompanied the first piece for the Diamond Jubilee Celebration collection, which was sold on QVC in January 1998.

Although it was sometimes difficult, Fenton was more than equal to the challenge of developing combinations of colors, shapes, and decorative treatments for QVC that would not be duplicated elsewhere in Fenton offerings. Fenton's repertoire of glass colors is necessarily constrained by chemistry and other technical factors, but the company's talented decorating designers were able to create a tremendous variety of decorations.

The first steps in creating items for QVC take place at Fenton. The production review committee consists of the following people: Frances Burton (Decorating), Bill Fenton, George Fenton, Nancy Fenton, Shelley Fenton Ash, Bob Hill (Mould Shop), Greg Meredith (Cold Metal), and Ken Moore (Hot Metal). In reviewing potential items, this group considers possible production or mould problems and pares down the list of items.

Bill Fenton and Shelley Fenton Ash interact closely with consultant Whitney Smith and the staff at QVC to further narrow down the list of possible products for an upcoming show. With the assistance of Nancy Fenton and the company's decorating designers and color chemists, Bill and Shelley sometimes get samples of key items ready for discussions with QVC staff members.

The entire product selection process is quite time-consuming, and a color combination or design idea may be reworked several times before everyone is satisfied and the item is scheduled for a future show. At any given time, Fenton and QVC are planning for shows that are many months away.

Production scheduling is an essential element of the Fenton operation, both for its regular line and for QVC items. Once an article is approved for a future QVC show, glass production and decorating time can begin to be anticipated and scheduled. As Fenton's sales grew overall during the 1990s, production capacity was stretched. A QVC order may be shipped in smaller quantities than planned or the broadcast time could be shortened.

Sometimes problems develop with an item after production is underway, necessitating its placement in a QVC show later on. On a few occasions, the problems just cannot be ironed out, and the item is pulled from production. When this happens early enough, another item may be selected. As the saying goes, "the show must go on," so adjustments are made as needed.

Bill Fenton appeared regularly on QVC starting in October 1988 and throughout the 1990s, and company President George Fenton and Vice-President Don Fenton were on several times also, particularly in 1998 and 1999. George also went to England and Germany for QVC broadcasts on which regular line Fenton items and a few special pieces were sold.

QVC crew members get all the product samples and progressives ready prior to the show.

QVC fans enjoy hearing the stories behind the items on the broadcast, and a great deal of preparation goes into any Fenton appearance on QVC.

Several complete sets of all the glassware scheduled for a show are available in the QVC studio during the broadcasts. Information is gathered about the Fenton employees responsible for particular items, and videotape clips are often used to give viewers an inside look at production techniques. Sets of Fenton glass "progressives," which show the individual steps and stages in making a piece, are often used as visual aids when Bill, Don or George are on the show.

A QVC broadcast is "live" television, and things sometimes go awry when items are shown on screen. On occasion, a fairy light has had its chimney upside down or a three-piece ginger jar comes up with a part missing. A mistake in the price sign for a pair of candlesticks once allowed buyers to purchase them at a real "bargain" price! During one of George Fenton's appearances, the battery on the QVC host's microphone suddenly gave out, and George had to keep on talking for a time until the QVC crew could fix the problem.

Beginning in 1997, Fenton and QVC started an on-going series of items called the Heirloom Collection. Each item was carefully developed by Nancy Fenton and key members of the Decorating Department. The decorating designs were carefully researched for historical authenticity and character, and they embodied elements from specific times in history, such as the Italian Renaissance or the English Tudor period (see Figs. 1376–1383).

Typical Heirloom Collection certificate.

The Heirloom Collection items were made in relatively small quantities, ranging from 250 to 1000. Heirloom Collection articles were individually numbered and accompanied by printed certificates. The Heirloom Collection pieces sold out very quickly on the QVC shows where they appeared, often within just a few minutes after the initial product overview at the beginning of the broadcast.

The New Century Collection, a group of seven distinctive items of Fenton Art Glass was sold on QVC during 1999 (see Figs. 1391–1397). The collection associated Fenton management and various groups of employees with historical qualities of importance to the glass industry: Discovery (Blowers); Quality (Finishers); Innovation (Handlers); Imagination (Decorators); Craftsmanship (Mouldmakers); Tradition (Pressers); and Vision (Fenton family). Shelley Fenton Ash created a special logo for the New Century Collection, and it was used on the bottom of each piece.

New Century Collection logo.

Two items–the pitcher highlighting Decorators (CV275 FJ) and the basket focusing on the Fenton family (CV283 BU)–were "Today's Special Value" items on QVC. The basket was accompanied by a booklet with color photos of Fenton family members. The pitcher (and all the other items in the New Century Collection) was packed with a printed card bearing photos and signatures of key Fenton employees in the various areas.

On two occasions–October 14, 1997, and November 13, 1998 (Bill Fenton's 75th birthday)–there were live QVC telecasts from the Fenton factory. The QVC broadcast crew arrived at Fenton several days prior to each show, and the days before the broadcast were filled with work. Two semi trucks filled with equipment and a brightly painted bus (containing the control suite) with satellite dishes on the roof) could be seen at the Fenton plant.

The "QVC Local" is a mobile television broadcast production studio.

Preparing for the on–site QVC shows was relatively easy. Once QVC and Fenton had determined the broadcast location in the Fenton factory, the QVC crew was responsible for setting up their equipment. Miles of cable had to be pulled into the Fenton plant, and there was plenty of heavy equipment to be unloaded and carried in. The hard working QVC crew set up lights and doublechecked their cameras and sound devices. When the two shows aired, everything went smoothly, and the QVC crew members appreciated all the things that Fenton employees did to make them feel welcome and to assist in their efforts.

Bill Fenton and QVC host Steve Bryant meet their fans in November, 1998.

Naturally, the QVC broadcasts were of interest to people in the immediate area of the Fenton plant, and some local newspapers covered the events, as did WTAP, the Parkersburg–area television station. The Fenton Gift Shop hosted "Meet Bill and Steve" events during the afternoon of each broadcast, and arrangements were made for the members of local Fenton collector clubs and others to see the broadcast site.

In 1997, the broadcast studio was set up in Fenton's Decorating Department. The decorators' normal work schedules were altered so that many would be working during the evening hours of the show. As QVC host Steve Bryant and Bill Fenton chatted and described the glass, Fenton decorators could be seen at work in the background. A roving camera in Hot Metal was used so that viewers could see glass production taking place throughout the evening.

The second broadcast took place on Bill Fenton's 75th birthday: Friday, November 13, 1998. The final item in the seven–piece "Diamond Jubilee Celebration" collection, commemorating Bill's 75th year, was the showpiece of the day. Designated QVC's "Today's Special Value," this vase was featured on a midnight–1 am broadcast segment. Bill and Steve did this broadcast from the center area of the Fenton Museum. Several showcases were moved, and the historic Fenton glassware displayed behind them related to the Fenton items which had been made especially for this show. The Fenton Museum is located directly above the Selecting area at the end of the lehrs, and arrangements were made to halt a noisy conveyer during the broadcast times.

Don Fenton did a two–hour show during the morning of November 13 from QVC's studios near Philadelphia. He remained there during the evening broadcast from the Fenton plant, just in case the satellite feed from the factory experienced technical problems.

Everything went off without a hitch, however, and Bill was in top form as he narrated video clips of glass production and discussed the items on the show. Most of Bill's family was on hand, and they crowded onto the set at the close of the show. QVC presented Bill with a special birthday gift, a silver Cartier tray on which an image of the Fenton plant in 1907 had been engraved.

Bill Fenton relaxes as "air time" approaches.

After the broadcast, everyone enjoyed birthday cake!

Chapter Forty–One
COLLECTING FENTON GLASS

Collectors have always had a great deal of enjoyment while acquiring Fenton glass and sharing stories and information with each other. Many say it works out this way: "It's fun to collect Fenton glass, and it's fun to be around fellow Fenton glass collectors."

The National Early American Glass Club, one of the first such clubs formed in the United States, was begun about 1933. During the 1960s, more glass collectors clubs began to be organized, uniting collectors in such areas as Carnival glass, stretch glass, and custard glass. In the 1970s, other newly formed clubs of glass collectors concentrated on the products of particular American glass companies. Some groups, such as the National Greentown Glass Association, were interested in a company which existed years ago, while other clubs focused on more recent glass-making firms, such as Cambridge, Duncan Miller, Heisey, or Imperial.

The Fenton Art Glass Collectors of America was founded in 1976 (for some history on this group, see *Fenton Glass: The 1980s Decade*, pp. 65–68). During the 1990s, two other organizations began, the National Fenton Glass Society and the Pacific Northwest Fenton Association. Each group has a regular newsletter and holds an annual convention (see the sidebar in this chapter for membership information on these clubs). The Fenton company has made souvenirs and other special glass items for each of these groups, and club members have had the opportunity to meet Fenton family members and employees at their meetings and conventions.

These national organizations were formed by Fenton collectors and are dedicated to learning more about Fenton glass. Each holds a national convention, and some have local chapters across the country. They are completely independent of the Fenton Art Glass Co. The company supplies information and other non–monetary support. The organizations are good sources of information as well as a great way to meet people with similar interests.

Fenton Art Glass Collectors of America, Inc.
P.O. Box 384
Williamstown, W.V. 26187

National Fenton Glass Society
P.O. Box 4008
Marietta, OH 45750

Pacific Northwest Fenton Association
8225 Kilchis River Road
Tillamook, OR 97141

Glass Messenger

In 1995, Fenton decided to launch its own publication for those interested in Fenton products. The Fenton Glass Messenger made its debut in early 1996. The sidebar on page one had this greeting for Fenton collectors: "Welcome to the Premier Issue of Glass Messenger from the Fenton Art Glass Company. This is a quarterly publication designed to be your window to the magical world of Fenton–an inside look at our new designs and products, as well as processes used by Fenton artisans to create handmade art glass. You'll also learn about Fenton employees, family and collectors."

The premier issue had a Family Signature Series piece on the front cover (3065 DP Asters on Dusty Rose Overlay pitcher with Lynn Fenton's signature). The lead story discussed the background of the Family Signature Series, and other stories were devoted to various colors and items then prominent in the Fenton line. A column called "Ask Clarence" invited readers to send in questions about Fenton glass.

From its inception, the Glass Messenger was a well–designed, colorful publication. News of forthcoming Fenton products can be found first in the Glass Messenger, and the articles reveal the stories behind the products and the people who make them. Personal profiles of Fenton family members and key employees can be found in each issue, along with information about various aspects of Fenton history and other tidbits of interest to Fenton glass collectors.

Now in its fifth year of publication, the Glass Messenger is produced by Lynn Fenton Erb and Associate Historian James Measell, who joined the company in August, 1997. Lynn and Jim plan the stories and layout of each issue, and several drafts are circulated among Fenton family members and others on the editorial team.

A local consulting firm handles the final layout, and color printing is done at the Richardson Printing Corp., a Marietta–based company that does much of Fenton's printing, including the various catalogs and supplements during the year.

Each year, subscribers to the Glass Messenger have the opportunity to purchase a special Fenton glass item. A personalized voucher, included with a regular issue of the Glass Messenger, enables current subscribers to order the item by contacting a Fenton retailer. During the past several years, the voucher has been included with the June issue. When new subscribers are processed later in the year, a voucher is automatically sent to them by the Fenton Customer Service staff.

Winter/Spring 1996
Premier Issue

GLASS
Messenger

A Publication for Friends and Collectors of Fenton Art Glass

In This Issue

The Signatures of Fenton

The Historic Collection

Fenton Miniatures

Creating a Meadow Beauty

Fenton Folk Art

Ask Clarence

Subscribing to the Glass Messenger

What's Coming

Special Fenton Events

Welcome to the Premier Issue of Glass Messenger from the Fenton Art Glass Company. This is a quarterly publication designed to be your window to the magical world of Fenton— an inside look at our new designs and products, as well as processes used by Fenton artisans to create handmade art glass. You'll also learn about Fenton employees, family and collectors.

Experience Dusty Rose Overlay, a celebrated Fenton technique. Overlay glass, dating back to the 1860s, is remade in a timeless color by Fenton. The cased glass pitcher is created by layering molten Dusty Rose over Milk Glass before the piece is blown, crimped and handled by skilled craftsmen. Fenton's Martha Reynolds designed the handpainted Asters pattern. As are all Fenton pieces, it is proudly made in America by Fenton artisans.

To subscribe to the Fenton Glass Messenger, call 1–800–249–4527 (304–375–6122 from outside the US) or contact: Fenton Glass Messenger, 700 Elizabeth Street, Williamstown, WV 26187 USA.

The fall 1996 issue of Glass Messenger announced the premier Subscriber Exclusive, "Roselle on Cranberry" (1533 JN). This basket was the first item made from a new mould designed by Jon Saffell. The hexagonal shape and crimping effect were different from other Fenton baskets. Martha Reynolds' decorating design, using a raised paste technique, produced a pronounced three–dimensional effect. These baskets have the signature of company President George Fenton and are individually numbered.

"French Rose on Rosalene" (9475 R6), the Glass Messenger Subscriber Exclusive for 1997.

A decorated vase, "French Rose on Rosalene" (9475 R6), was the Subscriber Exclusive for 1997. Rosalene, a heat–sensitive glass which contains pure gold, is one of Fenton's most popular and collectible colors. The mould used for this piece dates back to the early 1940s, when it was called "Melon" and carried No. 192. Martha Reynolds designed the rose motif, which is based on French aubusson carpets. The vase has the signature of Bill Fenton and is individually numbered.

For its 1998 Subscriber Exclusive, Fenton chose another popular glass color, Burmese. The "Morning Glories on Burmese" tulip vase (7255 UZ) has a realistic decoration by Frances Burton which depicts a

"Morning Glories on Burmese" (7255 UZ), the Glass Messenger Subscriber Exclusive for 1998.

hummingbird in search of nectar. The tulip vase mould dates from 1977. This vase has the signature of Frank M. Fenton and is individually numbered.

"Blue Harmony" was the name of the 1999 Subscriber Exclusive. This $7^{3}/_{4}$" vase (4026 VQ) begins with a bud of cobalt blue glass, and French Opalescent is gathered over the cobalt blue. When the piece is blown to its final shape and crimped, the cobalt blue is on the interior surface and fades into the French Opalescent.

Frances Burton and Martha Reynolds collaborated on the decoration design for the Blue Harmony vase, which has the signature of Don Fenton and is individually numbered. This piece was recognized with an Award of Excellence by *Collector Editions* magazine.

In June, 2000, the Glass Messenger carried a feature article on the next Subscriber Exclusive, the "Dancing Windflowers" basket in Lotus Mist Burmese (6831 ZM). This piece has the signature of Tom Fenton and, like the earlier Glass Messenger Subscriber Exclusives, is individually numbered.

This postcard shows an Exclusive Rep Event piece (handpainted Mulberry vase S1577 MD) as well as other items available in 1997: S6830 DK Dusty Rose Silverton basket (Don Fenton); S5165 PD Meadow Beauty Cat (Lynn Fenton); S6855 LE handkerchief vase (Tom Fenton); S9295 TS Rose slipper (Nancy Fenton); S9458 PX Plum Carnival Swan vase (Frank M. Fenton); and S1683 LS Aurora vase (Bill Fenton).

This postcard shows an Exclusive Rep Event piece (Royal Purple pitcher) as well as other items available in 1998: S5165 EM Cat (Nancy Fenton); S7640 PX Plum Carnival square box (Mike Fenton); S9458 GE Sea Green Satin Swan vase (George Fenton); and S4560 RU Ruby bell (Lynn Fenton).

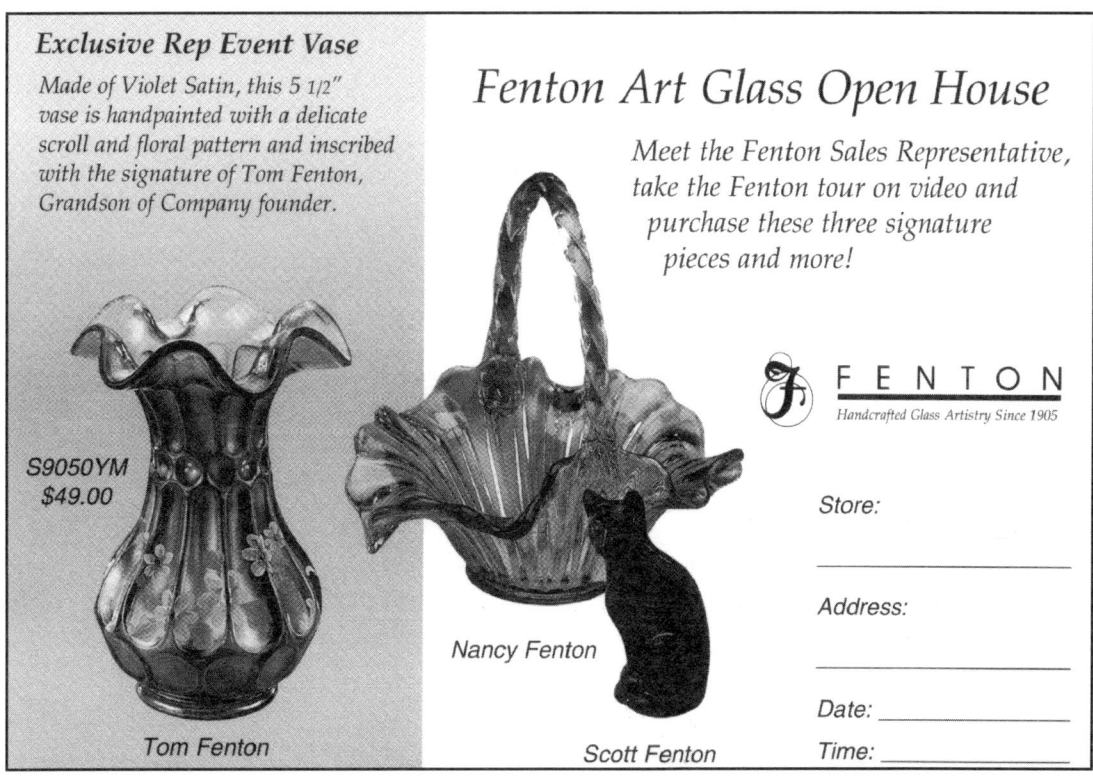

This postcard shows an Exclusive Rep Event piece (handpainted Violet Satin vase) as well as other items available in 1999: S6630 CP Empress Rose basket (Nancy Fenton) and S5065 KN 5" Cat (Scott Fenton).

This postcard shows an Exclusive Rep Event piece (handpainted French Opalescent vase) as well as other items available in 1999: S5151 XP Bear (Shelley Fenton) and S7693 US Melon vase (Frank M. Fenton).

In–Store Events

In addition to the various Fenton clubs and the Glass Messenger publication, many Fenton collectors add to their knowledge of Fenton glass and their collecting enjoyment by attending events hosted by Fenton dealers with the help of Fenton manufacturers representatives. There are two kinds of events, Family Signing Events and Rep Events, and both of these are associated with some special pieces of Fenton glass.

These kinds of events actually began in the late 1970s, when the Sage–Allen department store in New England sponsored a lecture on Fenton glass collecting by Roserita Ziegler, and Bill Fenton and Don Fenton were on hand to meet collectors and to sign Fenton glass.

Family Signing Events

The Family Signing Event, as it is now called, became a formal part of Fenton's sales programs in 1993. Since that time, various Fenton family members have visited many different Fenton dealers across the United States and in Canada, too. The schedules change slightly from year to year, but the Family Signing Events are typically held in the spring (just prior to Mother's Day) and in October–November. In 1999, for example, there were more than 75 Family Signing Events. The March and September issues of the Glass Messenger carry full listings of Family Signing Events, and many collectors have been able to meet a Fenton family member who has come to a Fenton dealer located near them.

In conjunction with the Family Signing Event program, Fenton developed a special piece of glass each year specifically for these events. This item could be purchased at the event itself, and many dealers also worked with their regular customers who wished to order pieces since they could not be present and had the item shipped to them (see Figs. 1402–1409 for all of these pieces).

The Family Signing Event piece for 1993 was a Lamb's Tongue basket (2731 RJ) in Rosalene glass. The supply of this basket was close to running short during the fall of 1993, so a Burmese pitcher with handpainted decoration (7464 7B) was also used during that time.

From 1994 through 1997, the Family Signing Event pieces were baskets. A Plum Opalescent Strawberry basket (2778 IP) was available in 1994, and a Cobalt Opalescent Snowflake basket (2786 KO) was marketed in 1995. The 1996 basket was Champagne Satin with a Sea Mist Green ring (7633 LW), and the 1997 Family Signing Event piece was a Plum Opalescent basket in the Button Arches pattern (4637 IP).

A Royal Purple Swirl vase (3056 UH) was the Family Signing Event piece for 1998. The popular Blue Burmese color was used in 1999, as collectors who came to Family Signing Events were able to purchase a Blue Burmese Daffodil vase (7793 UY).

Rep Events

In addition to the Family Signing Events, Fenton representatives and dealers often develop Rep Events, such as "Open House" occasions at a dealer's store. The Fenton video was often used at these events, and collectors were also able to purchase some items sold exclusively through the dealers hosting the event. These are called "Exclusive Rep Event" pieces.

The 1997 Exclusive Rep Event item was a handpainted Mulberry vase (S1577 MD), inscribed with the signature of George Fenton. For 1998, there were two Exclusive Rep Event pieces: a handpainted Sea Green Satin vase (S6858 3H) with Frank M. Fenton's signature and a Royal Purple pitcher (S1571 UH) with Bill Fenton's signature. There were two Exclusive Rep Event pieces for 1999: a handpainted Violet Satin vase (S9050 YM) with Tom Fenton's signature and a handpainted French Opalescent vase (S1646 FF) with the signature of Scott Fenton.

In addition to the Exclusive Rep Event piece, Fenton dealers were able to obtain some regular Fenton line items which were inscribed with the signature of a Fenton family member. These were pictured in color on postcards which the dealers sent out to their customer lists. These postcards are reproduced in this chapter with complete captions so that readers may determine the pieces which were offered in various years.

Come to Fenton!

If you're traveling north or south on Interstate Highway 77 in West Virginia, try to visit Fenton Art Glass in Williamstown. The company offers free tours of its glassmaking and decorating areas five days per week (8 am to 4:45 pm, M–F). You'll be "up close and personal," as a knowledgeable, enthusiastic guide takes a group of about 10 guests on a 40–minute tour. Schedules are subject to change, so you might want to call ahead: (304) 375–7772.

You can visit Fenton on their website: www.fentonartglass.com

Many Fenton dealers organize bus groups to bring collectors to Fenton. These trips are planned well in advance, and Fenton often organizes some special events for these visitors. A typical schedule allows for time to browse in the Fenton Gift Shop and the Fenton Museum as well as the tour of glassmaking and decorating.

INDEX

A

Aladdin Industrial Inc. 207 *illustrated* 135
American Christmas Tree (see Christmas Tree)
Angel bells *illustrated* 116, 148
Angel Ornaments *illustrated* 148
Angels 146 *illustrated* 148
Angels Aglow 188
Anniversary Bell *illustrated* 77
Anniversary items 153 *illustrated* 152
Aquamarine 27 *illustrated* 69, 73
Arbor Blossom on Petal Pink 22 *illustrated* 39
Asters and Butterflies *illustrated* 133
Asters on Dusty Rose Overlay 22 *illustrated* 61, 112
Autumn Gold 30 *illustrated* 54-55
Autumn Gold Opalescent 30 *illustrated* 54-55, 111
Autumn Leaves on Black 30 *illustrated* 48, 111

B

Baby gifts 153 *illustrated* 76
Baby's First Christmas 146 *illustrated* 148
Bailey (Singleton), glass made for 208
    illustrated 135-136
Bellflowers 23 *illustrated* 25, 73
Bell Medley 153
Bells *illustrated* 77, 121
Birds of Winter 146, 181 *illustrated* 146
Birth of a Savior Series 186 *illustrated* 114
Birthstone Bears 150
Blown Eggs (1991-1996) 179 *illustrated* 113
Blue Burmese 132, 200 *illustrated* 125-126
Blue Royale 23
Blush Rose on Opaline 162 *illustrated* 85-86, 112
Boutonniere Buddies 150 *illustrated* 151
Burmese 162 *illustrated* 97-99, 101, 103-104, 106-107, 123, 125, 132, 135, 138-139 (see also Connoisseur Collection)

C

Calendar Cats 150
Carnival glass 201-206 *illustrated* 127-131, 201-203
Carolyn's Collectibles, glass made for *illustrated* 136
Celeste Blue Stretch 23, 160, 162 *illustrated* 112, 161
Champagne Iridescent 146 *illustrated* 65
Champagne Opaline 146
Champagne Satin 22 *illustrated* 67, 69
Christmas 146, 149-150, 181-188 *illustrated* 71, 183

Christmas at Home Series 181
    illustrated 114, 181-183
Christmas Cactus *illustrated* 77
Christmas Rose *illustrated* 77
Christmas Star Series 184 *illustrated* 114, 185
Christmas Tree 146, 149 *illustrated* 71
Cobalt 23, 27 *illustrated* 73
Collectible Eggs 180 *illustrated* 115, 180
Collector Club pieces *illustrated* 144
Colonial Scroll on Royal Purple (see Royal Purple)
Columbus Quincentennial bells 200 *illustrated* 124
Connoisseur Collection 166-174
    illustrated 91-108, 168-171
Copper Rose 30
Cottage, handpainted 23 *illustrated* 48, 109
Covered animal dishes *illustrated* 120
Covered Hen egg plate *illustrated* 113, 120, 134
Cracker Barrel 208 *illustrated* 133, 209
Crackle glass 27, 30 *illustrated* 43
Cranberry 20 *illustrated* 21, 34-35, 45, 52, 74-75, 119
Cranberry Opalescent 20
    illustrated 20, 36, 57, 118, 125
Cranberry with Pansies (see Pansies on Cranberry)
Cranberry, decorated 20 *illustrated* 21, 45, 112

D

Designer Series Bells 194 *illustrated* 121, 194
Diamond Jubilee Collection (QVC) 211, 214
    illustrated 141
Diamond Optic Burmese (QVC) *illustrated* 138-139
Direct Mail Catalog Exclusives 197 *illustrated* 197
Doll figurines 200 *illustrated* 122
Dusty Rose 19-20, 22 *illustrated* 72

E

Easter 30, 146, 179-180, 192
Easter (1991) 179 *illustrated* 40
Easter (1992) 179 *illustrated* 41, 146
Easter (1993) 179 *illustrated* 49
Easter (1994) 179 *illustrated* 53
Easter (1995) 147, 179-180 *illustrated* 113, 147
Easter (1996) 179-180
Easter (1997) 180 *illustrated* 65, 69
Easter (1998) 180
Egg plate (see Covered Hen egg plate)

Eggs, blown (1991-1996) *illustrated* 113
Eggs, pressed (see Collectible Eggs)
Elizabeth Collection 27 *illustrated* 28
Empress Rose 19-20 *illustrated* 72
Exclusive Rep Event pieces 219 *illustrated* 217-218

F

Fall Lamp Special Limited Editions 195-196
 illustrated 123
Family Signature Series 175-178
 illustrated 109-112, 175-177
Family Signing Event pieces 220 *illustrated* 143
Fenton Art Glass Collectors of America, Inc. 144, 215
Fenton Gift Shop special orders *illustrated* 132
Field Flowers on Champagne Satin 22
 illustrated 67, 110
Floral Interlude (see Sea Green Satin)
Folk Art 192 *illustrated* 120, 193
French Opalescent *illustrated* 69
Fuschia 20, *illustrated* 50, 111

G

Gilded Star Flowers 150
Glass Messenger 215-216
Glass Messenger Subscriber Exclusives 217
 illustrated 143, 217
Gold Amberina 27, 164-165 *illustrated* 96
Gold Pearl 156 *illustrated* 81, 157
Golden Flax on Cobalt 23 *illustrated* 58
Golden Partridge 184 *illustrated* 115
Golden Pine Cones 150
Golden Winged Angels 186 *illustrated* 115, 186
Guardian Angel 150 *illustrated* 150

H

Happy Santas 146
Heart Optic 189-190 *illustrated* 118, 189
Heavenly Angels 149, 184 *illustrated* 149
Heirloom Collection (QVC) 211-213 *illustrated* 140
Historic Collection colors 154-165
Hobnail 146 *illustrated* 55, 57, 81
Hobnail, Milk Glass 27 *illustrated* 44, 56
Holiday Green 146
Holly Berries 184 *illustrated* 115
Holophane *illustrated* 136
Hydrangeas on Topaz Opalescent 163
 illustrated 110, 163

I

Ice Blue with Bellflowers (see Bellflowers)
Iced Pinecones 188 *illustrated* 115
Iridized Jade Opaline 146 *illustrated* 40
Iridized Opal, handpainted 146 *illustrated* 49
Irises on Misty Blue Satin 23 *illustrated* 66, 110, 112

J

Jade Opaline *illustrated* 38
Jade Pearl *illustrated* 41
Jewelry 195 *illustrated* 195
Jolly Snowman 188 *illustrated* 115
Joyce's Collectibles, glass made for 207
 illustrated 135

K

Kristen's Floral 30, 200 *illustrated* 59

L

Lenten Rose 186 *illustrated* 115
LifeStyles 30 *illustrated* 70
Light Amethyst Carnival 155-156 *illustrated* 80
Lilacs, handpainted 27 *illustrated* 46, 109, 111
Lotus Mist Burmese 165

M

Madonnas 146 *illustrated* 71, 148
Magnolia and Berry on Spruce 146
 illustrated 71, 111
Martha Stewart, glass made for 208 *illustrated* 134
Martha's Rose 30 *illustrated* 31, 73, 111
Mary Gregory 190 *illustrated* 119
Meadow Beauty 22 *illustrated* 61, 109
Meadow Blossom 22 *illustrated* 42
Medallion Collection 30, 153 *illustrated* 64
Memories in Glass 208 *illustrated* 208
Men's gifts 153 *illustrated* 76
Metropolitan Museum of Art 208 *illustrated* 136, 208
Milk Glass 27 *illustrated* 44, 56
Millennium Collection 196 *illustrated* 124
Mini-baskets 146 *illustrated* 146
Miniatures 195 *illustrated* 122
Misty Blue Iridescent 146 *illustrated* 65
Misty Blue Satin 23 *illustrated* 66
Moonlit Meadow 184
Morning Glories on Sea Mist Green 22
 illustrated 67

Fig.	Value	Fig.	Value	Fig.	Value	Fig.	Value	Fig.	Value	Fig.	Value	Fig.	Value
1039	$90	1096	$55	1153	$75R	1210	$30	1267	$75	1324	$125	1381	$225VR
1040	$80	1097	$75	1154	$70R	1211	$50	1268	$50	1325	$195	1382	$195VR
1041	$90	1098	$80	1155	$75R	1212	$50	1269	$50	1326	$225	1383	$185VR
1042	$90	1099	$80	1156	$70R	1213	$55	1270	$90	1327	$250	1384	$135
1043	$90	1100	$85	1157	$75R	1214	$75	1271	$295	1328	$175	1385	$125
1044	$90	1101	$85	1158	$85R	1215	$60	1272	$90	1329	$325	1386	$145
1045	$95	1102	$165R	1159	$75R	1216	$60	1273	$25	1330	$85	1387	$195
1046	$100	1103	$175R	1160	$65R	1217	$90	1274	$95	1331	$125	1388	$165
1047	$90	1104	$195	1161	$75R	1218	$50	1275	$35	1332	$95	1389	$165
1048	$90	1105	$175	1162	$65R	1219	$110	1276	$45	1333	$50	1390	$95
1049	$65R	1106	$50	1163	$75R	1220	$50	1277	$65	1334	$65	1391	$175
1050	$165R	1107	$150	1164	$85R	1221	$65	1278	$85	1335	$275	1392	$225
1051	$55R	1108	$175	1165	$125	1222	$95	1279	$75	1336	$55	1393	$150
1052	$80R	1109	$165	1166	$95	1223	$60	1280	$65	1337	$60	1394	$175
1053	$60R	1110	NP	1167	$45	1224	$55	1281	$175	1338	NP	1395	$165
1054	$85R	1111	$95	1168	$45	1225	$35	1282	$150	1339	$45	1396	$195
1055	$85R	1112	$95	1169	$50	1226	$225	1283	$135R	1340	$50	1397	$225
1056	$85R	1113	$75	1170	$50	1227	$150	1284	$135R	1341	$45	1398	$125
1057	$95R	1114	$85	1171	$50	1228	$90	1285	$85	1342	$45	1399	$175
1058	$95R	1115	$125	1172	$175	1229	$90	1286	$85	1343	NP	1400	$195R
1059	$55R	1116	$85	1173	$65	1230	$70	1287	$125	1344	$50	1401	$165
1060	$85R	1117	$135	1174	$325	1231	$55	1288	$85	1345	$85	1402	$75
1061	$65R	1118	$50	1175	$375	1232	$39	1289	$120	1346	$98	1403	$65
1062	$60	1119	$85	1176	$350	1233	$95	1290	$75	1347	$85	1404	$75
1063	$45	1120	$85	1177	$365	1234	$79	1291	$95	1348	$195	1405	$85
1064	$52	1121	$250R	1178	$120	1235	$60	1292	$95	1349	$75	1406	$85
1065	$42	1122	$195R	1179	$50	1236	$80	1293	$110	1350	$75	1407	$95
1066	$50	1123	$285R	1180	$165	1237	$130	1294	$40	1351	$65	1408	$120
1067	$50	1124	$195R	1181	$95R	1238	$50	1295	$50	1352	$95	1409	$95
1068	$60R	1125	$150R	1182	$50	1239	$100	1296	$45	1353	$95	1410	$95
1069	$45R	1126	$195R	1183	$60	1240	$250R	1297	$35	1354	$125	1411	$150
1070	$65VR	1127	$45	1184	$50	1241	NP	1298	$24	1355	$95	1412	$35
1071	$45R	1128	$195R	1185	$275VR	1242	$115	1299	$24	1356	$40	1413	$225
1072	$50R	1129	$95R	1186	$195VR	1243	$40	1300	$20	1357	$85	1414	$175
1073	$52R	1130	$135R	1187	$175VR	1244	$115	1301	$20	1358	$85	1415	$150
1074	$40R	1131	$75	1188	$325VR	1245	$338	1302	$18	1359	$150	1416	$50
1075	$40R	1132	$95R	1189	$225VR	1246	$60	1303	$24	1360	$225	1417	$125
1076	$45R	1133	$95	1190	$195VR	1247	$115	1304	$45	1361	$225	1418	$80
1077	$45R	1134	$95	1191	$225VR	1248	$68	1305	$45	1362	$175	1419	$150
1078	$50R	1135	$95	1192	$55	1249	$55	1306	$75R	1363	$165	1420	$85
1079	$50R	1136	$100	1193	$98R	1250	$60	1307	$50	1364	$85	1421	$125
1080	$50R	1137	$100	1194	$195R	1251	$0	1308	$125	1365	$85	1422	$95
1081	$50R	1138	$85	1195	$250R	1252	$65	1309	$65	1366	$110	1423	$85
1082	$50R	1139	$100	1196	$70PR	1253	$350	1310	$95	1367	$125	1424	$75
1083	$62R	1140	$100	1197	$95	1254	$90PR	1311	$75	1368	$165	1425	$175
1084	$50R	1141	$65	1198	$90	1255	$45	1312	$95	1369	$150	1426	$50
1085	$55R	1142	$55	1199	$115	1256	$75	1313	$90	1370	$75	1427	$50
1086	$54R	1143	$55	1200	$55	1257	$100	1314	$85	1371	$120	1428	$50
1087	$50R	1144	$60	1201	$90	1258	$43	1315	$65	1372	$135	1429	$50
1088	$60R	1145	$60	1202	$105	1259	$112	1316	$50	1373	$125		
1089	$60R	1146	$150	1203	$85	1260	$90	1317	$55	1374	$135		
1090	$120VR	1147	$60	1204	$45	1261	$75	1318	$35	1375	$165		
1091	$85VR	1148	$75R	1205	$30	1262	$52	1319	$35	1376	$195VR		
1092	$95	1149	$80R	1206	$36	1263	$135R	1320	$35	1377	$175VR		
1093	$90R	1150	$75R	1207	$90	1264	$40	1321	$35	1378	$200VR		
1094	$55	1151	$75R	1208	$295	1265	$50	1322	$35	1379	$175VR		
1095	$55	1152	$65R	1209	$60	1266	$50	1323	$35	1380	$295VR		

Fig.	Value	Fig.	Value	Fig.	Value	Fig.	Value	Fig.	Value	Fig.	Value	Fig.	Value
641	$34	697	$35	754	$25	811	$40	868	$115R	925	$115R	982	$165R
642	$34	698	$78	755	$195	812	$42	869	$150R	926	$175R	983	$195R
643	$14	699	$20	756	$20	813	$85	870	$150R	927	$95R	984	$185R
(644	$23)	700	$40	757	$24	814	$90	871	$350R	928	$75R	985	$575R
645	$23	701	$60	758	$25	815	$95	872	$65	929	$85R	986	$185R
646	$22	702	$195	759	$32	816	$65	873	$295R	(930	$185VR)	987	$225R
647	$20	703	$120	760	$28	817	$65	874	$20	931	$145VR	988	$210R
648	$20	704	$195	761	$195	818	$45	875	$55	932	$185VR	989	$750VR
649	$32	705	$24	762	$36	819	$38	876	$55	933	$80R	990	$375R
650	$19	706	$24	763	$32PR	820	$28	877	$42	934	$375VR	991	$195R
651	$22	707	$28	764	$32	821	$45PR	878	$28	935	$75R	992	$175R
652	$10	708	$28	765	$325R	822	$185VR	879	$10	936	$95R	993	$750VR
653	$20	709	$24	766	$50	823	$200VR	880	$32 -	937	$45R	994	$125
654	$14	710	$24	767	$36	824	$195VR	881	$24	938	$210VR	995	$85
655	$20	711	$24	768	$39	825	$250VR	882	$125R	939	$125R	996	$95
656	$12	712	$24	769	$120	826	$595VR	883	$75	940	$150VR	997	$150
657	$4	713	$24	770	$32	827	$50	884	$100	941	$85R	998	$85
658	$65	714	$24	771	$36	828	$45	885	$95	942	$150VR	999	$135
659	$45	715	$25	772	$32	829	$135	886	$40	943	$65R	1000	$150
660	$75	716	$25	773	$48	830	$60	887	$32	944	$175R	1001	$120
661	$36	717	$20	774	$60	831	$42	888	$32	945	$120R	1002	$165
662	$48	718	$20	775	$325R	832	$36	889	$45	946	$150VR	1003	$125
663	$70	719	$20	776	$65	833	$32	890	$50	947	$120R	1004	$95
664	$45	720	$24	777	$50	834	$75	891	$125R	948	$95R	1005	$100
665	$32	721	$22	778	$40	835	$45	892	$135R	949	$195VR	1006	$110
666	$52	722	$22	779	$28	836	$85	893	$135R	950	$295VR	1007	$100
667	$57	723	$20	780	$40	837	$125	894	$195R	951	$375VR	1008	$175
668	$35	724	$16	781	$24	838	$100	895	$175R	952	$175VR	1009	$110
669	$48	725	$20	782	$32PR	839	$95	896	$375R	953	$285VR	1010	$85
670	$42	726	$24	783	$65	840	$450R	897	$165R	954	$150VR	1011	$125
670A	$28	727	$32	784	$36PR	841	$60	898	$32	955	$175VR	1012	$165
671	$88	728	$24	785	$36	842	$85	899	$50	956	$150VR	1013	$135
672	$52	729	$18	786	$38	843	$595VR	900	$22	957	$120VR	1014	$100
673	$78	730	$18	787	$28	844	$120R	901	$350R	958	$295VR	1015	$85
674	$28	731	$30	788	$295R	845	$120R	902	$18	959	$325VR	1016	$125
675	$52	732	$28	789	$195	846	$110R	903	$50	960	$235VR	1017	$100
676	$85	733	$29	790	$195	847	$120R	904	$35	961	$775VR	1018	$95
677	$102	734	$42	791	$225	848	$295R	905	$150	962	$150VR	1019	$105
678	$118	735	$30	792	$32	849	$325R	906	$325R	963	$300R	1020	$125
679	$95	736	$35	793	$24	850	$95	907	$62	964	$240R	1021	$110
680	$55	737	$20	794	$32	851	$175R	908	$50	965	$210R	1022	$95
681	$110	738	$20	795	$36	852	$95	909	$32	966	$235R	1023	$105
682	$65	739	$20	796	$36	853	$24	910	$40	967	$950VR	1024	$115
683	$85	740	$20	797	$38	854	$65	911	$80	968	$195R	1025	$135
684	$50	741	$20	798	$24	855	$40	912	$70	969	$175R	1026	$75
685	$105	742	$36	799	$48	856	$100R	913	$29	970	$225R	1027	$150
686	$65	743	$50	800	$275R	857	$45	914	$350VR	971	$195R	1028	$125
687	$45	744	$75	801	$75	858	$45	915	$160R	972	$825VR	1029	$125
688	$52	745	$36	802	$65	859	$395	916	$150R	973	$165R	1030	$85
689	$92	746	$50	803	$165	860	$55	917	$95R	974	$120R	1031	$105
690	$75	747	$240R	804	$36	861	$65	918	$150R	975	$205R	1032	$110
691	$60	748	$36	805	$36	862	$36	919	$150R	976	$335R	1033	$115
692	$70	749	$38	806	$36	863	$55	920	$95R	977	$275VR	1034	$85
693	$27	750	$42	807	$40	864	$45	921	$450R	978	$700R	1035	$135R
694	$32	751	$36	808	$32	865	$150R	922	$425R	979	$275R	1036	$75
695	$27	752	$28	809	$42	866	$535VR	923	$400R	980	$205R	1037	$85
696	$42	753	$24	810	$45	867	$175R	924	$225R	981	$165R	1038	$85

Fig.	Value	Fig.	Value	Fig.	Value	Fig.	Value	Fig.	Value	Fig.	Value	Fig.	Value
245	-$28	302	-$115	359	-$30	415	-$395	472	-$45	527	-$22	584	-$25
246	-$24	303	-$75	360	-$60	416	-$28	473	-$45	528	-$22	585	-$28
247	-$48	304	-$14	360A	-$50	417	-$60	474	-$65	529	-$28	586	-$25
248	-$28	305	-$65	361	-$54	418	-$50	475	-$40	530	-$28	587	-$18
249	-$65	306	-$275	362	-$15	419	-$36	476	-$55	531	-$22	588	-$24
250	-$40	307	-$20	363	-$15	420	-$36	477	-$32	532	-$23	589	-$14
251	-$32	308	-$32	364	-$36	421	-$120	478	-$36	533	-$45	590	-$28
252	-$45	309	-$9	365	-$15	422	-$28	479	-$45	534	-$45	591	-$56
253	-$14	310	-$35	366	-$50	423	-$45	480	-$28	535	-$50	592	-$56
254	-$32	311	-$25	367	-$60	424	-$75	481	-$54	536	-$28	593	-$28
255	-$45	312	-$18	368	-$12	425	-$60	482	-$28	537	-$22	594	-$50
256	-$95	313	-$25	369	-$28	426	-$24	483	-$65	538	-$26	595	-$50
257	-$79	314	-$24	370	-$12	427	-$95	484	-$28	539	-$22	596	-$28
258	-$65	315	-$32	371	-$12	428	-$20	484	-$28	540	-$28	597	-$10
259	-$95	316	-$20	372	-$50	429	-$65	485	-$85	541	-$105	598	-$10
260	-$65	317	-$35	373	-$95	430	-$120	486	-$50	542	-$95	599	-$10
261	-$48	318	-$22	374	-$75	431	-$52	487	-$36	543	-$265	600	-$10
262	-$32	319	-$23	375	-$275	432	-$85	488	-$48	544	-$64	601	-$28
263	-$39	320	-$32	376	-$60	433	-$395	489	-$18	545	-$75	602	-$28
264	-$36	321	-$28	377	-$18	434	-$35	490	-$28	546	-$28	603	-$12
265	-$20	322	-$12	378	-$36	435	-$36	491	-$25	547	-$22	604	-$12
266	-$40	323	-$20	379	-$14	436	-$29	492	-$42	548	-$75	605	-$20
267	-$70PR	324	-$22	380	-$25	437	-$29	493	-$60	549	-$40	606	-$12
268	-$115	325	-$20	381	-$20	438	-$36	494	-$16	550	-$28	607	-$12
269	-NP	326	-$36	382	-$45	439	-$70	495	-$15	551	-$46	608	-$65
270	-$38	327	-$42	383	-$45	440	-$29	496	-$15	552	-$65	609	-$85
271	-$55	328	-$42	384	-$45	441	-$45	497	-$16	553	-$215	610	-$90
272	-$55	329	-$30	385	-$20	442	-$55	498A	-$7	554	-$45	611	-$95
273	-$350	330	-$18	386	-$75	443	-$28	498B	-$295	555	-$32	612	-$65
274	-$60	331	-$275	387	-$35	444	-$55	499	-$95	556	-$75	613	-$75
275	-$36	332	-$28	388	-$18	445	-$275	500	-$90	557	-$28	614	-$65
276	-$60	333	-$18	389	-$36	446	-$18	501	-$18	558	-$40	615	-$150
277	-$30	334	-$35	390	-$24	447	-$24	502	-$28	559	-$28	616	-$27
278	-$28	335	-$32	391	-$34	448	-$85	503	-$55	560	-$43	617	-$32
279	-$28	336	-$28	392	-$22	449	-$36	504	-$45	561	-$32	618	-$16
280	-$48	337	-$30	393	-$34	450	-$45	505	-$50	562	-$63	619	-$18
281	-$28	338	-$28	394	-$36	451	-$27	506	-$28	563	-$53	620	-$26
282	-$46	339	-$85	395	-$195	452	-$34	507	-$65	564	-$250	621	-$24PR
283	-$10	340	-$42	396	-$225	453	-$34	508	-$42	565	-$54	622	-$30
284	-$10	341	-$90	397	-$195	454	-$95	509	-$75	566	-$32	623	-$69
285	-$10	342	-$120	398	-$24	455	-$65	510	-$55	567	-$70	624	-$60PR
286	-$28	343	-$115	399	-$48	456	-$65	511	-$55	568	-$32	625	-$24
287	-$45	344	-$34	400	-$15	457	-$27	512	-$45	569	-$26	626	-$24
288	-$28	345	-$35	401	-$26	458	-$45	513	-$55	570	-$11	627	-$24
289	-$48	346	-$65	402	-$9	459	-$85	514	-$45	571	-$22	628	-$15
290	-$28	347	-$75	403	-$40	460	-$65	515	-$45	572	-$7	629	-$12
291	-$10	348	-$56	404	-$18	461	-$45	516	-$36	573	-$28	630	-$20
292	-$10	349	-$60	405	-$24SET	462	-$65PR	517	-$54	574	-$27	631	-$35
293	-$10	350	-$45	406	-$18	463	-$34	518	-$50	575	-$22	632	-$95
294	-$295	351	-$56	407	-$20	464	-$34	519	-$36	576	-$18	633	-$32
295	-$105	352	-$45	408	-$24PR	465	-$35	520	-$36	577	-$92	634	-$25
296	-$85	353	-$32	409	-$20	466	-$20	521	-$39	578	-$85	635	-$24
297	-$59	354	-$30	410	-$20	467	-$45	522	-$52	579	-$265	636	-$15
298	-$48	355	-$30	411	-$24	468	-$65	523	-$42	580	-$95	637	-$15
299	-$45	356	-$30	412	-$85	469	-$92	524	-$42	581	-$28	638	-$15
300	-$75	357	-$30	413	-$435	470	-$24	525	-$52	582	-$40	639	-$45PR
301	-$80	358	-$30	414	-$425	471	-$48	526	-$22	583	-$65	640	-$95

FENTON GLASS: THE 1990's DECADE
Edited by James Measell
2000-2001 Price Guide
(Compiled by Robert E. Eaton)

Over 1,000 color figures are listed in this guide with estimates of retail value on today's market. Also listed is a rarity rating or Rare(**R**), Very Rare(**VR**), and Not Priced(**NP**). The indication PR denotes that the price listed is for a pair of items.

A price paid at an auction or seen tagged on an item at a shop or antique show is not necessarily what it is worth. An auction price is one often paid after heated competition between two determined collectors. A dealer's tag is based upon his or her personal knowledge of the collector market and a necessary business markup from his own original purchase price.

Prices listed in this guide are based upon three major factors—color, condition, and collectibility:

COLOR—many pieces shown in this book were made in several colors. The price listed is for the exact item illustrated. Another color might be worth more or less. Also, a rating or "VR" doesn't necessarily mean that the same piece is very rare in a different color.

CONDITION—prices are listed for items in undamaged condition with good color and/or indescence.

COLLECTIBILITY—a piece is collectible if people want it badly enough to compete! Much Fenton glass is very collectible.

Neither the author nor the publisher will be responsible for losses incurred as a result of quoting prices in this book.

Fig.	Value	Fig.	Value	Fig.	Value	Fig.	Value	Fig.	Value	Fig.	Value	Fig.	Value
1	-$15	36	-$70	71	-$48	106	-$24	140	-$25	175	-$20	210	-$135
2	-$21	37	-$70	72	-$35	107	-$19	141	-$22	176	-$65	211	-$85
3	-$29	38	-$100	73	-$45	108	-$25	142	-$25	177	-$20	212	-$55
4	-$20	39	-$50	74	-$40	109	-$32	143	-$9	178	-$42PR	213	-$42
5	-$20	40	-$45	75	-$55	110	-$22	144	-$9	179	-$42	214	-$42
6	-$20	41	-$55	76	-$35	111	-$17	145	-$26	180	-$35	215	-$60
7	-$20	42	-$45	77	-$89	112	-$17	146	-$9	181	-$48	216	-$120
8	-$26	43	-$32	78	-$375	113	-$15	147	-$26	182	-$45	217	-$65
9	-$35	44	-$85	79	-$295	114	-$17	148	-$58	183	-$42	218	-$65
10	-$20	45	-$45	80	-$75	115	-$11	149	-NP	184	-$32	219	-$70
11	-$20	46	-$265	81	-$65	116	-$24	150	-$42	185	-$95	220	-$36
12	-$18	47	-$52	82	-$75	117	-$21	151	-$9	186	-$85	221	-$65
13	-$39	48	-$110	83	-$32	118	-$45	152	-$9	187	-$105	222	-$85
14	-$25	49	-$45	84	-$50	119	-$9	153	-$25	188	-$80	223	-$45
15	-$39	50	-$55	85	-$48	120	-$9	154	-$42	189	-$48	224	-$36
16	-$25	51	-$39	86	-$450	121	-$9	155	-$9	190	-$48	225	-$25
17	-$35	52	-$35	87	-$265	122	-$15	156	-$24	191	-$46	226	-$36
18	-$19	53	-$115	88	-$75	123	-$14	157	-$20	192	-$30	227	-$25
19	-$68	54	-$125	89	-$42	124	-$8	158	-$45	193	-$35	228	-$20
20	-$25	55	-$50	90	-$36	125	-$8	159	-$32	194	-$45	229	-$45
21	-$30	56	-$52	91	-$37	126	-$8	160	-$35	195	-$42	230	-$60
22	-$265	57	-$46	92	-$36	127	-$42	161	-$25	196	-$195	231	-$25
23	-$295	58	-$42	93	-$42	128	-$18	162	-$32	197	-$28	232	-$39
24	-$65	59	-$450	94	-$34	129	-$23	163	-$25	198	-$36	233	-$275
25	-$42	60	-$70	95	-$32	130	-$45	164	-$19	199	-$48	234	-$20
26	-$285	61	-$75	96	-$25	131	-$24	165	-$25	200	-$60	235	-$24
27	-$450	62	-$60	97	-$23	132	-$45	166	-$85	201	-$36	236	-$32
28	-$45	63	-$45	98	-$55	133	-$26	167	-$26	202	-$18	237	$16
29	-$52	64	-$65	99	-$56	134	-$26	168	-$36	203	-$32	238	-$20
30	-$48	65	-$45	100	-$60	135A	-$26	169	-$56	204	-$20	239	-$14
31	-$35	66	-$58	101	-$32	135B	-$26	170	-$35	205	-$9	240	-$45
32	-$45	67	-$60	102	-$52	136	-$45	171	-$60	206	-$18	241	-$24
33	-$30	68	-$85	103	-$24	137	-$45	172	-$20	207	-$16	242	-$42
34	-$40	69	-$45	104	-$65	138	-$43	173	-$24	208	-$210	243	-$14
35	-$40	70	-$40	105	-$45PR	139	-$25	174	-$26	209	-$85	244	-$30

Fig.	Value	Fig.	Value	Fig.	Value	Fig.	Value
451	$ 75	479	$ 75	507	$ 50	535	$ 120
452	40	480	350 (VR)	508	75	536	450 (VR)
453	65	481	45	509	60 pr.	537	28
454	80	482	65	510	50 (R)	538	65
455	45	483	65 (S)	511	85 (S)	539	150
456	45	484	24	512	125	540	75
457	75	485	45	513	55	541	55
458	50	486	195 (S)	514	35	542	75
459	55 (R)	487	95 (VR)	515	250	543	350 (R)
460	40	488	95	516	450 (R)	544	45
461	195	489	80	517	45	545	45
462	45	490	50	518	275 (S)	546	150
463	55	491	22	519	450 (VR)	547	45
464	35	492	125 (R)	520	550 (VR)	548	125
465	100	493	42	521	95 (R)	549	50
466	25	494	23	522	650 (VR)	550	650
467	45 pr.	495	75	523	300 (VR)	551	85
468	30	496	40 set	524	200 (R)	552	195 (R)
469	25	497	30	525	150 (VR)	553	45 ea.
470	95	498	30	526	300 (R)	554	60
471	250 (R)	499	25	527	550 (VR)	555	45
472	150 (VR)	500	25	528	925	556	40
473	175	501	25	529	50	557	35
474	450 (VR)	502	25	530	325	558	85 (S)
475	425 (VR)	503	30	531	325 (S)		
476	60	504	85	532	85		
477	65	505	260 (R)	533	290		
478	175	506	80	534	110		

Additions and Corrections to *Fenton Glass: The Second Twenty-Five Years*

p. 8. The sketch at lower left depicts Fenton's Dancing Ladies covered bon bon or candy jar.

p. 25, figs 1 and 3. The numbers in parentheses are "ware numbers" instituted in July, 1952. Before that, Fenton used either mould numbers or pattern numbers.

p. 25, figs. 2, 4 and 5. This color was originally called Satin Rose, and the name was later changed to Rose Satin (today's collectors call the color "cranberry opalescent satin").

p. 26. Although most of Northwood's Chinese Coral is red–orange, some pieces are indeed similar to Fenton's "Flame." See the illustrations in Heacock, Measell and Wiggins' *Harry Northwood: The Wheeling Years, 1901–1925*, especially pp. 141–142.

p. 59, figs 476-477. Beaded Melon was No. 711.

p. 59, fig. 485. Not Fenton, this atomizer was probably made by Duncan Miller for the T. J. Holmes Co.

p. 61, fig. 510. This is the No. 4303 Lamb's Tongue mayonnaise.

p. 63, fig. 536. This vase was called Sung Ko.

Fig.	Value	Fig.	Value	Fig.	Value	Fig.	Value
275 –	$ 225	319 –	$ 75 (S)	363 –	$ 150	407 –	$ 175
276 –	450	320 –	45	364 –	30	408 –	165
277 –	250	321 –	55	365 –	135	409 –	32
278 –	28 each	322 –	120	366 –	150	410 –	275
279 –	48	323 –	25	367 –	105	411 –	165
280 –	75 (S)	324 –	50	368 –	75	412 –	325
281 –	45	325 –	55	369 –	85	413 –	150
282 –	35	326 –	70 (S)	370 –	75	414 –	275
283 –	35 each	327 –	75 pr.	371 –	80	415 –	120
284 –	85	328 –	225	372 –	79	416 –	175
285 –	65	329 –	200 pr.	373 –	24	417 –	225
286 –	36	330 –	28	374 –	60	418 –	195
287 –	32	331 –	28	375 –	50	419 –	165
288 –	75	332 –	62	376 –	35	420 –	65
289 –	75	333 –	98 set	377 –	52	421 –	60
290 –	250 (VR)	334 –	45	378 –	185 (R)	422 –	60
291 –	32	335 –	85 (R)	379 –	50	423 –	125
292 –	75	336 –	125	380 –	135	424 –	100
293 –	70 (S)	337 –	24	381 –	65	425 –	75 (R)
294 –	75	338 –	95	382 –	225	426 –	135 (R)
295 –	36	339 –	40	383 –	95	427 –	295 (VR)
296 –	36	340 –	35	384 –	100 pr.	428 –	85 (VR)
297 –	50	341 –	60	385 –	85	429 –	160
298 –	30	342 –	550 (S)	386 –	75	430 –	75 (R)
299 –	55 (S)	343 –	65	387 –	225	431 –	75 (R)
300 –	65	344 –	20 each	388 –	36	432 –	65
301 –	36	345 –	65	389 –	25	433 –	65
302 –	40	346 –	135	390 –	30	434 –	150
303 –	45	347 –	18	391 –	45	435 –	100
304 –	30	348 –	30	392 –	65	436 –	100
305 –	75 (S)	349 –	45	393 –	145	437 –	165
306 –	195 (S)	350 –	40	394 –	165	438 –	250
307 –	225	351 –	35	395 –	150	439 –	195
308 –	135	352 –	85	396 –	135	440 –	135
309 –	140 (R)	353 –	40	397 –	63	441 –	85
310 –	295 (R)	354 –	35	398 –	75	442 –	65
311 –	95	355 –	40	399 –	75	443 –	95
312 –	80	356 –	75	400 –	65	444 –	25
313 –	50	357 –	65	401 –	75	445 –	185
314 –	79	358 –	42	402 –	85	446 –	60
315 –	42	359 –	65 (VR)	403 –	75	447 –	125
316 –	36	360 –	28	404 –	80	448 –	75
317 –	195 (VR)	361 –	18	405 –	65	449 –	50
318 –	40 each	362 –	18	406 –	65	450 –	40

Fig.	Value	Fig.	Value	Fig.	Value	Fig.	Value
97	$ 155 (S)	143	$ 20	187	$ 85	231	$ 80
98	40	144	225 (R)	188	48	232	85 (S)
99	24	145	335 (VR)	189	55	233	18
100	95 pr.	146	130	190	120	234	22
101	85	147	22	191	28	235	20
102	195	148	75	192	125 (S)	236	22
103	65	149	40	193	175 (S)	237	22
104	80	150	125 (S)	194	125 (S)	238	100
105	175	151	40	195	32	239	32
106	75 (R)	152	40	196	250 (S)	240	55
107	65	153	32	197	90	241	175 (S)
108	125	154	32	198	75 (R)	242	95 (S)
109	55	155	32	199	95	243	55
110	45	156	125	200	32	244	225
111	75 pr.	157	20	201	32	245	75
112	65	158	25	202	110 pr.	246	175
113	35	159	65	203	28	247	85
114	18	160	125	204	45	248	85
115	35	161	85	205	35	249	125
116	45	162	65	206	165 pr.	250	95
117	35	163	28	207	150	251	45
118	28	164	55	208	55	252	35
119	36	165	24	209	165 pr.	253	100
120	18	166	65 (R)	210	110	254	150
121	15	167	95	211	35	255	85
122	20	168	150	212	45	256	75
123	20	169	50	213	35	257	32
124	250 set	170	150	214	125 ea.	258	85 pr.
125	55	171	25	215	95	259	18
126-8	175 set	172	125	216	54	260	60
129	75	173	65	217	60	261	175
130	28	174	20	218	70	262	150
131	35	175	150	219	59	263	175 (R)
132	22	176	20	220	35 ea.	264	75
133	15	177	75	221	55	265	42
134	12	178	35	222	75	266	28
135	15	179	45	223	75	267	19
136	12	180	150 (S)	224	65	268	55
137	35	181	65 (S)	225	35	269	28
138	45	182	100	226	55	270	28
139	35	183	18	227	150 (S)	271	65 pr.
140	35	184	75	228	40	272	28
141	20	185	65	229	30	273	20
142	32	186	25	230	65	274	32

FENTON GLASS: THE SECOND TWENTY-FIVE YEARS
by William Heacock
1998 Price Guide (Compiled by Robert E. Eaton, Jr.)

Over 550 color figures are listed in this guide with estimates of retail values on today's market. Also listed is a rarity rating of Scarce (S), Rare (R) and Very Rare (VR).

A price paid at an auction or seen tagged on an item at a shop or antique show is not necessarily what it is worth. An auction price is one often paid after heated competition between two determined collectors. A dealer's tag is based upon his or her personal knowledge of the collector market and a necessary business markup from their own original purchase price.

Prices listed in this guide are based upon three major factors—color, condition and collectibility.

COLOR—many pieces shown in this book was made in several colors. The price listed is for the exact item illustrated. Another color might be worth more or less. Also, a rating of "VR" doesn't necessarily mean that the same piece is very rare in a different color.

CONDITION—prices are listed for items in undamaged condition with good color and/or iridescence.

COLLECTIBILITY—a piece is collectible if people want it badly enough to compete! Much Fenton glass is very collectible!

Neither the author nor the publisher will be responsible for losses incurred as a result of quoting prices in this book.

Fig.	Value	Fig.	Value	Fig.	Value	Fig.	Value
1	$125 (R)	25	$300 (R)	49	$95	73	$20
2	250	26	68	50	20	74	20
3	110	27	550 (VR)	51	35	75	160 (S)
4	150	28	65	52	160	76	140
5	375	29	225	53	175	77	85 pr
6	135	30	85	54	225 (R)	78	300 (R)
7	125	31	185 pr.	55	60	79	175
8	245	32	75	56	55	80	145 (S)
9	295 (R)	33	250 (S)	57	35	81	79
10	175	34	175 (S)	58	30	82	55
11	275 (R)	35	145	59	45	83	30
12	150	36	120	60	50	84	50
13	135	37	125	61	28	85	35
14	195	38	450 (S)	62	20	86	38
15	195 pr.	39	40	63	30	87	45
16	95 (R)	40	125	64	32	88	85
17	125 (R)	41	110 (R)	65	32	89	85
18	265 (S)	42	128 pr.	66	25	90	150 (S)
19	310 (S)	43	450 (R)	67	32	91	300 (S)
20	65	44	25	68	40	92	24
21	215	45	28	69	30	93	35
22	200	46	35	70	40	94	24
23	90	47	35	71	135	95	24
24	135 (R)	48	65	72	48	96	20

Morning Mist 27 *illustrated* 29, 73, 109
Mother and Child pendant 191 *illustrated* 191
Mother's Day 191 *illustrated* 191
Mountain Berry on Gold Overlay 23
    illustrated 61, 112
Mulberry 27, 162-163 *illustrated* 37, 87
Museum Collection (QVC) 210

N

Natalie ballerina 200 *illustrated* 126
National Fenton Glass Society 144, 215
Nativity 184, 186 *illustrated* 184
Nativity Set 187-188 *illustrated* 117, 187
New Century Collection (QVC) 213 *illustrated* 142
Northwood Art Glass 208 *illustrated* 136

O

Ocean Blue *illustrated* 49
Opaline 146 *illustrated* 85-86
Opaline with Blush Rose *illustrated* 85-86
Ornamental Magic 186 *illustrated* 115

P

Pacific Northwest Fenton Association 144, 215
Pansies on Cranberry 20 *illustrated* 52, 74, 110-111
Pansies, handpainted 27 *illustrated* 61, 63, 109
Pearly Sentiments 20 *illustrated* 33
Periwinkle on Blue Burmese *illustrated* 126
Persian Pearl 156 *illustrated* 81, 159
Petal Pink 20, 22 *illustrated* 39, 50
Pink Crackle 30 *illustrated* 43
Pink Pearl 22 *illustrated* 41
Pinstripe Collection 30 *illustrated* 70
Plum 27 *illustrated* 46, 68
Plum Carnival 27, 204, 206 *illustrated* 129-130
Plum Opalescent *illustrated* 136, 143-144
Plum Overlay 27
Plum Slag 146 *illustrated* 53
Poinsettia Glow 150, 184 *illustrated* 71
Poinsettias *illustrated* 115
Praying Children 187 *illustrated* 136
Primrose, handpainted 22 *illustrated* 51
Provincial Floral on Cranberry 20
Puddle Parade *illustrated* 53

Q

QVC and Fenton 211-214 *illustrated* 137-142

R

Radiant Angel 184, 186 *illustrated* 116, 185
Red Carnival 201, 204-205
    illustrated 111-112, 127, 201-203
Renaissance Angel ornament 188 *illustrated* 115
Richardson (David), glass made for 210
    illustrated 136
Romance Collection 153 *illustrated* 65
Rosalene 132, 200 *illustrated* 109, 126
Rose Garden 20 *illustrated* 75
Rose Magnolia 20, 22, 160 *illustrated* 51, 81
Rose Pearl 22 *illustrated* 47, 49
Rosebuds on Rosalene *illustrated* 126
Rosso (Helen and Phil), glass made for 208
    illustrated 135
Royal Hobnail *illustrated* 57
Royal Purple 30, 164 *illustrated* 93, 112, 125, 140-141
Rubina Verde 23, 27, 163 *illustrated* 90, 125
Ruby 146

S

Salem Blue 23 *illustrated* 77
Sandwich Historical Society *illustrated* 136
Santa figurines 186-188 *illustrated* 116
Sapphire Blue Opalescent 154-155 *illustrated* 78
Schwarz-Bear 200 *illustrated* 199
Sea Green Satin 23, 163-164 *illustrated* 91-92, 109
Sea Mist Crackle 30 *illustrated* 43
Sea Mist Green 22-23 *illustrated* 24, 62, 67
Sea Mist Green Satin 22, 30 *illustrated* 38
Sea Mist Opalescent 22 *illustrated* 23, 38
Sea Mist Slag 146 *illustrated* 53
Secret Slipper 153 *illustrated* 150
Shell Pink 20, 146 *illustrated* 40
Showcase Dealer Exclusives 196 *illustrated* 125, 196
Silver Crest 27 *illustrated* 28
Snowberry 149-150 *illustrated* 71
Special Products, 207-210
    illustrated 132-136, 144, 207-210
Spruce Carnival 204 *illustrated* 131
Spruce Green 23, 146 *illustrated* 71, 111
Star Flowers on Gold Pearl 156 *illustrated* 81, 158
Starflowers on Cranberry Pearl *illustrated* 110
Stewart (Martha), glass made for 208 *illustrated* 134

Stiegel Blue Opalescent 155 *illustrated* 79-80
Stiegel Green Stretch 160 *illustrated* 82-83
Sweetbriar on Plum Overlay 27 *illustrated* 68, 110

T

Thistle 23, 27 *illustrated* 24, 110
Topaz Opalescent 146, 163 *illustrated* 88-89, 135
Topaz Opalescent with Hydrangeas 163
    illustrated 88-89
Tranquility 27 *illustrated* 73, 112
Trellis 20, 22 *illustrated* 22, 61
Twilight Blue 23 *illustrated* 25, 42
Twilight Crackle 30 *illustrated* 43
Twilight Tulips 23 *illustrated* 25, 42
Twining Berries 150 *illustrated* 71, 109, 111

U

Unicorn 150 *illustrated* 150

V

Valentine's Day 189
Victorian Bouquet on Black 30 *illustrated* 60
Vining Garden on Sea Mist Green 22 *illustrated* 61
Vining Hearts, handpainted *illustrated* 47
Vintage, handpainted 27 *illustrated* 46, 112
Violas on Petal Pink 22 *illustrated* 50
Violet 27
Violet Satin 27, 164 *illustrated* 94-95, 112
Violets on Iridized Opal *illustrated* 41
Violets on Rosalene *illustrated* 126

W

Walrath (Mary C.), glass made for 207 *illustrated* 136
Watercolors 20 *illustrated* 33
White Magnolia on Spruce Green *illustrated* 110
White Pearlized, handpainted *illustrated* 40
Willow Green Opalescent 165
Winterberry *illustrated* 77
Woodland Frost 150, 186 *illustrated* 71

Y

Yellow Ribbon bell 200 *illustrated* 124, 199